VALENTINA LUJÁN

To be happy
is for
the brave

... and you're braver than you think

Valentinamente_feliz

To **Lázaro and Simón**, for being my greatest challenge and source of courage.

To you who bought this book, because you had the ambition and the courage not to settle for a half-lived life.

To you, who woke up without enthusiasm for several days, felt uneasy, and sought out options and information to live better.

To you who are willing to work on becoming your best self, because you shape families, couples, organizations, societies, and a happier world.

To you, who are brave and willing to be happy, even though it may feel uncomfortable at first.

To you, who hold this book in your hands, thank you for believing in me, but above all, **thank you for believing in yourself.**

Copyright © 2025 by Valentina Luján

All rights reserved.

Published and Distributed in Canada by Live Life Happy Publishing.
www.livelifehappypublishing.com

All rights reserved. No part of this book may be reproduced by any mechanical, photographic, or electronic process, or in the form of a phonograph recording: Nor may it be stored in a retrieval system, transmitted, or otherwise be copied for public or private use- other than for "fair use" as brief quotations embodied in articles and reviews without prior written permission of the publisher. If you use any of the information in this book for yourself, which is your constitutional right, the author and the publisher assumes no responsibility for your actions.

Library of Congress Cataloging-in-Publication Data

Valentina Luján

To Be Happy Is for the Brave: And You're Braver Than You Think

Categories: Positive Psychology > Courageous Happiness > Science-Backed Well-Being > Transformative Habits > Empowered Change > Tools for Fulfillment > Commitment to Joy > Bravery in Action

ISBN 978-1-998724-08-6 Hardcover

ISBN 978-1-998724-07-9 Electronic

ISBN 978-1-998724-06-2 Paperback

Cover Design: Valentina Luján

Live Life Happy Publishing

PUBLISHER'S NOTE & AUTHOR DISCLAIMER

This publication is designed to provide accurate and authoritative information concerning the subject matter covered. It is sold to understand that the publisher and author are not engaging in or rendering any psychological, medical or other professional services. If expert assistance or counselling is needed, seek the services of a competent medical professional. For immediate support call your local crisis line. The following book could contain actual events and experiences that the author has encountered in their life. However, some names and specific locations have been changed or omitted to protect the privacy and confidentiality of the individuals involved. The changes do not alter the story's integrity or its messages.

GRATITUDE

Toño: Thank you for helping me truly dream BIG and for being my adventure companion.

Mom: Thank you for teaching me the superpower of intuition and the magic of keeping both wings in flight and feet on the ground simultaneously.

Dad: Thank you for showing me that unconditional love exists, the value of freedom, the peace of integrity, and the power of sports.

To my siblings: Thank you for training me for life and teaching me that the path is an individual one.

Tal Ben-Shahar: Thank you for your wisdom, simplicity, and friendship — and most of all, thank you for that chance meeting in November 2019. You changed my life forever!

Colleagues from HSA and the Revolution of Happiness in Action: Thank you for being a safe space for support, consultation, camaraderie, ideas, honesty, and learning.

INTRODUCTION

Do you want to be happy or happier, but you don't know how? If you answered yes, this book is for you. Do you feel that happiness is confusing, distant, and almost impossible for you? Or do you think you're living a mediocre life, just getting through your days, coasting along... and you're fed up? If you answered yes, this book is also for you.

The purpose of this book — and the field of Happiness Studies — goes beyond providing scientific information. Above all, it's about promoting conscious and intentional transformation to help you live better. I am convinced that you want to be happy and live a fulfilling life, but maybe you don't know how or where to start.

I'd love to tell you that I climbed Everest or that I survived some extraordinary event, but the reality is that my life is pretty average. It was precisely through an ordinary experience that my greatest superpower was awakened: courage.

I must tell you that here you will NOT find a magical formula or a light at the end of the tunnel. Anyone who promises to make you happy or tells you to follow their light to feel fulfilled is LYING. This book aims to be a bridge between serious scientific research and the practicality of life, offering you real, actionable tools to care for your mental, physical, and emotional health, find purpose, and build fulfilling relationships — ultimately helping you live better. This book is designed to show you that happiness is possible if you work to build it.

Happiness isn't something you search for, achieve, or that just happens to you, nor is it something anyone can give you. Happiness is a complex construction and therefore requires effort and strategy. It's a long-term process, which can sometimes feel uncomfortable. That's why be brave is essential to achieving it.

Here, I share why courage is the trigger that allows a person to freely choose to build their happiness (understood as the ambitious idea of living fully) — and why you are braver than you think.

We have all faced adversity in different forms. When faced with it, there are two paths: you either break or you grow stronger. Which one will you choose? The beauty of life is creating a life that, despite its dose of adversity, feels worth living to you. To achieve this, we can lean on the Science of Happiness, which, backed by scientific methods, increases your chances of success when you commit to working on your happiness.

As you read this book, I want you to remember that you don't need a trauma-filled life to make courage worthwhile. We are all brave simply because we've overcome countless challenges and discomforts. Just think about everything you do today that once scared you. Inside you already lies what you need; you are braver than you think — you just need to reconnect and redirect.

The most striking expression of unhappiness is suicide. According to data from the Pan American Health Organization, every 40 seconds, someone dies by suicide worldwide, and for each person who succeeds, 20 more have attempted it.

Currently, depression rates are on the rise, and it is estimated that by 2030, depression will be the leading cause of disability worldwide. It is urgent to provide reliable and accessible options to prevent both suicide and depression. And what better vaccine than

INTRODUCTION

to teach (without romanticism) and inspire people to formally and consciously work on building their happiness and a fulfilling life?

What is happiness? Should everyone build happiness? What does it take to be happy? Is happiness a personal responsibility? Is there a formula for happiness? Does being vulnerable make me strong or weak? What is courage? Do you live for yourself or to meet others' expectations? Can you be happy in the face of life's inherent adversity? Is feeling comfortable in my own skin possible or just a utopia — and what does it depend on?

This book aims to bridge science, academia, accessible communication, and entertainment. I am convinced that learning to be happy and working on it can be fun. So here, you'll find scientifically backed information and tools to give you a solid path. In other words, if you decide to build your happiness, you can work on it with a high chance of success, avoiding the loss of self-belief, disillusionment, or self-sabotage when your efforts don't yield immediate results.

If, on the other hand, you think that reading this book alone will make you happy, you are mistaken. Building a fulfilling life requires decisions and hard work. If you're unwilling to do that, keep merely surviving your days — but don't complain about your unhappiness because you're choosing it. No one can take away your ability to decide how you respond to what happens to you.

I am an extrovert. I love connecting and interacting with people, but life simply wouldn't give me enough time to share my message with as many people as I want if I did it only by speaking one-on-one, in person...

That's why I wrote this book — to shout three things to the world:
1. To be happy is your **respons-ability**: You have the ability to respond to happiness.
2. You need **courage** to build your happiness.
3. You can **learn** to be courageous and to be happy.

This book's sole purpose is to offer you knowledge and information. I am just your travel companion; I am not a certified psychotherapist. Therefore, this book does not intend to replace the advice or guidance of specialists such as doctors, coaches, psychiatrists, or other qualified professionals.

Regardless, thank you, thank you, thank you for resonating with my message that "to be happy is your respons-ability" and for trusting me, no matter your story or the life circumstances you are facing today. From the depths of my heart, I hope this book helps you be courageous and start building your happiness (long-term well-being) for and by yourself.

WHO I AM

I am a woman of challenges and hard work. I was born in Mexico City on June 17, 1983. Yes, I'm a Gemini! I embody duality (however that seems to you). I grew up in León, Guanajuato, Mexico, in a "quirky" family — or perhaps too liberal by provincial standards.

I lived there for 20 years, playing golf and being an honor-roll student (I had a good memory), until I returned to Mexico City, seeking the pollution, adrenaline, and prosperity it offers. I am an extrovert, and being surrounded by people energizes me. I love meeting people who are very different from me.

I love learning, and I am a sports and travel enthusiast. I have lived for short periods in the United States, Spain, Canada, and France, always knowing that my home is Mexico. I've left behind friends — who are still like family — in each of these places. I love working; I've been doing it since I was 14 years old. I believe work nourishes the soul — it's not just about making money.

From a young age, I promised myself that I would never be financially dependent on anyone, and at 41, I'm on track. I don't prac-

INTRODUCTION

tice any religion, but I deeply believe in God. A God who listens to me and loves granting my requests. A God of whom you and I are a part. My soul trusts that the world is a safe place to live, though my rational mind often finds evidence to the contrary.

I love animals and nature, and I have deep respect for Mother Earth. My most important values are freedom, integrity, and happiness; I use them as a compass for my daily decisions. I'm not afraid of growing older; I enjoy challenging stereotypes and believe that age is more about attitude than a number.

I am surrounded by wonderful and brave people, starting with my husband, Toño, and my children, Lázaro and Simón, with whom I have the privilege of sharing my daily journey. My friends are a treasure to me, and I've realized that their common trait is courage. They inspire me!

My greatest fear is that my children's physical integrity might be violated. My deepest wish is for my children to feel and know that they are responsible and capable of building their happiness freely, being their most authentic selves, without the need to please others.

I have a natural inclination toward altruistic causes related to children and women. I help whenever I can. Bossy or violent people unimpress me. Not sleeping well affects me a lot. I sleep with earplugs. Sleep, for me, is sacred — both mine and others.

I know my body is my loyal companion, a machine, and my primary tool — not an ornament. Money is a means, never an end.

Abundance goes far beyond money or material possessions. I'm scattered and tend to open several doors at once, but I never leave things unfinished. I love champagne and good food, but I don't like cooking. I am passionate about order and cleanliness, though not to the point of OCD.

I believe there's a big difference between "playing to win" and "playing not to lose." I've learned that making my mind a safe and kind place takes a lot of work. My nightstand is full of books and a spray of aromatherapy. My worth is based on my generosity, wisdom, and compassion — not on academic titles or designer bags — although I'll probably keep collecting diplomas because I love structured learning.

I'd rather visit a stationery store than a perfume shop. Saying "no" doesn't come hard to me, but I'm still working on my excessive bluntness. I only watch TV when something is recommended to me or during the Olympics.

My exploration of the world of happiness began in my adolescence when I felt profoundly unhappy. My dissatisfaction with life led me to seek alternatives to give my existence meaning. At 13, I started attending self-awareness workshops, therapy sessions, and conferences. I began reading, asking questions, questioning everything, and trying to decipher the concept of happiness.

But happiness felt abstract, ethereal, uncertain, confusing, and sometimes distant — until I discovered the Science of Happiness. That's when everything gained structure, meaning, tangibility, and closeness. Happiness became something real and achievable if I put in the required effort.

That's why I'd love to share a bit of my journey with you today — and maybe save you a few falls along the way. I'll clarify: there are no shortcuts. That's why to be happy is for the brave!

I'm excited for this book to reach countless corners of the world. If you like it or find it helpful, pass it to someone you want to help live better. I love living!

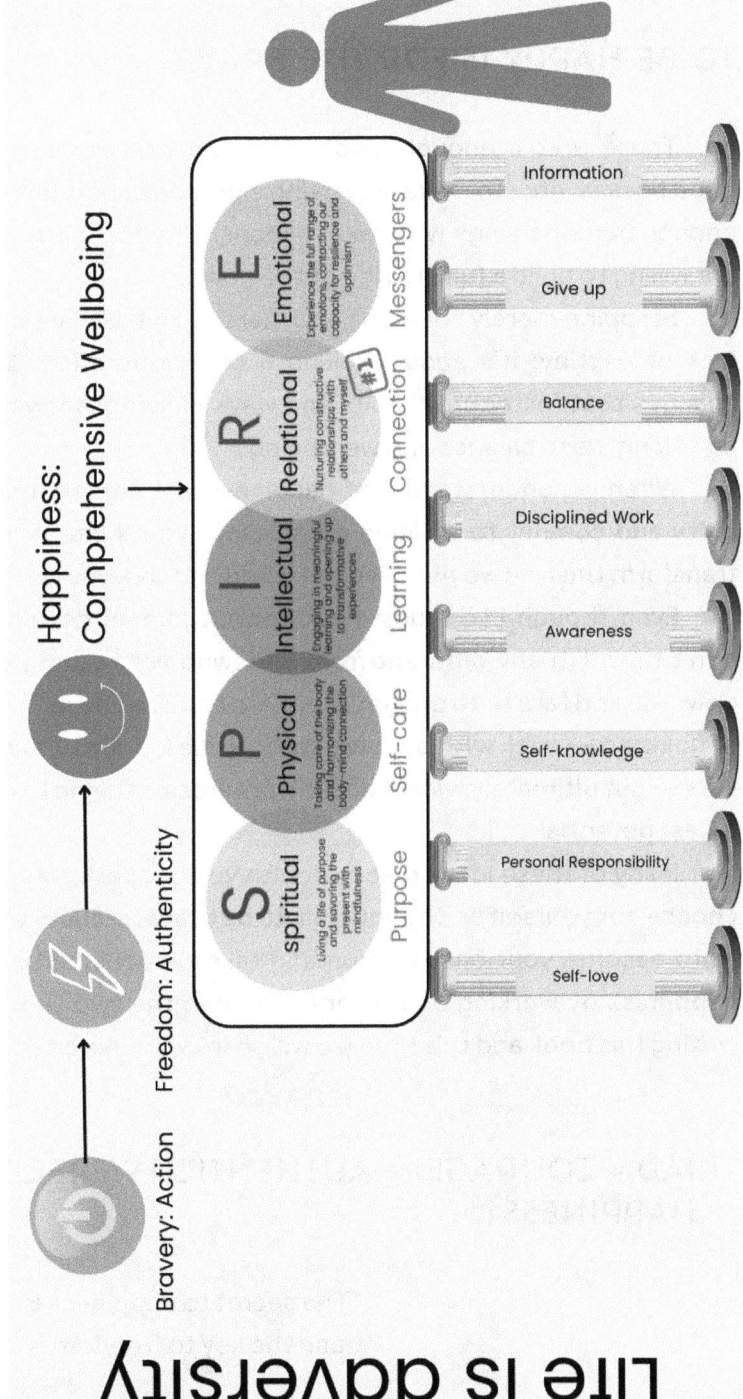

TO BE HAPPY IS FOR THE BRAVE

There aren't enough good governments, good husbands, good bosses, etc., to make every single person happy. But there are enough human beings who take responsibility for themselves and are willing to build a fulfilling life of their own.

Stopping merely surviving and starting to truly live isn't about luck or destiny; it's about making a conscious effort to create changes that foster new habits and ways of living, allowing you to build long-term balance and well-being.

When we understand that happiness is a **personal responsibility** and commit to building it consciously and intentionally, we transform the way we perceive the world and the way we live.

Even though I've studied a lot about human development, I don't think I'm any different from you, who are reading this right now. You and I are both on a journey here to learn and in the process of doing so — each with our own story, values, priorities, and interests — but ultimately, works of art in progress, striving to reach our fullest potential.

If any of these ideas resonate with you or spark your desire to **choose**, for yourself and by yourself, to **be brave**, **reclaim your power** to become your best version and take **responsibility for your happiness** by working on it every day, then the two years I spent writing this book and this time we will share will have been worth it.

TRIAD = COURAGE -> AUTHENTICITY/FREEDOM -> HAPPINESS

> "The secret to happiness is freedom,
> and the key to freedom is courage."
> **THUCYDIDES**

INTRODUCTION

To be happy is for the brave. Daring to strengthen your courage muscle is the catalyst that allows you to live authentically and freely, and therefore, to be truly happy. Happiness, authenticity (the freedom to be), and courage all require action.

My friend Leonardo Curzio, a distinguished journalist and academic in Mexico, says: "Freedom belongs to those who work for it." And I believe that happiness also belongs to those who work for it.

To be happy and feel comfortable in your own skin, two things are essential:

1. That you live authentically, embracing your essence and breaking away from those expectations and ready-made scripts that awaited you the day you were born.
2. That you have freely decided to do the intentional, conscious work required to build long-term well-being and shape a life that, to you, is worth living.

This journey will take you into uncomfortable zones, difficult decisions, and challenging crossroads, like questioning your concept of loyalty and deciding whether it's more important to please others or to be true to yourself.

Ultimately, you'll embark on a lifelong journey where you are the protagonist. It will be filled with frustrations, joys, disappointments, challenges, successes, mistakes, satisfactions, and more. But it will undoubtedly be exciting and will put you in the driver's seat of your life.

Fear will show up more often than you'd like. But remembering that it happens to all of us and that you are braver than you think (for having overcome so many experiences and for being willing to feel all the uncomfortable or painful emotions that come with being human) will give you the strength to act in alignment with yourself despite feeling afraid.

TO BE HAPPY IS FOR THE BRAVE

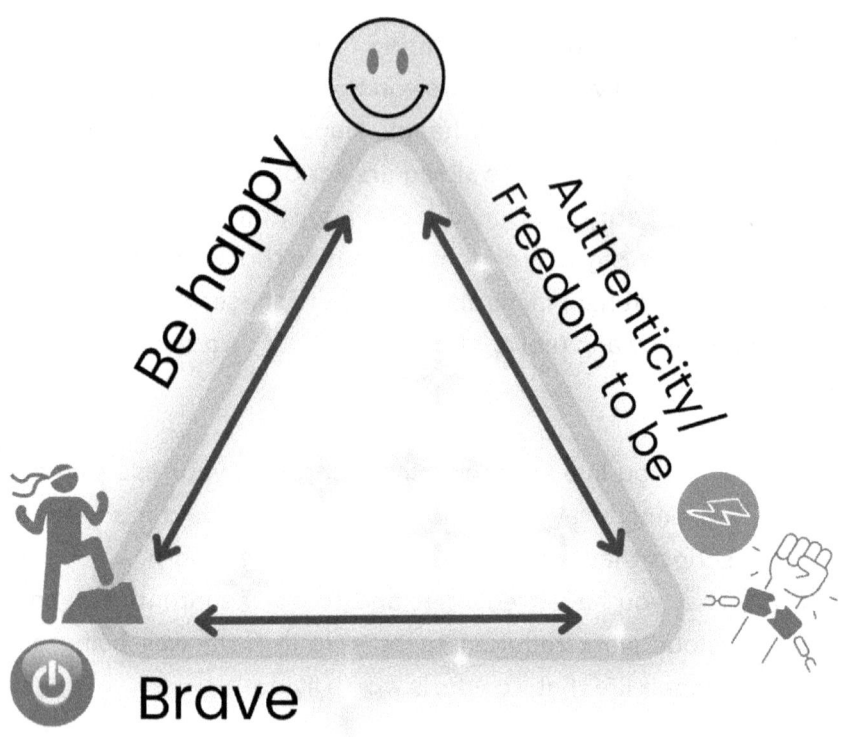

01 ADVERSITY: LIFE

BEING HAPPY

> "Everything can be taken from a man but one thing: the last of the human freedoms to choose one's attitude in any given set of circumstances, to choose one's own way."
> VIKTOR FRANKL

There are 3 important rules for being happy:

1. Understand what happiness is. To build something, you first need to conceptualize it — that is, to know what it is.
2. Accept life's unhappiness. This is what my teacher, Tal Ben-Shahar, calls the first step. If you're waiting for a life free of adversity to be happy, you will end up dying unhappy.
3. Reality, reality, reality. Life is what it is, not what you want it to be. And with the truth — no matter how difficult — we can all cope.

These three rules are essential for effectively managing your expectations about this book, happiness, and life. Sometimes, when circumstances are tough, happiness boils down to resilience.

TO BE HAPPY IS FOR THE BRAVE

Free yourself from the magical thinking of a happy, perfect, and challenge-free life. Earth is a school planet, where you came to learn. No one escapes uncertainty, pain, difficulty, and risk — which can often be uncomfortable. So when you face adversity, rejoice because it means you are alive.

Adversity manifests in any undesirable situation. Some experience it through illness, financial crisis, earthquakes, hurricanes, pandemics, war, depression, persistent anxiety or panic, divorce, abandonment, unemployment, betrayal, extreme stress, the death of a loved one, discomfort, motherhood, etc. Therefore, adversity is part of everyone's life. Yes, even those you have idealized! Without exception, we all face adversity.

Here is a QR code linking to the conversation I had with my teacher, Dr. Tal Ben-Shahar. I'd love for you to get to know him, or listen if you already do — none of his words are wasted. Enjoy it!

In each section of this book, you will also find the "Building My Happiness" segment with essential questions to help you achieve your goals.

Building My Happiness: **The 3 Rules and Me**

1. What does happiness mean to me?
2. Am I waiting for my life to be perfect to be happy?
3. To what extent do I allow myself to flow with life's unhappiness?
4. Today, what conditions am I placing on my happiness?
5. Do I believe I tend to be objective about reality?

A LOW BLOW

To be happy, it's essential to make yourself the priority and to choose for yourself and by yourself. Without that, it's impossible to build a state of well-being where you can say, "Life is amazing" or "I feel comfortable in my own skin; I wouldn't trade places with anyone." Own your life and stop asking for permission or opinions on how to live it.

If you don't feel at peace, don't seize the opportunity to experience your reality, and don't do what you believe is right, it will be difficult to build happiness.

From this experience, I learned four crucial things:

1. Loyalty to myself comes first.
2. If I learn to be with myself, I will never feel alone.
3. I decide the importance people or situations have in my life.
4. Peace and serenity are the bare minimum for happiness.

As I told you, my greatest superpower awakened through a common experience: courage. Now, let me tell you something:

I was in middle school, about 13 or 14 years old. That age when your friends mean everything to you — they're your entire world — and your only goal is to belong, to feel appreciated and loved by your peers.

I was part of a group of eight to ten friends. Many people called us "the popular girls," but I preferred to call us "extroverted." Among them, two were my best friends. One of them, Ema, was like the sister you would choose in childhood — we had even gone to the same elementary school. The other, Marisol, had become a close friend in just two years, sharing a friendship filled with affection, loyalty, and fun.

One day, after recess, I found a letter on my desk. I got excited because we often exchanged little tokens of friendship and surprised each other. I remember sitting down to read it calmly while the rest of my classmates returned to the room. I was filled with excitement and curiosity about what it would say.

As soon as I started reading, my stomach turned. I felt dizzy and rushed to the bathroom to vomit—a wave of overwhelming discomfort spread through my body. The school coordinator came to ask what was wrong.

– I feel sick; I want to go home – I need my mom to come and pick me up.

–What's wrong?

– I feel really bad; maybe I ate something that made me sick.

The letter, written in teenage words, said, " We don't want to be your friends anymore. You're the worst person in the world. You want the boys we like to notice us. You always want all the attention. You're such a drama queen, flirtatious, and selfish. Blah, blah, blah.

I got home and, without any explanation, went straight to my room. I remember spending the whole day there, crying and crying and crying. It was a Thursday, so I didn't go to school on Friday.

ADVERSITY: LIFE

Thousands of thoughts raced through my mind — including whether life was even worth living with that level of pain.

I thought to myself, if I tell my mom and she decides to confront them or get involved, how embarrassing. Or if she asked me if I wanted to change schools, I'd feel scared — and I didn't want to change schools. I liked studying there.

I spent the whole day in my room, still in my pajamas, feeling utterly hopeless, crying, with the situation replaying endlessly in my mind. My heart felt crushed — no, shattered. I experienced a deep sadness like I had never felt before. It was an incomparable sense of loss mixed with feelings of rejection and abandonment.

I ran out of tears to cry, and my eyes ached. On Saturday night, I realized I had only one day left to decide what to do because on Monday, I would have to either go back to class or confront my mom with the truth.

I had several choices. I could apologize so they would accept me back into the group. But the price of apologizing for something I hadn't done felt like betraying myself just to belong, and I knew that would hurt even more.

After hours of reflection, I concluded: If this matters too much to me, I'll be giving away all my power and well-being to others — specifically to Ema and Marisol, who wrote the letter. I thought: I can let this define my life and become a tragedy, or not. Of course, it hurt. Of course, my daily school life would change. But surely there was something I could do... at the very least, survive.

It goes without saying how important friendships are, especially during adolescence. I remember being extremely anxious about recess. In class, I could pay attention and get through it. But during recess? The whole group had stopped talking to me. The thought of being alone and everyone else noticing that I'd been excluded was distressing. I felt like an outcast.

I thought: A book! I'll bring a book. That entire week, I took books with me. During recess, I ate my lunch and read. Gradually, I started making friends with girls from other groups. In fact, during those days, I met the person who would become my best friend for many years. She had just moved to the city — and the school. She didn't have any friends, and neither did I. The Universe brought us together.

Months passed, and the incident faded. One by one, the other girls in the group who had stopped talking to me began apologizing. One day, after returning to the classroom from a flag-raising ceremony, Ema and Mariana handed me a letter. Immediately, I felt a pit in my stomach, and adrenaline surged through my body. I relived that awful day in my mind and thought, "Another one of their cursed letters..."

But no. To my relief, it was a letter apologizing for everything that had happened and the hurt they had caused me.

Today, however, I thank them for that harsh blow, because the feeling — and the lesson — of deciding to live for myself and not surrender my power was a turning point in my life. I discovered another superpower: **I am responsible for my life!**

All human beings always have the ability to choose who we want to be in the face of what happens to us (no matter how painful it is). At that time, I didn't have all the knowledge to back up that statement. Sometimes, I even doubted that it was possible.

But empirically, that's what happened. I consciously analyzed my options:

- **Play the victim** and feel like life owed me something because I hadn't even been interested in their crushes. Blame them and paint them as villains, or cry and beg to be accepted back. That's not who I am.

- **Take responsibility**. Acknowledge my part, learn from it, make an action plan, execute it, feel capable, and reinterpret the stories that hurt me in a way that adds value to my life. I chose: As long as I'm good with myself, I've already won.

It was difficult, yes. It hurt a lot at first, but each day, it hurt a little less, and about a week later, it stopped being hard. I even remember enjoying the experience of being alone and realizing that I was enough company for myself. I chose to believe that something good would come from it and that they were the ones missing out on my company, affection, and friendship.

I accepted their apologies, though I no longer cared between you and me. I had processed the situation, and they were no longer relevant to me. We went from being best friends, traveling with each other's families, to all of that disappearing. I didn't carry any resentment because I didn't hate them. I never thought of getting revenge, because that would have meant channeling energy and time toward them that they didn't deserve. To me, they were dead, so I made new friends.

That's when it clicked for me that to be happy, you need two things: live for yourself and feel at peace.

Back then, I didn't have the structure and knowledge I have now, but I think I began walking the path of self-discovery and learning that has brought me to where I am today. If there was a retreat, I went. If there was an emotional art workshop, I signed up. I kept a journal and did many introspection exercises. I started to know myself really well. I read books like The Little Prince or Chicken Soup for the Teenage Soul, which has short stories that, in four or five pages, recount adversity and its resolution. I became interested in personal development and took the risk of confronting my own shadow. That's why I say to be happy is for the brave.

Building My Happiness: **Identifying Low Blows**

1. What are some of the low blows I've experienced in my life?
2. What emotions do I associate with those experiences?
3. Why did those experiences leave such a mark on me?

PATHS

> "Pain + Reflection = Progress."
> RAY DALIO

Accepting adversity as an unavoidable part of life allows you to face it with an attitude of challenge rather than despair, fostering a happier and healthier approach to existence. When faced with adversity, you either break or grow stronger. There are only two paths:

1. The Victim Role / Post-Traumatic Stress Disorder (PTSD)
   Why me? You resign yourself, suffer, blame others, depend on others, feel incapable, believe life owes you something, and the same things happen to you repeatedly.
2. Personal Responsibility / Post-Traumatic Growth (PTG)
   What is this teaching me? You recognize your part, learn, capitalize on the event, create an action plan, feel capable, execute, see options, and believe that you are the architect of your life.

Your path depends on your inner freedom — that power to choose, which no one can take from you, even in the worst circumstances. Viktor Frankl, a psychiatrist and survivor of World War II concentration camps, said that freedom gives human existence intention and meaning.

You exercise this inner freedom with every choice you make, no matter how insignificant it seems. All these choices combined create your reality, your present. **Yes, you create your reality.** So if you like your life, congratulations. And if you don't, I invite you to reclaim your power for and by yourself, and start making different, conscious choices.

This is important because only by being aware of the superpower that is your inner freedom can you use it whenever you want.

You can always choose: whether to be kind or not, whether to exercise or spend hours in front of the TV, whether to exercise out of guilt and shame (to change your body) or out of self-love and gratitude (to care for it), whether to sit up straight and take care of your spine or not, whether to surround yourself with people who inspire you or who drain you, what kind of work you dedicate your time to, what kind of profiles you follow on social media, how you spend your money, how you use your time, whether you give thanks or not, whether you smile or not, whether you complain frequently or not, where you place your attention, whether you take things personally, what you listen to, what you watch, what you read, what you prioritize in your life, etc.

Everything is a choice, and the key lies in making more and more conscious decisions.

If you're waiting for adversity to disappear from your life to be happy, you'll end up dying unhappy. Adversity is an inherent part of life. When you accept this, you'll start seeing it as a challenge, something to be curious about, rather than a problem, burden, tragedy, obstacle, or inevitable misfortune.

This is how, from a very young age, I began my journey of self-discovery and personal growth — a journey that, years later, led me to formally study happiness. Today, I know that this process continues and will last a lifetime.

Building My Happiness: Facing the Adversity in My Life

1. Describe an adverse situation you want to work on (it doesn't matter if it's current or from the past). Analyze and write down the situation in detail.
2. How have I faced that situation up until now?
3. How would I act from the victim mindset? (Why me?)
4. How would I act from a personal responsibility mindset? (What is this teaching me?)
5. So far, which path have I chosen — the victim role or personal responsibility?
6. Do I choose to continue with this path, or to change it?
7. What would a courageous attitude look like in this situation?
8. Who do I want to be from now on in response to what is happening or has happened to me?
9. What can I do differently to face this situation more effectively?
10. What is the first step I commit to taking, based on my insights?

PERSONAL RESPONSIBILITY

> "I'm a great believer in luck. I've found that the harder I work, the more luck I have."
> THOMAS JEFFERSON

ADVERSITY: LIFE

Recognizing your power to choose how you respond to circumstances empowers you to change them if you don't like them. Taking responsibility for your life puts you in control of your reality, offering you the ability to improve it. Personal responsibility is the greatest spark of hope.

Responsibility (respons-ability) is the ability you have to respond to what happens to you. Responsibility is the greatest generator of hope — that belief in a better future — because it puts you in charge of your reality and gives you the possibility to change it.

Responsibility will lead you to empowerment and freedom.

This is important because recognizing that your actions and decisions have brought you to where you are today allows you to act and decide differently to change your circumstances (if you're not happy with them) and build a better life.

If you believe that your situation depends on external factors or other people, then all you can do is wait for a stroke of luck for those factors or people to change so that your situation improves.

RESPONSIBILITY AS A GENERATOR OF HOPE

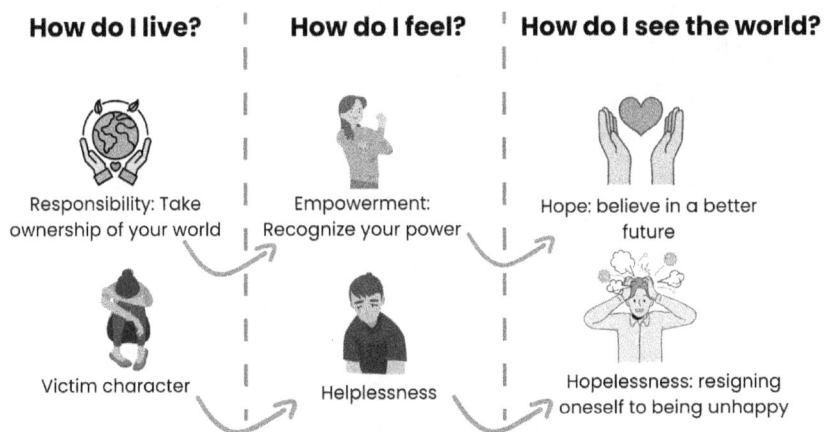

Recognize yourself as the protagonist of your life. Be aware that you create your reality, even when it doesn't seem like it. Only then can you reclaim your power, for and by yourself, and take different actions to generate a different outcome.

Albert Einstein, the most important scientist of the 20th century, defined insanity as "doing the same thing over and over again and expecting different results."

Responsibility means having the ability to respond. The word "responsibility" comes from the Latin responsum, which is a form of the verb respondēre, made up of the prefix re- (repetition) and the verb spondere (to promise, to offer). Personal responsibility is feeling capable of building your own life — having the ability to face what happens to you.

If you're happy with the life you have now, you can celebrate and feel proud. And if you're not, you can choose to start building a different life today, for and by yourself.

Do you feel like life owes you something? Are you carrying a story you told yourself for 20 or 30 years because your parents didn't attend your school events when you were a child? Do you often think that for things to be different, others have to change, not you? When you say, "I don't like this," do you feel disempowered, incapable of changing it, and unsure where to start — or do you immediately see resources, possibilities, and plans?

Are you asking, "Why me?" or "What is this teaching me?" Do you live in the past, ruminating on suffering (in any form), while life — and the opportunity to be happy today — passes right in front of you?

A victim is someone who chooses to be innocent at the cost of being powerless. The victim surrenders all their power by saying: "Oh, I didn't know." "I can't." "The circumstances overwhelm me." "Everyone else is to blame." "It wasn't me." "I bear my cross." "I asked nicely, but they didn't understand." "That's not meant for me." At first glance, it seems to offer benefits, but the price is extremely high. The victim believes that everything and everyone decides their life except them — circumstances, fate, the government, or other people. They blame everything else and refuse to take a leading role in creating their own life.

The danger of living in the victim role is that if you dislike your life, you are condemning yourself to it forever, because it will be nearly impossible to change it.

This is extremely important because, while taking on the role of a spectator in your life may give you the apparent advantage of not being responsible for failures, it also robs you of the ability to create changes and adjustments that could lead to greater well-being. In other words, choosing not to take the helm of your life condemns you to unhappiness.

Often, this is a subconscious process that takes time and effort to recognize. It's not that someone wakes up one day and consciously decides to give their power away to their boss, partner, parent, or government. Rather, at some point, they learned this behavior, and because they've done it for so long, they can't see any other option.

If you identify with the victim role, let me tell you two things:

1. We've all worn the victim costume at some point. Depending on the stories we tell ourselves about what happened to us, we wear different versions of the victim costume throughout our lives. The key is not to make the victim costume a way of life.
2. You can always choose. You have the power to take off that costume and act from personal responsibility. Every day is a new opportunity, and you can create different conditions.

The important thing is that now you know you create your reality. I sincerely hope that you're willing to start this journey of responsibility so you can live a life of fulfillment and happiness, for and by yourself.

Alright! I understand that I need to take responsibility for myself and my life, but... how do I do that? Question yourself! Asking these questions can help you determine whether you're wearing the victim costume. And if you are — beware!

Whenever you feel like you're slipping into the victim role, identify the decisions and actions you took that contributed to the situation. Instead of asking, "Why me?", ask: "What is this teaching me?" "What good can come from this?" "What can I do about it?"

My teacher, Dr. Tal Ben-Shahar, often says in class:

"Not everything happens for the best, but there are people who always make the best out of what happens."

In other words, you never lose — you either win or learn.

Taking responsibility for your life is essential if you want to be happy and live fully. From my 41-year journey, this decision has liberated and empowered me. If I had to choose one word to describe my life, it would be responsibility.

I consider it so important and try to embody it so fully that during one session, while working on life purpose with my dear Carmen — a therapist whose wisdom and honesty spark deep questioning — she asked me:

"If you were about to die and had the chance to give humanity one piece of advice — a phrase that could be heard in every corner of the Earth — what would it be?"

My answer was: "To be happy is your responsibility."

In that moment, I realized that contributing to a world where more people understand and feel responsible for building their happiness is part of my life's mission. In many ways, I feel that this is what I was born to do.

That's why #ToBeHappyIsYourResponsibility is my Valentinamente Feliz project's slogan, hashtag, or phrase. I invite you to follow me on my YouTube channel, Instagram, LinkedIn, and other platforms.

In this QR code, enjoy a conversation I had with Tal in Cartagena, Colombia, about this topic. I'm sure it will be helpful to you!

Building My Happiness: **Identifying the Victim Within Me**

1. How do I perceive myself within the context of my life?
2. Am I the protagonist of my story?
3. Do I feel like I am driving my life, that I am in charge of it?
4. Do I feel capable and believe that I can put in the effort to change what I don't like about my life?

You have personal responsibility if you answered "yes" to these last four questions. You are aware that you are building your life, and you very likely believe that your future can be better than your present because it depends on you to make it so.

DOING AND TRUSTING

"You can't connect the dots looking forward; you can only connect them looking backward. So you have to trust that the dots will somehow connect in your future. You have to trust in something — your gut, destiny, life, karma, whatever. This approach has never let me down, and it has made all the difference in my life."
STEVE JOBS

Act with determination in the areas you can control, but also learn to let certain aspects of life unfold naturally, recognizing that not everything is within your control.

The key lies in recognizing your sphere of action and impact and focusing your efforts there, while allowing systems, life, and energies beyond your control to play their part — trusting that, no matter what happens, everything is working for your highest good in the long run.

This is crucial for maximizing your ability to manifest the life you dream of, co-create the relationships you long for, and make assertive choices.

There are two ways to create your reality: through action and through conscious allowance — letting things happen. While you need to take ownership of your life and actively work to build your happiness, you must also recognize that you can't control everything and that you are not an isolated being. This is where trusting life, the universe, energy, God, or whatever concept resonates with you, comes into play.

Later, in Chapter 2, I'll share a scientific study on what determines happiness. But for now, I'd like to give you a recommendation based on my personal experience and life philosophy (since I can't provide scientific backing for this):
Trust life. The Universe's timing is perfect. No one can push a river.

Here's a QR code linking to an interview with Yordi Rosado and Martha Higareda on their show, "De Todo un Mucho." In it, we talk about doing and trusting, among many other interesting topics.

Building My Happiness: **Identifying My Doing and Trusting**

1. Do I know how to identify the areas where I can have an impact according to my circumstances?
2. How controlling do I consider myself? (1 being very little, 10 being extremely controlling)
3. Do I feel that I trust easily?
4. When an unexpected event of medium-to-low importance happens, do I flow with it easily, or do I get stuck on it for several days?

THE VACCINE

There is a psychological vaccine for difficult times: happiness. When a person has worked to build the habits, systems, and structures necessary to feel satisfied and fulfilled, they will still face adversity — because they are alive (and that's inevitable). However, they will have the tools to navigate adversity and see it as a challenge or opportunity rather than as a problem or tragedy.

Therefore, actively working on your happiness is an effective vaccine against suicide and depression.

This is important because it's never too late to start building long-term well-being. The ideal approach is to focus intentional efforts on the areas that, thanks to science, we know will yield the best results in terms of happiness.

Some of These Tools or Antibodies Can Be:

- Having strong, meaningful relationships.
- Enjoying good health.
- Living with a sense of purpose.
- Continuously learning about topics that interest you.
- Developing an optimistic outlook on life and/or a growth mindset.
- Having mechanisms to manage painful or uncomfortable emotions and promote pleasant emotions.
- Maintaining a recovery and rest program.
- Using screens mindfully, with screen-free spaces and times.
- Practicing the habit of gratitude.

Building My Happiness: **Recognizing My Antibodies**

1. Check off the tools from the list above that you believe you already have. Then, circle ONE tool from the list that you want to start working on to build your "vaccine" against adversity.

ANTIFRAGILITY

Antifragility is essential for happiness. It is the intersection between life's inherent adversity and the ultimate goal of human existence: happiness. It is the place where the sweet and the bitter aspects of life meet.

This is important because if you're waiting for life to be free of adversity to be happy, you'll end up dying unhappy. So remember:

- Learn to fail or fail to learn.
- A mistake is just one way of not doing something.
- Start making mistakes.

Growing from adversity and trauma — in other words, becoming antifragile — requires conscious effort, practice, and time.

You've probably heard of resilience, the physics concept that describes how an object or system returns to its original shape after being subjected to an external force that temporarily altered it.

The idea of antifragility takes resilience a step further — some call it Resilience 2.0 — suggesting that when the force acting on an object stops, the object doesn't just return to its original shape, it comes back stronger and improved.

And guess what? This principle applies not just to certain objects but also to some human systems and organizations.

Nassim Taleb, a Lebanese-American researcher, financial expert, and professor at New York University, introduced this concept in 2012 in his book, Antifragile. More than a decade later, this concept remains relevant in everyday life and helps us understand that life is inherently adversarial, yet you can still be happy if you become antifragile.

ANTIFRAGILITY

As we've mentioned, when facing adverse situations, there are two possible outcomes: Post-Traumatic Stress Disorder (PTSD) — where we break down, crumble, and feel defeated. Post-Traumatic Growth (PTG) — where we emerge stronger and improved.

The good news is that the simple awareness that growth is possible through adversity already makes you somewhat resilient because it gives you hope.

Trauma is the way events are processed, not the events themselves. That's why the same event can be traumatic for one person and not for another. Often, things become traumatic because they are processed in isolation — hidden away, accompanied by shame, guilt, or rejection.

While it's true that some events have a greater potential for trauma than others, all levels of trauma are valid and deserve respect. In other words, trauma is not comparable.

Of course, we can't talk about a "traumometer" or any device that measures levels of trauma, since the pain or damage from your experiences depends on how you interpret them or the stories you tell yourself. These interpretations are influenced by complex variables like past experiences, beliefs, interests, lessons learned, values, etc.

Creating interpretations that challenge your lineage, history, and reality — and telling yourself stories that add value — is one way to build antifragility and well-being. That's why to be happy is for the brave.

One of the factors that greatly enhances your antifragility is having quality relationships with people who matter to you or being part of a community where you feel identified, can contribute, and feel nourished. Likewise, having a solid system for managing your vital energy and recovery strengthens your antifragility.

Building My Happiness: **Becoming Antifragile**

1. Identify and describe an adverse situation you are facing.
2. List the resources you have to face this adversity: Relationships, skills, money, experience, etc.
3. List all the potential benefits you can gain from this difficulty: (Try not to analyze or judge your ideas. The goal is to end up with a long list.)
4. Take a moment to recognize the lessons and benefits this experience has given or will give you:
5. How will I be better once this situation has passed?

GROWTH MINDSET

> "Fail often and fail fast."
> TAL BEN-SHAHAR

As I mentioned, when faced with adversity and failure, there are two paths: you can either feel defeated and beat yourself up, or you can learn and grow. Your mindset is the decisive factor in unlocking your potential. That's why it's essential to cultivate a growth mindset and avoid a fixed mindset. This is important because the good news is that a growth mindset can be developed. This image clearly illustrates the difference between a growth mindset and a fixed mindset.

ADVERSITY: LIFE

We can't talk about a growth mindset without mentioning Dr. Carol S. Dweck, who, in her book Mindset, shares the distinctions between the two types of mindsets.

People with a fixed mindset perceive failure and mistakes as a threat — a manifestation of a lack or weakness. They want to protect their perceived "amount" of intelligence, talent, or personality at all costs. They use a lot of energy worrying about how they are perceived, trying to decipher what others think of them, and projecting a certain image. They fear taking risks and focus more on the problem than the solution. Instead of describing an action (I failed), they internalize it and make it part of their identity (I am a failure).

On the other hand, people with a growth mindset see failure and mistakes as an opportunity to learn and grow. They are not afraid of making mistakes and constantly ask themselves: "How can I grow and improve?" When they encounter failure, they take action and are decisive. They believe that everyone has tremendous potential and is on a path of growth. This mindset makes success more familiar to them.

I remember when Luis García, a well-known Mexican soccer player and sports commentator, came on my podcast. During the interview, he told me about the development process of palm trees. Palm trees have rings on their trunks, each representing a growth phase. To form each ring, the tree must break and fracture internally to grow. This very breaking is what makes it incredibly flexible so that, when hurricanes hit the coast, it bends but does not break.

I invite you to give meaning to adversity, knowing that your fractures will help you grow and make you flexible and resilient against future storms.

Here's a QR code so you can enjoy my conversation with him:

Building My Happiness: **Identifying My Mindset**

1. Which of the two types of mindsets do I identify with the most? Why?
2. Do I recognize where I learned to perceive failure the way I do?
3. Would I like to change or improve my perspective based on what I've discovered?
4. What commitment do I make to myself today?

02 HAPPINESS

HAPPINESS WITHOUT SECRETS

If I told you that to be happy is your responsibility — the most important one — what would you think? Happiness is not a matter of magic or luck, nor are there formulas or shortcuts. Happiness is not just fleeting moments, nor is it a single decision. Happiness doesn't just happen, isn't something to seek, find, or achieve. And finally, happiness doesn't have to be that distant, confusing, abstract, and unreachable thing that you don't truly understand.

Happiness is earned and worked for. Happiness is built. Happiness begins with a personal decision and continues with a lot of intentional, conscious, and consistent effort — which, by the way, no one can do for you, no matter how much they love you. Being happy is possible, and it's for the brave.

It's important to internalize these clarifications because people build their reality through words. Believing that happiness is something to be found, or that it's a matter of luck, condemns you to unhappiness by putting you in a passive, defenseless role, preventing you from taking action. Misconceptions about happiness make it harder for you to roll up your sleeves and stop wasting time waiting for happiness to appear magically or be granted by someone else. You search for things you know exist — like your keys or a pair of shoes — but searching for something that doesn't exist because you haven't built it yet is a different matter entirely.

To be happy requires two types of research:

- External (re-search): This comes from the science of happiness; it is generic and objective.
- Internal (me-search): This involves self-knowledge, introspection, and reflection; it is individual and subjective.

Reading and knowing a lot about happiness will not make you happier. That's like expecting to get well just because you bought the medicine (my dad sometimes does that, ha ha ha!). The reality is that to be happy, you have to act, apply, experiment, fail, get frustrated, get excited, evaluate, observe, try again, adjust, and start over. Happiness, like health, good relationships, and most things that are worth it, requires action after making a decision.

We are all capable of building happiness. So don't call it a dream — call it a plan. Stop seeing happiness as an ethereal, romantic, and distant concept, and make it close and tangible through ACTION. Confidence is fueled by action.

Sometimes, thinking about the complexity of happiness and all the efforts required to build it can feel overwhelming. But it is far more overwhelming to resign yourself to living a mediocre or unhappy life.

I became interested in happiness as a child. I used to wonder why some people seemed happy and fulfilled, while so many others were frustrated, just surviving day to day. I also observed myself and reflected on why I felt happy some days and not on others... so, at around 13 years old, I began this journey of self-discovery — understanding what worked for me, what excited me, when and why

I felt certain emotions. It's a path I've been on for nearly 30 years, and today I know it will last a lifetime.

One of the most important things I've learned is that there are as many experiences of happiness as there are people on Earth. Happiness will have different smells, images, textures, and flavors for each person.

However, tools, information, and general concepts offered by the Science of Happiness can increase your chances of success when you consciously build long-term well-being.

The field of flourishing and personal development is dual. The objective side consists of the Science of Happiness and its scientific methods. The subjective side involves the art of applying this information based on your interests, values, culture, goals, strengths, and life story. Because we are all different, what brings me great well-being might cause you anxiety. Therefore, each of us must build our own personal formula for happiness, where experimentation is essential.

Building My Happiness: **Getting Familiar with Happiness**

1. What idea resonates with me? Why?
2. What idea can help me make happiness feel close and achievable for me?
3. What adjustment am I ready to make now to build well-being in my life?
4. What is my commitment to myself (something executable, easy, and measurable)? Write it down, specify a time of day, and decide how often you will do it.

BEING HAPPY VS. FEELING HAPPY

"Feeling happy" is experiencing momentary joy, like when something good happens. "Being happy" runs deeper — it means living a fulfilling and meaningful life. Being truly happy requires continuous effort and conscious decisions to build a life that you genuinely enjoy and that satisfies you.

Understanding the difference between being happy and feeling happy is vital to avoid unhealthy habits or addictions that only seek fleeting moments of happiness.

Being happy is a complex, ambitious, and long-term idea, while feeling happy refers to a (temporary) state of mind associated with contentment and pleasure. It's important to consciously distinguish and experience both concepts to avoid falling into vices or illusions and to contribute to building your happiness.

The immediacy of modern life makes "feeling happy" more popular, causing us to lose sight of the ultimate goal of human existence: "being happy."

Not feeling happy all the time is normal, and that's okay — you are human. Happiness and being happy are not just about moments. While the concept does include happy moments (emotional well-being and pleasure), it also encompasses four other areas of well-being spiritual, physical, intellectual, relational. "Feeling happy" focuses solely on emotional well-being, while "being happy" embraces all five types of well-being, referring to a state of fulfillment and flourishing.

In today's world — which idealizes immediacy, shortcuts, digital filters, minimal effort, comfort, and cosmetic surgeries over effort, willpower, and habits — "feeling happy" is overvalued compared to "being happy." This explains current rates of depression.

The mindset of "let's have a good time now and deal with the consequences later" prevails. For example, drinking alcohol excessively without considering the hangover and damage to your body afterward.

It is crucially important to understand the differences between these ideas to avoid addictions and harmful habits that arise from hedonistic illusions. These illusions suggest that the more frequently and intensely you feel pleasure and euphoria, the more likely you are to be happy (long-term well-being). This is completely false.

I have spoken at many forums before skeptical and resistant audiences. Many express that the idea of happiness is a utopia or that it sounds utterly absurd, superficial, or silly — some even say it's easy to talk about happiness when you're not worried about paying next month's rent.

From this, I draw a crucial idea: we lack a clear concept of happiness. When we talk about happiness, it is essential to distinguish between "Being Happy" and "Feeling Happy."

We are fortunate that the Spanish language allows us to make this distinction ("estar feliz" vs "ser feliz"), which is far from minor. In English, for example, the verb "to be happy" is used for both concepts, making the idea quite confusing. Therefore, I insist — let's start with this clarification.

"Feeling happy" is a (momentary) state of mind associated with pleasant emotions like optimism, joy, contentment, peace, excitement, and enthusiasm. It is linked to the production of dopamine and adrenaline.

"Being happy" is a much more ambitious concept. It involves having the courage to build the systems, structures, and habits necessary for a fulfilling life — a life that you enjoy, that holds deep personal meaning, and where you find tangible learning, health, and connection with the people who matter to you. This is a lifelong process associated with the production of serotonin and oxytocin.

I've created a table for you to clarify these differences:

Feeling Happy	Being Happy
Pleasure	Serenity and fulfillment
Short term	Long term
Incites to receive	Incites giving
Can be addictive	Non-addictive
Dopamine	Serotonin
Loneliness	Connection
Hedonistic	**Uncomfortable**
Result	Process
Cannot be all the time	Yes, it can be all the time
Intensity	Consistency

These ideas might seem contradictory. When you are "feeling happy", you experience pleasant emotions, whereas in "being happy", you embrace the full range of emotions, including uncomfortable or painful ones. However, these concepts are complementary, and the key lies in balancing both (whatever that means for you at this moment in your life).

While it is important to have moments of joy and celebration, being happy involves effort and work, which can be painful and uncomfortable.

Saying that happiness consists of moments is incorrect. Happiness is not about fleeting emotional highs. Instead, it refers to the robust and solid construction of a fulfilling life where flourishing is possible.

When we talk about happiness in this book, we are referring to "Being Happy", not "Feeling Happy."

Being happy is achievable through small, intentional, and conscious efforts sustained over time. These efforts help you build positive habits in the different areas of your life as a whole person — spiritual, physical, intellectual, relational, and emotional.

For example, imagine I'm at a close friend's birthday party. The food and music are perfect, I'm having an amazing time, and I'm experiencing a moment of deep connection with people I truly care about.

Suddenly, I receive a call on my phone with the bad news that a close family member has been in an accident and is being taken to the hospital.

Obviously, I am no longer **feeling happy**. My mood of pleasure and joy shifts to worry, pain, anguish, anxiety, fear, and even sadness. Undeniably, I am in a state of alertness, and my body fills with adrenaline and cortisol. But I am still happy, because all the structures I have built in my life for long-term well-being and meaning are still present. I am still in good health, I know and work on my sense of purpose, I live in the present and focus on one task at a time, and my relationships with the people I love and who love me still exist. I also have tools to manage my emotions, and my curiosity for learning new things continues to develop skills that make me feel capable and empowered.

> Building long-term well-being is an investment. In other words, it's an effort that requires giving up immediate rewards (pleasure) for a greater return later (well-being). It also involves experimentation, frustration, uncomfortable emotions, resilience, etc., which might reduce "feeling happy" in the short term to build a greater sense of "being happy" in the medium and long term. In a modern world where immediacy is increasingly popular and essential, investment

> processes can be uncomfortable. That's why, to be happy is for the brave.

A common question I receive is: "As a happiness expert, are you always happy?" The answer is: NO. If I were always happy, I would be denying my human condition.

Simply by living, we all experience the full range of emotions — from the ones we love feeling to the ones we hate feeling. Yes, feeling is part of being human!

So, of course, I'm not always happy. Sometimes I feel sad, sometimes I have worries, I fall into anxiety and start doing things non-stop, I feel fear, I make mistakes, I get angry, and very often I feel tired. I experience all states of mind, just like anyone else — and I believe that contrast makes life interesting. It would be boring to be happy all the time.

Where I am different from many people is that, after 25 years of studying human behavior and working on my self-awareness and personal development, I've learned tools to quickly navigate through difficult moments and capitalize on the learning experience. I've also learned how to experience these moments less frequently.

Building My Happiness: **Identifying When I Am or Feel Happy**

1. Can I distinguish between "Feeling Happy" and "Being Happy"?
2. In what situations do I feel happy?
3. Have I ever experienced a moment when I wasn't happy but still felt that I was happy overall? If yes, describe when.
4. Which of my activities do I think produce dopamine?
5. Which of my activities do I think produce serotonin?

6. Which idea from this section resonated the most with me?
7. What commitment will I make to live better based on my insights from this section?

WHAT IS HAPPINESS?

> "For me, the only satisfying definition of happiness is fulfillment."
> **HELEN KELLER**

Happiness equals Fulfillment. Happiness is feeling fulfilled in your own skin. **"Being happy" is an individual and complex construction** of long-term well-being. It's a process that leads you to consider that, in general terms, your life is good enough to be worth living.

That's why I repeat: **Happiness doesn't just happen, isn't found, isn't achieved, and can't be given to you by anyone else**. Happiness is built. Happiness isn't just about moments. Happiness isn't a single decision; rather, it begins with a decision and continues with a lot of personal work (which requires many more decisions). **To be happy is not a matter of magic or luck, it's a matter of effort and merit.**

Understanding what happiness is represents the first step toward being happy. So now, what is happiness?

Imagine a drawer filled with all sorts of things: mail, keys, tools, rubber bands, food, a book, hand cream, glasses — a little bit of everything. Someone asks you to find something important and valuable in that drawer but doesn't tell you what it is, what it looks like, or what it's for. Do you think it would be easy to find it? Of course not! It would be incredibly difficult because you don't know what you're looking for.

Happiness works in a similar way. Happiness is something we all want to bring into our lives, but very few of us can describe it. That's why happiness seems abstract, distant, confusing, and ambiguous, and why very few of us can materialize it.

Your words create your world. Yes! Your creation of reality is limited by the extent of your vocabulary. If I say a word in Thai, it likely won't mean anything to you because you have no concept to associate it with.

This is why it's essential to define happiness so that you have a clear concept to work from.

Happiness isn't something you seek or find; it's something you build. Talking about finding happiness implies that it already exists and that you've simply lost it — like searching for your keys because you know they're in your house but you can't access them at the moment. But how can you find something that doesn't exist because you haven't built it yet?

My teacher, Dr. Tal Ben-Shahar, describes happiness as: "The well-being of the whole being."

Building My Happiness: **Understanding Happiness**

1. In my own words, what is happiness?
2. What is my greatest insight from reading this section?
3. Do I feel like I'm on the right path to being happy?
4. What does this new vision or perspective on happiness inspire me to do?
5. How can I start building a happier, calmer, and more fulfilling life?

YOU CAN LEARN TO BE HAPPY

Remember: happiness doesn't just happen — you have to build it.

The Science of Happiness offers tools and scientific knowledge that, when applied correctly, increase the likelihood of living a fulfilling and happy life. You don't have to settle for unhappiness; you can take concrete actions and educate yourself in well-being and mental health practices to actively improve your quality of life.

Did you know you can learn to be happy? Happiness is achievable. It starts with a decision and continues with intentional and consistent work. Being happy isn't automatic — it requires your willpower.

Some researchers say we are born with a negativity bias, while others say we aren't. But the reality is that today you can learn to be happy. The Science of Happiness provides scientific information and tools to live better. When you choose to apply them, you will have a high chance of success.

This information matters because you no longer have to resign yourself to being unhappy or spending your days tired, unenthusiastic, and lacking meaning. Now you know something that can be a turning point in your life.

You can take action to stop merely surviving and start building a fulfilling and happy life. You are totally capable!

Studying to understand what happiness is, learning how it works, and working every day to build a fulfilling life — (note, not a perfect one, but perfect in its imperfection) — is the only way I've found to wake up every day with enthusiasm, even on the bad days.

WHAT YOU THINK HAPINESS IS

A ─────────── B

What people tell you happiness is

What it really means to build your happiness

Have you ever taken a course in math, history, biology, cooking, decorating, or nutrition?

Have you ever taken a course on relationships, purpose, presence, parenting, emotions, or happiness?

I tend to believe that humans do not have a natural inclination to be happy and that we are born with a negativity bias. That is, our brains are wired to focus on dangers, crises, and areas for improvement because this is what allowed us to survive as a species for thousands of years.

To simplify: if a caveman focused on enjoying the sunrise, a wildcat could come along and eat him! All of his attention had to be on survival, which meant focusing on dangers, problems, and opportunities to stay safe.

However, today it is important to know that you can learn to be happy and build long-term well-being. In other words, you can unlearn the programs you were born with or grew up with and learn to live with purpose, presence, health, connection, and joy. And for this, there is the Science of Happiness.

> Building My Happiness: **Learning to Be Happy**
>
> 1. Do I think I am someone who naturally feels satisfied? Why?
> 2. Do I usually focus on what needs improvement or on what meets my expectations?
> 3. Can I identify the variables or factors that make it difficult for me to feel fulfilled with my life?
> 4. How do I feel knowing that I can learn to be happy?
> 5. Identify a daily learning experience by answering the question: What did I learn today? This can help you focus on your progress and promote a sense of satisfaction with your day.

THE SCIENCE OF HAPPINESS

> "Science is the great antidote to the poison of enthusiasm and superstition."
> ADAM SMITH

The purpose of scientific studies on happiness is to help people live better lives. Many individuals have dedicated their lives to studying well-being, and it's the sum of their contributions that has given the study of happiness structure, methodology, and scientific recognition today.

Understanding the Science of Happiness is important because if you've spent years wanting to be happy but didn't know how, you can now use these sciences to "play it safe" and start building your happiness.

Did you know that the Science of Happiness and Happiness Studies exist? The term "Science of Happiness" commonly refers to Positive Psychology. Still, many scientific disciplines contribute to human well-being, such as: sociology, anthropology, neuroscience, psychiatry, nutrition, education, medicine, history, economics, philosophy, sports Medicine. Other formal fields of study also contribute to Happiness Studies, including: literature, film, visual Arts, music, photography.

All these areas provide scientific information and tools that increase your chances of building long-term well-being when you decide to apply them.

Stop surviving, choose to be happy, explore these sciences, and work on building habits that make you feel fulfilled in your own skin.

When people refer to the "Science of Happiness," they are usually talking about Positive Psychology because it has made a significant contribution to the field of well-being and human flourishing.

Approximately 25 years ago, Martin Seligman, the father of Positive Psychology, met with Ray Fowler and Mihaly Csikszentmihalyi, experts in the field, in Akumal, a bay in the Riviera Maya, Mexico, where hundreds of turtles come to nest each year. These scientists rented houses and spent several weeks with their families, developing the theoretical framework of what would become Positive Psychology.

As Seligman stated in his 1998 inaugural address at the annual meeting of the American Psychological Association (APA):

"Ideally, psychology should help document what types of families produce healthier children, what types of work environments promote greater satisfaction among employees, and what types of policies result in higher civic engagement."

Thus emerged a new branch of psychology focused on the present and future (not the past) and the "why" and "how" of flourishing. Positive Psychology does not ignore problems but broadens the perspective to focus on strengths and current resources. Most importantly, it offers scientifically proven information and tools. If we choose to apply them, they help us build our best version and live more fully.

In March 2022, in Miami, Florida, the first Happyning event took place. It was organized by me and three other volunteers from the Happiness Studies Academy (HSA) Business Club Event Committee to promote the application of the SPIRE Model in what we call "The Happiness Revolution in Action." The event also facilitated connections among HSA members from over 60 countries. It was a two-day program held just before the World Happiness Summit (WOHASU).

The Universe gave me a wonderful gift during this event. Martin Seligman was the keynote speaker at WOHASU, and his presentation was amazing. Like a true nerd, I bought several of his books and patiently waited in line to have them signed, hoping for a photo with him.

To my surprise, a volunteer asked the first 10 people in line to step into a small meeting room. My excitement skyrocketed when I realized we were about to have a private class session with Martin Seligman! We had the opportunity to ask questions and converse with him for over an hour. Yes, just as you read it!

During the session, I asked him a question that has been crucial for my journey with Valentinamente Feliz:

"What do you think about approaching happiness as a personal responsibility?"

Thankfully, I had the presence of mind to record his response with my phone. Here's a QR code for you to watch the video.

After that incredible experience, the entire trip was worth it. I felt like I was floating, filled with deep gratitude. It was a sign from the Universe telling me: "Keep going. You're on the right path."

At the end of the session, I invited Martin Seligman and his wife, Mandy, to join us for the gala dinner to close the Happyning event. I also mentioned my husband Antonio's interest in providing tools to the 10,000 talented youth in the schools he runs. Seligman gave me his email and asked me to send him the event details.

I left, pinching my arm to remind myself that I wasn't dreaming, and immediately sent him the information.

The Happyning closing dinner began, and as an organizer, alongside my three colleagues, I had to make sure everything was ready. Although we were a small group (just the four HSA team members, a few members of the HSA Alumni Business Club, and around 70 HSA students and alumni), it was a special evening, filled with vibrant and authentic energy. And yes, the Seligmans showed up.

The moment for the graduation ceremony arrived, where we handed out diplomas to those who had completed their Happiness Studies Certification. At the end, Tal Ben-Shahar, my mentor, formally announced the first postgraduate program in Happiness Studies, a collaboration between the Happiness Studies Academy and Centenary University in New Jersey, USA.

It was then that Dr. Martin Seligman gave an emotional speech, recognizing Tal's career and celebrating his commitment to the scientific study of happiness. He honored Tal as the new "Master Teacher of Happiness." The audience, though small, erupted in applause, cheers, and celebration. Antonio, my husband, and I hugged each other with excitement.

Although Positive Psychology is a relatively new field, having been formally established in 1998 with Seligman's declaration, it has been built upon the contributions of several theorists and psychologists over time. Beyond Behaviorism (with Ivan Pavlov, John B. Watson, and B. F. Skinner) and Psychoanalysis (with Sigmund Freud), many pioneers significantly contributed to the rise of Positive Psychology, including:

- William James (1842-1910): Considered one of the fathers of modern psychology, he explored topics like consciousness, emotion, and will.
- Abraham Maslow (1908-1970): Known for his Hierarchy of Needs, he highlighted the importance of self-actualization and human potential. In 1954, he wrote a chapter titled Toward a Positive Psychology.
- Karen Horney (1885-1952): The first scientist to emphasize the importance of focusing on goodness, light, kindness, love, and positivity while acknowledging the shadow side. A pioneer in writing therapy, she underscored the role of culture and social environment in human development.
- Aaron Antonovsky (1923-1994): Known for his Sense of Coherence Theory, which explores how people handle stress and the importance of research questions.
- Ellen Langer (1947): Known for her work on mindfulness and its impact on health, well-being, and aging. She was the first to research the factors that lead to a more fulfilling life.
- Carl Rogers (1902-1987): Founder of client-centered therapy, emphasizing self-acceptance and personal growth.

- Viktor Frankl (1905-1997): Author of Man's Search for Meaning, my favorite book. He developed logotherapy, which focuses on finding meaning and purpose as a driving force in life.
- Erik Erikson (1902-1994): Developed the Theory of Psychosocial Development, exploring the challenges and crises people face at different life stages.
- Philip J. Stone (1936-2006): A social psychology expert known for integrating technology into research and for studying interpersonal dynamics and strengths. He collaborated closely with Gallup.
- Albert Bandura (1925-2021): Known for his Social Learning Theory, highlighting modeling and self-efficacy in shaping human behavior.
- Mihaly Csikszentmihalyi (1934-2021): Famous for his research on flow states — those optimal experiences where people feel fully immersed and engaged in an activity.

This scientific rigor gives greater credibility to the Science of Happiness compared to self-help content. Because these tools are tested and validated, they offer higher chances of success when applied, helping to avoid losing confidence in oneself. One of the ideas that resonates with me most about the distinction between Positive Psychology (focused on health, strengths, and potential) and Traditional Psychology (focused on illness, problems, and crises) is that your focus is a choice.

Yes, you can choose! You can choose to see the glass as half-empty or half-full. The situation doesn't change, but you can change where you focus your attention.

Knowing that science validates your ability to choose where to focus to work on your flourishing is a simple yet **powerful idea**.

Shifting from "I'm broken and missing something" to "This works, and how can I improve it?" is empowering and optimistic.

That's why to **be happy is for the brave**. Always remember:

#BEINGHAPPYISYOURRESPONSIBILITY

Building My Happiness: **Discovering the Science of Happiness**

1. Were you aware of the Science of Happiness? What does your answer tell you?
2. What is working in my life today? What do I have? Remember that even if you are going through a crisis, feel everything is gray, and believe nothing is working right now, there is always something that does work — ALWAYS. Find it!
3. What do I have and do today that, if I didn't have or do, I would miss dearly?
4. What fields of study or knowledge have helped me on my journey of flourishing?
5. How does knowing that there is a science that can help me learn to be happy make me feel?
6. How can the Science of Happiness help me live better?

SPIRE MODEL

The SPIRE Model is a scientific framework for building long-term holistic well-being (happiness). It's important to understand it to have a clear structure that serves as a guide or map to build your happiness.

Personally, when I learned about this model, I felt closer and more empowered to be happy — as if happiness became possible and tangible for me. There was a clear path!

The SPIRE Model tells us that all human beings, regardless of gender, age, culture, interests, education level, or socio-economic status, have five areas or types of well-being in our lives that we can work on to live better. These areas are interconnected and interdependent.

For example, if I choose to walk for 15 minutes with my partner or dog after eating to benefit my physical health, I will also be improving my relational well-being (whether with my partner or pet) and my spiritual well-being by being present. Additionally, I may benefit my intellectual well-being if I choose to listen to an audiobook during the walk.

Of the scientifically grounded models for building well-being, I especially identify with the SPIRE Model created by my teacher, Dr. Tal Ben-Shahar, in collaboration with Maria Sirois and Megan McDonough, because of its simplicity and practicality.

This model consists of five areas, which we will explore in depth in the following sections.

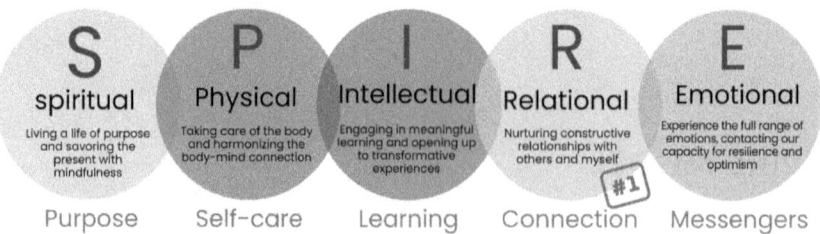

Tal Ben-Shahar, Megan McDonough y María Sirois

HAPPINESS

The SPIRE Model's 12 Principles

1. The **ultimate goal** in life is and should be the well-being of the whole person.
2. Everything is **interconnected**. A purposeful life is a spiritual life.
3. Ordinary experiences are elevated to extraordinary **through mindfulness**.
4. **The mind and body** are connected.
5. A healthy life requires attending to our **nature**.
6. **Curiosity** and openness help us make the most of what life offers.
7. Engaging in meaningful **learning** fulfills our potential as rational beings.
8. **Relationships** are crucial for a fulfilling life.
9. The foundation of healthy relationships with others is a **healthy relationship with myself**.
10. All **emotions are legitimate**, acceptable, and part of being human.
11. Emotions are the result of our **thoughts and actions** and, in turn, inform our thoughts and actions.

Building My Happiness: **Applying the SPIRE Model**

1. Do I feel that having a model or framework as a foundation for building my happiness brings me closer to the possibility of being happy?

2. Can I name an action I took today with the intention of benefiting one area of SPIRE, which, upon reflection, also benefited several others?

3. Which idea from this section resonated the most with me?

SPIRITUAL WELLBEING - PURPOSE AND PRESENCE

Living with clarity about what holds deep meaning for you makes you incredibly antifragile. If you spend most of your time doing what you love and are good at, with a meaningful purpose, you will not merely survive your days — you will feel like life isn't long enough to fulfill all you want to do.

Knowing your core **values** and living in alignment with them fills your days with purpose. Experiencing the present moment with all your senses helps you find meaning in your life, no matter how ordinary it may seem. Helping and serving others can provide you with a sense of purpose and transcendence.

Success is about achieving goals aligned with your purpose. Grounding your dreams and identifying medium- and long-term projects that excite you and guide your efforts helps life feel meaningful. Having a sense of purpose helps you respond rather than react, making your life more strategic. Studies show that people with purpose live 8 to 10 years longer than those who lack it.

Spiritual well-being is connected to your **sense of purpose**, finding **deep meaning** for yourself, and enjoying life in the **present**. The process of defining your purpose is not just mental but also emotional and spiritual. Purpose is a profound resource worth taking the time to cultivate, as it helps you endure and contribute to the world.

Purpose is the direction in life, the intention that always lies ahead of you and guides your goals. It helps prevent a life of aimlessness, disinterest, and confusion. Today, more than ever, we need to cultivate a sense of purpose, magnify the reasons we have to live, and counteract the rising rates of mental health issues such as depression and suicide.

A purpose and a goal are different concepts. A goal can be achieved, while a purpose is ongoing. It acts as a compass, guiding how you allocate your limited resources, like time, money, effort, and patience, in ways that benefit your long-term well-being and happiness.

For example, having the purpose of being an involved and loving parent can never truly be "completed," but it will guide your decisions until the day you or your child is no longer present.

My purpose is to inspire more people daily to take responsibility for building their happiness and work toward it.

This idea makes my heart race and motivates me to make the necessary efforts to continue sharing information and tools that help others live better. It gives meaning to failure, exhaustion, the investment of time and money, mistakes, uncomfortable emotions, and more.

As I said, my purpose is unlikely to ever be "finished." However, it serves as a compass that guides my decisions while strengthening my identity as an expert in the Science of Happiness and as an imperfect human being who enjoys life's journey (with all it entails) and loves sharing it with others.

Purpose is a deeply personal and internal journey, and no one can define what it looks like for you. A sense of purpose is not an objective truth but a subjective experience, and as such, **it can change**. In fact, as you naturally mature, it should evolve.

Having a purpose also reduces impulsiveness, encouraging people to think in medium- and long-term perspectives instead of focusing solely on immediate gratification. When we think of spirituality, we often associate it with religion. However, having a spiritual life does not require adhering to any religion.

Many people find spirituality in religious frameworks, but many others, including those who don't believe in God, lead deeply spiritual lives. They have clarity about what brings meaning to their lives and live with a sense of purpose in the here and now.

The relationship between your identity and purpose is direct and bidirectional. Your self-concept influences your purpose, and at the same time, your purpose shapes your identity through the decisions you make and the person you become.

Five Ways to Build Purpose in Life
1. Maximize your strengths: Use your talents and skills.
2. Discover what brings meaning to your life: Focus on what matters most to you.
3. Clearly identify your core values.
4. Live in the present: Be here and now.
5. Dream and plan: Set clear projects and imagine big possibilities.

Building My Happiness: **Exploring My Spiritual Well-Being**

1. Why do I want to keep living?

2. Do I practice any religion? If yes, has it helped me live better?

3. Write an initial draft of your life purpose in less than five lines. You can adjust the wording over time until it feels perfectly aligned.

4. Do I generally feel like I live in the present?

STRENGTHS

"You don't choose your passions; they choose you."
TAL BEN-SHAHAR

Recognizing the things in which you naturally excel and those that ignite your passion will help you unlock your true potential. Focusing on enhancing your strengths rather than correcting your weaknesses will lead you to excellence and allow you to enjoy what you do far more.

Can you imagine waking up every day to do things you love and at which you perform extraordinarily well? It is possible!

Defining a clear purpose aligned with your preferences and talents — what Marcus Buckingham called performance strengths and passion strengths, respectively — makes it possible for you to spend most of your time engaged in activities that you not only do well but also love doing. This brings even more meaning to your life.

That point where your skills and passions intersect is what Sir Ken Robinson calls "your element." Identifying your element is incredibly useful, as it allows you to direct your efforts with alignment and maximize your long-term spiritual well-being.

Ken Robinson believed that anyone who dedicates their time to activities where their interests and talents converge is practically guaranteed success and happiness — and I agree.

When we talk about **performance strengths**, we refer to activities where you naturally excel, even if you don't particularly enjoy them. These are tasks where your talents and natural abilities shine through, things that you find easy to learn, or areas where you have already experienced success and earned awards, recognition, certifications, or diplomas.

When we talk about **passion strengths**, we refer to those activities you love doing, even if your performance isn't necessarily outstanding. These are the tasks that, just thinking about them, fill you with energy and vitality. They connect with your most authentic essence, activities you deeply enjoy, moments when you feel truly alive, or tasks you would continue doing even if you weren't paid for them.

By finding the intersections between these two types of strengths — performance strengths and passion strengths — you will discover your zone of **maximum potential**. These are the areas where you can make your greatest contribution to the world.

When someone chooses to spend their days in this zone, a virtuous cycle is created. They feel excited and energized to engage in those tasks, and because their natural talents are at play, it is very likely that they will achieve positive results. This positive feedback from their environment will further motivate them to continue pursuing those activities.

The following diagram illustrates what Marcus Buckingham calls the zone of maximum potential or contribution.

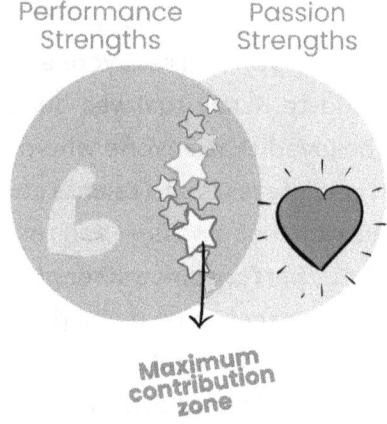

Research shows that the most effective way to achieve excellence is by focusing on your strengths. The old approach of concentrating solely on your weaknesses can, at best, lead to a mediocre or moderately satisfactory result. It cannot lead to your best version, because your natural abilities and talents are not found there.

While we shouldn't ignore our areas for improvement, we also shouldn't let them rob us of the opportunity to shine. **The suggestion is to leverage your strengths and manage your weaknesses**.

HAPPINESS

If you have the fortune to choose how you spend your time, ideally you should do so based on this approach. If, for any reason, you can't, then try to identify both the tasks you enjoy the most and those you enjoy the least in your current work, and aim to spend most of your time on activities that generate the most energy and joy for you.

Sometimes, even thinking about making adjustments to your professional or work activities can cause anxiety and fear. In those moments, remember three things:

1. You can't expect a different life by doing the same thing.
2. Everything passes.
3. To be happy is for the brave.

It's those short-term uncomfortable decisions made in pursuit of medium- and long-term benefits that will help you live better, making you feel like the owner and creator of your life. A life that, while it may never be perfect, will certainly be worth living in its perfect imperfection.

Building My Happiness: **Connecting with My Strengths in Action**

1. Write down 15 activities that have brought you significant satisfaction in your life, whether because you enjoyed the process of doing them or because you were pleased with the result.
2. Choose 5 activities and identify the personal characteristics that contributed to your success in each.
3. What patterns do you notice?

Recognizing my strengths

Identify the strengths you consider you have from the list

Presence	Growth	Sacrifice	Confidence
Achievement	Orientation	Imagination	Security
Wisdom	Appreciation	Individuality	Self-sufficiency
Passion	Balance	Integrity	Serenity
Innovation	Persuasion	Kindness	Service
Adventurous	Command Ability	Sociable	Spontaneity
Authenticity	Strives for excellence	Strategy	Beauty
Harmony	Curiosity	Autonomy	Inclusion
Execution	Leadership	Openness	Influence
Disciplin	Mastery	Creativity	Intuition
Control	Objectivity	Forgiveness	Loyalty
Community	Positivity	Humility	Ethical
Choice	Love	Kindness	Nobility
Belief	Vitality	Prudence	Patience
Awareness	Congruence	Self-regulation	Acceptance
Joy	Integrity	Humor	Gratitude
Knowledge	Originality	Frankness	Spirituality
Fun	Diversity	Negotiation	Takes Risks
Assertiveness	Service	Strategy	Adaptability
Honesty	Self-love	Self-esteem	Courage
Organization	Order	Focus	Change Agent
Openness	Compassion	Clarity	Analytical Ability
Good Storyteller	Structure	Communication	Good Listener
Resilient	Tenacity	Consistency	Flexibility
Respect	Tolerance	Proactive	Generosity
Responsibility	Transformation	Empathy	Faith
Valor	Independence	Freedom	Initiative
Grace	Efficiency	Persistence	Gentleness
Friendship	Justice	Boldness	Learning

Ask three people who know you well which strengths from the list they believe you possess. What differences do you notice between the strengths you perceive in yourself and those that your loved ones see in you? What do these differences tell you? What are your insights or discoveries?

If you want to explore further, you can take the VIA Institute Strengths Test or the Clifton Strengths Assessment by Gallup — both are available for free on their websites.

Finding my Element or Maximum Contribution Zone

Identifying Your Talents or Performance Strengths

- What am I good at?
- Where do my natural talents and abilities lie? What is much easier for me to learn?
- In which areas of my life have I experienced success so far (awards, certifications, recognitions, etc.)?

Identifying Your Passions or Passion Strengths

- What excites me to do?
- What fills me with energy?
- What do I love to do?
- What connects with my essence?
- When do I feel most alive?
- What tasks would I do even if I weren't paid for them?

Finding the Intersections

Look for activities or areas that appear on both lists to identify your element or zone of maximum potential, as defined by Sir Ken Robinson or Marcus Buckingham.

Applying My Strengths to My Activities

- Which of my strengths align with the activities I currently do in my life?
- What does my previous answer tell me? What does it invite me to do?
- How could I spend more time today on activities that combine my talents and passions?
- Which weaknesses have I focused on that have limited my potential to shine?
- How can I manage my weaknesses to allocate most of my resources to enhancing my strengths?

MEANING

> "The meaning of life is to give life meaning."
> VIKTOR FRANKL

"Meaning" is a word that I personally find difficult to conceptualize. It feels abstract, like everything and nothing at the same time… it doesn't serve me much. But when I ask myself: "What is important to me?", I can immediately respond and identify meaning.

Having clarity about what is truly important to you allows you to make decisions in line with your essence and to build purpose. How can you prioritize what brings you meaning if you don't know what is important to you?

Diversity among human beings is a constant. For some, purpose is found in family, others in work, a project, a charitable cause, a sporting activity, religion, and so on. And that's okay — diversity enriches us. The simple act of clearly identifying what is important to you is a significant step toward your happiness because it enables you to make decisions aligned with those values.

Another way to increase your purpose is to find deeper meaning in your current work. During my Happiness Studies Certification, while reviewing the research by Amy Wrzesniewski, a professor at Yale University, I learned that the same activity can be viewed as a job, a career, or a calling, depending on the perspective and intention with which you approach it.

- **Job/Employment:** An activity you perform to receive a paycheck or achieve an immediate result.
- **Career:** An activity you see as a means to an end, performed to achieve a promotion, gain more recognition, or obtain a benefit in the medium term.
- **Calling/Vocation:** An activity you pursue to bring meaning and transcendence to your life and the lives of others.

For example, if I view recording a podcast simply as a way to produce content and stick to a schedule, it's a job. If I see the same activity as a way to gain more exposure so I can get hired for more speaking engagements and consulting projects, it's a career. But in reality, for me, it is a way to massively share what I feel fortunate to know, with the hope that it inspires listeners to work hard to build a fulfilling life for and by themselves. That makes it a personal calling. All three perspectives are valid. However, the last one fills your effort with meaning and justifies any fatigue, additional time, or financial investment required to carry out that task. Living your activities as callings makes you highly antifragile.

Once again, it's not an all-or-nothing situation. Viewing all your activities as callings would be exhausting while seeing them all as jobs would be superficial and boring. Therefore, balance is key.

Identify those activities that are callings for you or transform the activities where you spend most of your time into callings. At the same time, recognize the activities you perform as jobs or careers and live them with intention.

On another note, it's proven that service, helping others, and solidarity provide purpose to our lives because they offer a sense of transcendence. Some authors even suggest that success should not be measured by the money you make but by the number of lives you improve during your lifetime.

On a personal level, I prefer a holistic measure of success that goes beyond the obvious, as illustrated in the following diagram:

WHAT SUCCESS LOOK LIKE?

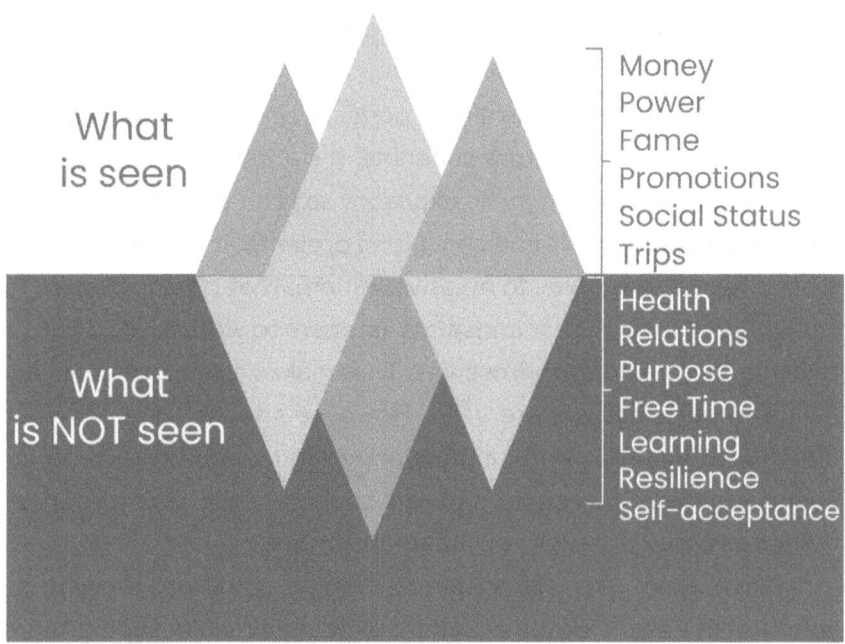

HAPPINESS

If you want to work on your purpose and are looking for something disruptive, I invite you to explore the "No Barriers" foundation (an organization that helps people achieve dreams through team work and shared humanity) on Youtube and reflect on what is truly important to you at this moment in time and space.

Building My Happiness: **Finding My Meanings**

1. What is the most important thing to me? Be honest.
2. What do I think "should" be the most important thing to me? Why?
3. What do my previous answers tell me?
4. Did you include yourself in your answers?
5. Is there alignment between the time, energy, and resources I dedicate to what is most important to me? Why?
6. What do I commit to doing based on my answers?

Building My Happiness: **Finding Meaning in My Activities**

7. What activity do I spend the most time on?
8. Do I experience it as a job, career, or calling?
9. How can I reframe it to turn it into a "calling" that excites me?
10. What other important activities do I perform, and how do I experience them?
11. Would I like to reframe these and change the intention with which I do them?

VALUES

What are the most important values to you? Do you share these values with your partner or your work culture? What values do you want to be part of your children's and family's identity? Have you ever asked yourself these questions?

Connecting with your values is like having a compass to guide your life. Having clarity on your core values — the ones you want to govern your life — allows you to walk with serenity and integrity, strengthening your antifragility.

If you identify which values are important to you, consider yourself fortunate because you have a GPS (navigation system), a list of criteria or filters that will serve as a reference when making important or difficult decisions. You will be able to make peace with the idea of letting go of opportunities, people, situations, beliefs, or ideas that no longer add value to your life. This will create space for those aligned with your current vision of the world and your values, bringing you closer to your best self.

Will it be easy? No. That's why to be happy is for the brave.

For example, if your core values are "A" and "R," when you receive a job opportunity, you can ask yourself if it aligns with "A" and "R" and if it will contribute to your life purpose and overall happiness. If the answer is yes, it's worth considering.

HAPPINESS

Building My Happiness: **Identifying My Core Values**

Exercise to choose your top 2 values in 2 steps:

1 Identify the values that are important to you from this list and mark them.

Acceptance	Joy	Kindness	Love
Authenticity	Self-discipline	Autonomy	Well-being
Goodness	Compassion	Commitment	Trust
Consideration	Creativity	Dedication	Determination
Discipline	Empathy	Enthusiasm	Equity
Balance	Hope	Excellence	Loyalty
Flexibility	Generosity	Gratitude	Honesty
Honor	Humility	Inclusion	Independence
Integrity	Justice	Leadership	Loyalty
Freedom	Open-mindedness	Optimism	Patience
Peace	Perseverance	Positivity	Prudence
Punctuality	Purity	Righteousness	Reflection
Respect	Responsibility	Wisdom	Sacrifice
Satisfaction	Serenity	Service	Simplicity
Sincerity	Solidarity	Self-improvement	Temperance
Tenacity	Tolerance	Transparency	Courage
Courage	Truth	Versatility	Willpower
Gratitude	Honesty	Innovation	Inspiration
Motivation	Security	Sensitivity	Solidarity
Wisdom	Serenity	Service	Sobriety
Sophistication	Solidarity	Self-improvement	Sustainability
Transparency	Union	Unity	Appreciation
Courage	Truthfulness	Virtue	Vision

2 Compare the values you selected in pairs and choose the one that resonates with you the most until you are left with the 2 values that resonate the most with you. These 2 values will serve as your daily compass. For example, if you marked "solidarity" and "gratitude," which one would you choose if you had to pick just one? Continue eliminating until you are left with only 2 values.

3 What are those 2 values?

4. Do I feel that I share values with my partner and/or the work culture I am part of?
5. What are the values I want to be part of my children's and family's identity?
6. Do I consider people's values when deciding whether or not to connect with them?
7. What environments, groups, or spaces that promote my core values can I identify?
8. What do these findings invite me to reflect upon or do?

PRESENCE

Focusing all your attention elevates ordinary experiences to extraordinary ones. Meditation is simply directing your focus to one thing, such as your breath or a sound, and returning to that focus each time you get distracted. This practice can significantly improve your mental and emotional state. Being present helps you escape the weight of the past and the anxiety of the future.

Living in presence allows you to derive maximum satisfaction from your human experience. Recognize your ability to elevate the ordinary to the extraordinary simply by giving your full attention, all your senses, to an object, stimulus, task, emotion, or thing. Meditation is focusing on one thing at a time. Meditation is the practice of a thousand new beginnings, and its value lies in noticing when your attention drifts away from the object of focus and intentionally bringing it back. For me, the power of meditation lies in its ability to create emotional and mental states parallel to your reality, regardless of what that reality may be, since **your brain doesn't distin-**

guish between reality and imagination. Connect with your breath. It is said that what a bath is for the body, meditation is for the mind.

Living inundated by stimuli and in a culture that promotes multitasking (doing multiple tasks simultaneously) prevents you from focusing your attention on the present. We often find ourselves thinking about the past or the future, without realizing that the only thing we truly have is the present moment.

I once heard something from Eckhart Tolle that blew my mind: "If the past torments you, return to the present, because the past can only survive in your absence, not in your presence. Presence only happens in the present." Therefore, the importance of living in the here and now lies in the levels of satisfaction and well-being you experience.

I am glad that every day the practice of mindfulness is becoming more popular, providing people with tools and resources to develop this skill. It has even been shown to be effective in treating many disorders, such as anxiety, panic, obsessive-compulsive disorder, and others.

When we hear about meditation, we often think of the famous idea of "clearing the mind" or imagine a monk standing on his head at dawn. The reality is that meditation is (as simple or complex as) focusing your attention on one thing, whether it's your breath, counting, music, bodily sensations, movement, etc. The practice of meditation, like most things that are worthwhile, requires a process that builds new connections in your brain and strengthens the skill, making it more familiar and easier each day.

One idea that was liberating for me regarding meditation was learning, through the words of my teacher Tal Ben-Shahar, that there is no such thing as good or bad meditation – it simply is.

All human beings can meditate if we decide to commit the will and discipline it requires. There are many technological applications (i.e., Headspace or Calm), expert profiles on social media, or free content on YouTube that can support you in developing the habit of meditation.

Both meditation and the practice of mindfulness are tools to achieve presence. The two differences I find are:

1. Mindfulness (informal meditation) requires engaging all your senses with an external stimulus, while meditation (formal) involves turning off some of the senses to focus on an internal stimulus.
2. Meditation requires formality in the sense that it needs a specific moment, while the practice of...

Mindfulness, on the other hand, can be practiced informally. Simply experience whatever you are doing with presence, giving your mind enough time to rest (approximately 3 minutes): walk, shower, enjoy your meals, observe nature, shop, etc. Both practices build presence.

The four rules of meditation are:

1. Rest your mind on one thing.
2. Bring your attention back. It is the practice of a thousand new beginnings.
3. Breathe slowly, gently, and deeply.
4. Avoid judgment. There are no good or bad practices.

Remember, the goal is to have no goal beyond a deep and honest experience. The practice will contribute to your mental hygiene.

Personally, I find that the greatest value of meditation lies in reaching states of calm and creativity quickly and easily because the mind and body do not distinguish between reality and imagination. During meditation, you can visualize yourself doing something unimaginable to your conscious mind (like skydiving, making peace with your worst enemy, traveling to magical places, or even a sexual fantasy with your favorite celebrity) and experience the emotions and physical reactions exactly as if you had lived it in the real world.

For me, meditation **is a way to connect with the wisdom of my soul from a conscious state**. I even believe that this is where the power of prayer lies.

Sometimes we overthink life so much that we forget to actually live it. Personally, connecting with my breath has been a very powerful tool to enter states of presence and calm. That is, I close my eyes and observe the characteristics of my breath: temperature, speed, rhythm, scent, texture, the parts of my body that move, etc.

I use this practice as a preventive tool to prepare my mood or environment (for example, before a workshop, session, conference, negotiation, or complex experience) and as a reactive tool to handle a crisis (for example, finding patience when I've run out, drawing on reserves of vitality when I'm exhausted, taking those precious seconds to think clearly in the middle of an unexpected event, or being creative).

Here are three exercises to build presence:

1. Imagine a square. Visualize tracing the left vertical side as you inhale, the top horizontal side as you hold your breath, the right vertical side as you exhale, and the bottom horizontal side as you hold your breath out. If you have asthma, avoid this exercise.
2. Hold a flower in your right hand and a candle in your left hand. If you don't have them available, just imagine it. Close your eyes, inhale as you smell the delicious fragrance of the flower, and exhale as you blow on the candle flame. Repeat this at least 10 times, or until you reach the state of calm you seek.
3. Take a cookie, a piece of fruit, or any food you enjoy. Close your eyes and savor each bite, paying attention to the taste, the texture, and the parts of your mouth that are stimulated by the contact with the food. Do this slowly, without rushing.

I invite you to breathe, live in the present, and deeply connect with your human experience.

HAPPINESS

Building My Happiness: **Living in Presence**

1. Do I often find myself thinking about the past or the future?
2. Have I tried meditating before? If you answered yes to the previous question: How many times? Have I tried building a habit of meditating (at least 4 times per week)?
3. If you have tried: Did I succeed? What contributed to the result?
4. Observe: Look around and take in your surroundings, becoming aware of the present moment. Record it. How do I feel?
5. Feel: Approach your current emotion with curiosity and give yourself permission to feel it, whatever it may be. Record it. How do I feel?
6. Breathe: Inhale while feeling the temperature of the air and extend your exhalation. Notice which parts of your body move. Record it. How do I feel in one word?
7. Accept: Acknowledge who you are at this moment, trust in your progress and evolution, and celebrate yourself. Record it.
8. How do I feel?
9. Absorb: Slow down and absorb what you see, hear, taste, and touch during a moment of your day. Record it.
10. How do I feel in one word?
11. What do I take away from my answers?
12. What commitment do I make to myself?

DREAMS

> "The future belongs to those who believe in the beauty of their dreams."
> ELEANOR ROOSEVELT

Having dreams and medium- to long-term projects gives direction to your daily decisions. Dreams are realized through a combination of ambition, imagination, talent, and effort. Having dreams is a sign of self-love and well-being because it implies a sense of worthiness, value, and belonging.

Dreams give you direction, and while you can always change your mind, dreams keep you on track. It is important that your dreams strike a balance in difficulty. They should be engaging and challenging, but also feel achievable. And most importantly, **you are NEVER late!**

To achieve your dreams, four things are important:

1. Opportunities need to find you prepared.
2. Have a detailed plan that specifies resources, timelines, responsibilities, risks, Plan B, Plan C, and Plan D.
3. Focus on the step in front of you, because often, looking at the whole staircase can be frustrating or overwhelming.
4. Feel passion for your dream.

It's common for your dreams to scare you, to the point of paralyzing you. But remember, there is nothing grand about shrinking yourself to avoid overshadowing others or to avoid having to justify failure. Make mistakes often and quickly, following the advice of my mentor, Tal Ben-Shahar. Fight for your dreams (with everything that implies), reinvent yourself, enjoy the process, inspire... and in doing so, you'll give those around you permission to fight for their dreams, too.

> Building My Happiness: **Getting Closer to Dreaming**
>
> 1. Do I allow myself to dream? If yes, what are my dreams? If no, why is that?
> 2. What can I do about it?
> 3. What can I do to be more prepared to build my dreams?
> 4. Do I have a plan to build my dreams? If not, how can I create one? If I had to focus on the next step without looking at the staircase (other than for inspiration).
> 5. What would that step be? What commitment do I make to myself?

PHYSICAL WELLBEING - HEALTH

> "Sometimes your joy is the source of your smile, but sometimes your smile can be the source of your joy."
> THICH NAHT HANH

The mind and body are connected; your thoughts and emotions impact your physical health. What the voice keeps silent, the body screams. Remember: your longevity is determined 75% by the decisions you make. **Your body is a tool, not an ornament**. Care for your body for yourself and by yourself; you owe nothing to anyone.

Physical well-being involves building health and self-care habits to keep your body functioning optimally. We promote physiological and psychological well-being when we exercise, eat healthily, foster physical contact, learn to breathe properly, and give our body time to rest and recover.

We rarely stop to think that our body is our primary vehicle and armor, and it has been with us since our first day on this planet and will remain with us until our last breath. Beyond specific physical details tied to beauty stereotypes and cultural expectations, your body is your unconditional companion on this journey through life. Regardless of your hair type, eye color, weight or build, height, or whether you have the curves and muscles you desire, I invite you to be conscious of your relationship with your body. From a place of gratitude (not criticism), reestablish your bond with it. This will allow you to communicate with it more effectively, understand it, and give it what it needs at any moment to continue providing you with excellent service.

Have you ever had a physical discomfort and couldn't think of anything else? Have you heard the phrase, "You don't value your health until you lose it"? The reality is that we need to feel healthy to function in daily life. Often, we take our health for granted, assuming we will always be healthy, without giving importance to building healthy habits that keep our bodies vital and functioning properly.

It used to be thought that the mind and body were separate. We would go to psychiatrists and psychologists to address issues from the neck up, and to doctors, physiotherapists, and nutritionists to address issues from the neck down. Today, there is ample scientific evidence confirming the opposite: **the mind and body are intimately connected**, making integrated treatment advisable when addressing afflictions.

For recommendations, it's always good to use the best examples possible, which is why I want to talk about the "Blue Zones" — communities where people are the healthiest and live the longest. In the research conducted by Dan Buettner and a National Geographic team, they sought to answer a question: What can we learn from them?

The answer consists of these three aspects:

1. How long you live is determined 25% by your genes and early experiences (ages 0 to 7) and 75% by the decisions you make and your environment.
2. Deep, meaningful relationships give a sense of belonging and determine your health and well-being.
3. Proximity to nature also promotes well-being.
4. Once again, remember your power to choose to build a better life. The small choices you make regarding nutrition, exercise, physical contact, sleep habits, breathing, and stress management will determine the quality of service your body can provide.

Building My Happiness: **Exploring My Self-Care**

1. Do I care for my body because I love it and am grateful for it, or because I dislike it and want to change it?
2. What thoughts arise from knowing that 75% of my longevity depends on my decisions?
3. Have I experienced the connection between my body and mind?
4. If you answered yes, In what way?
5. Have I ever gotten sick after experiencing a moment of adversity?
6. What commitment do I make to myself after these reflections?

NUTRITION AND MICROBIOTA

> "Nutrition has a profound impact on virtually all major causes of disease in Western societies."
> DAVID SERVAN-SCHREIBER

Healthy nutrition significantly contributes to the optimal functioning of your body. Food isn't just what you eat, but also what you see, hear, feel, smell, and the people and energies around you. You can always make small adjustments to your daily diet to improve your nutrition.

Recently, the gut has been considered the true brain of the body, as it was discovered that the gut microbiota regulates the brain's biochemical activity and, therefore, your mood.

Your body is the engine, and food is the fuel. The quality of your body's performance will largely depend on the quality of the fuel you give it.

Although I am not a nutritionist, and the intention of this book is not to delve technically into the field of nutrition or spark debate about different perspectives or practices, I do want to draw your attention to the importance of healthy nutrition and remind you of your power to consciously choose what you put into your body.

Every metabolism is different, so not all foods affect everyone the same way. Therefore, I wouldn't suggest a specific diet, but I would like to recommend some general aspects you can consider on your path to physical well-being, should you wish to improve your nutrition. These include:

- Diversity of foods = diversity of nutrients.
- Avoid foods high in saturated fats.
- Reduce your intake of sugars, especially refined ones.
- Aim to eat fresh or preservative-free foods.

- Stop eating when you're 80% full, not when you're stuffed.
- Eat slowly and savor the flavors and textures of your food.

Of course, if you have a specific medical condition, an eating disorder, or want a detailed dietary plan, consult a nutrition specialist.

Additionally, recent research has shed light on the microbiota — the world of microorganisms living in your body, in perfect balance with each other and with you. The gut microbiota is the most numerous group and, therefore, the most important for health. In terms of numbers, the microorganisms in your gut outnumber your own cells, making you a "superorganism."

The gut microbiota is essential because there **is a close relationship between happiness and the bacteria in our body**. The gut communicates constantly with the brain. These tiny organisms, which we can call our little pets, as Nazareth Castellanos says, act on the nervous, endocrine, and immune systems and regulate your brain's biochemical activity, thus influencing your mood. For example, did you know that 90% of serotonin, commonly called the body's happiness hormone, is produced in the gut, while only 10% is produced in the brain?

Most microbes are our friends; however, if they grow beyond their normal range, they can invade your system and cause inflammation, depression, and other illnesses. You can help balance your microbiota by taking care of your diet, following some of the previously mentioned suggestions, such as avoiding ultra-processed and industrialized foods, refined sugars, and saturated fats, as these can confuse gut receptors.

Remember, your body is an interconnected system, so healthy social interactions also influence microbial health, as do the air you breathe and your quality of rest. Physical exercise also positively impacts microbial diversity and increases the abundance of beneficial bacteria.

Finally, remember that food is not just what you eat but also what you hear, see, feel, smell, and experience. Therefore, I invite you to be mindful of the ideas you use to nourish your brain, the sounds and words you choose for your ears, the energy and people you want to surround yourself with, considering how they make you feel. Be aware of the social media profiles, TV programs, and images you consume, especially when you wake up and before going to bed. Consider the places you frequent.

Just like you can choose between eating a fresh apple or a chocolate-covered churro, you can choose to wake up to news and tragedies or to gratitude for life's blessings. You choose to nourish your life with things that will benefit you in the long term or things that won't. Whatever your choice is, please make it consciously! Be responsible.

Building My Happiness: **Exploring My Nutrition**

1. Do I believe my body has optimal vitality and functioning for my age?
2. Do I consider that my current nutrition contributes to my overall well-being?
3. Which of the general recommendations in this section resonated with me and would I like to start incorporating into my life?
4. How am I going to support my gut microbiota?
5. What is the most meaningful takeaway from this section?

EXERCISE

> "Exercising isn't like taking antidepressants; rather, not exercising is like taking a depressant. Your body is made to move."
> TAL BEN-SHAHAR

There is a wealth of scientific research demonstrating the benefits of exercise. It reduces the risk of diabetes, heart disease, inflammation, and more. It improves memory, creativity, concentration, self-esteem, libido, the immune system, and longevity, among many other aspects.

Our human nature calls for movement. Historically, we covered long distances and carried various materials to survive. Our bodies were not designed for a sedentary lifestyle, for spending entire days sitting in boardrooms, or for having food delivered at the push of a button. I invite you to redefine movement and engage in physical activity as self-care, with gratitude, rather than judgment or criticism.

According to the WHO, 31% of adults worldwide do not engage in the recommended physical activity. In adults, physical inactivity is a major risk factor for cardiovascular diseases, type 2 diabetes, dementia, and certain types of cancer, such as colon and breast cancer.

Making exercise a habit can be a challenge for some people, especially if their family or school life did not promote its importance during childhood. This challenge becomes even harder when the goal of exercise is distorted by focusing on unattainable beauty standards, instead of using it as a way to promote health for all body types.

Integrating movement into your daily activities is a good starting point. You can carry your grocery bags, park farther from entrances to walk more, adopt a pet for companionship on walks, or take the stairs instead of the elevator. Alternatively, you can choose to practice a sport or start an exercise routine you enjoy, making it easier to turn into a habit without facing overwhelming resistance each time you plan to move, which might otherwise lead to giving up and losing confidence in yourself. Remember, before solidifying a new habit, people try an average of seven times.

The reality is that you don't need to spend a lot of time exercising; 20 minutes a day is enough. You can explore the well-known HIIT (High-Intensity Interval Training), which involves raising and lowering your heart rate. In a short period of intense activity, you can achieve the full range of exercise benefits your body needs.

Professor Michael Babyak from Duke University concluded that **30 minutes of aerobic exercise, three times a week, has the same effect as the best antidepressant** on the market for treating depression. Even six months after the study, people who exercised were four times more likely to remain psychologically healthy compared to those who took antidepressants.

As Tal says, exercise isn't like taking antidepressants; not exercising is like taking depressants because your body is designed to move. Leading a sedentary life frustrates your body's natural need for physical activity. And since the mind and body are connected, it also frustrates a natural need of your mind.

I would never suggest abandoning antidepressant treatment in favor of exercise alone. Only the patient, in consultation with a specialist, can determine the best course of action. However, there is extensive scientific evidence suggesting physical activity as an effective psychological and psychiatric intervention for treating depression, dysthymia (prolonged mild depression), attention deficit, anxiety, etc.

Exercising frequently enhances happiness (long-term well-being), and happiness promotes movement, creating a virtuous circle. Is it easy? No. That's why to be happy is for the brave.

Building My Happiness: **Exploring My Relationship with Exercise**

1. In my childhood, did I experience a family or school culture oriented toward exercise?
2. Can I recognize the value of exercise for my well-being?
3. What is the main reason I do (or would do) exercise?
4. What does my previous answer reveal?
5. What type of activity or sport appeals to me?
6. When I do exercise, do I do it because I love myself or because I hate myself?
7. How could I redefine movement and become physically active?
8. What commitment do I make to myself regarding exercise?

SLEEP

Sleep is a fundamental pillar for the health and overall well-being of any person, and its importance cannot be overstated. A healthy adult under normal conditions should sleep between 8 and 10 hours per day. During sleep, the body works to repair and rejuvenate tissues, synthesize proteins, and release growth hormones crucial for development and recovery. Additionally, sleep is essential for the optimal functioning of the immune system, helping fight illnesses and keeping us healthy. On the other hand, lack of sleep can weaken the immune system, making us more susceptible to infections and chronic diseases.

From a cognitive perspective, sleep plays a crucial role in memory processing and learning. During deep sleep and REM (Rapid Eye Movement) stages, the brain processes and consolidates information acquired during the day, facilitating long-term memory and improving problem-solving skills and creativity. Without adequate sleep, our cognitive abilities significantly decline, affecting concentration, judgment, and decision-making.

Sleep also profoundly impacts our emotional and mental health. Proper rest is associated with a better mood, greater resilience, better stress management, and a lower predisposition to emotional disorders like depression and anxiety. Lack of sleep can lead to mood swings, irritability, and increased emotional reactivity. Additionally, quality sleep improves emotional regulation, allowing us to better manage difficult situations and maintain a positive outlook.

In the realm of physical well-being, adequate sleep is linked to better performance and increased energy. Athletes and physically active individuals rely on sleep for muscle recovery and preparation for future activities. Sleep also regulates hormones that control appetite and metabolism.

Therefore, prioritizing sleep and establishing healthy sleep habits are essential actions to maintain holistic balance across the five types of well-being in the SPIRE model, not just physical well-being. Here is a chart with some tips that may help you improve your sleep quality:

HAPPINESS

Building My Happiness: **Sleeping Better**

1. Do I sleep between 8 and 10 hours daily?
2. Describe your bedtime routine. What can I improve?
3. What are my beliefs about sleep? Where do they come from?
4. What do I commit to doing to improve my sleep quality based on my findings?

TOUCH

> "A hug is a perfect way to show love."
> RICHELLE E. GOODRICH

Consensual physical contact requires connecting with another human being (regardless of the type of relationship), which takes time. However, in this modern world of immediacy and digital connection (instead of face-to-face connection), it seems increasingly difficult to give ourselves the time to truly connect. And if we add the trauma effects left by the pandemic, things become even more challenging.

Hugs lasting more than 20 seconds or kisses of at least 6 seconds are a wonderful source of oxytocin, the connection hormone. In fact, John and Julie Gottman claim that couples who kiss before going to work live 4 years longer.

The scientifically documented benefits of consensual physical contact are irrefutable:

- Relieves pain by releasing opioids that increase circulation in soft tissue.
- Strengthens the immune system.
- Significantly promotes cognitive and motor development in children.
- Helps with anxiety, depression, eating disorders, and overall mood improvement.
- Promotes trust and, therefore, improves communication.
- Heals feelings of loneliness, isolation, fear, and anger due to the production of oxytocin.
- Relaxes muscles, relieves tension, and reduces blood pressure and heart rate.
- Brings you to the present moment and focuses your attention.

Some of my favorite studies are those related to the importance of physical contact, whether through hugs, massages, or sexual intimacy. Ultimately, they all agree on the significance of physical contact for human well-being, as it is a fundamental requirement of our nature.

One event that triggered various studies in this area happened in a U.S. hospital. It was observed that neonates (randomly assigned) in one of two intensive care units gained weight and strengthened much faster than babies in the other unit. A doctor was intrigued by this phenomenon, but when reviewing the care records, everything seemed to follow protocol in both units. He decided to observe at night and discovered what was happening. To his surprise, he witnessed a nurse in the unit holding each baby, gently massaging them for a few minutes, and rocking them to sleep. The nurse thought she would be fired for breaking protocol, but the opposite happened. Her brave, loving intuition led to these practices being adopted in that hospital and many others, prompting future research on physical contact in both animals and humans.

Virginia Satir, a renowned author, social worker, and psychotherapist, said that we need 4 hugs a day to survive, 8 for maintenance, and 12 to grow. The reality is that feeling supported and comforted when times are tough makes a big difference. Simply rubbing a body part after bumping it shows the power of physical contact. Therefore, I encourage you to seek out that comfortable and comforting physical contact frequently, in a way that is intentional and culturally appropriate.

According to Martin Seligman in his book What You Can Change and What You Can't, increasing physical contact helps treat 70% to 95% of sexual dysfunctions, and spending more time hugging and cuddling increases levels of pleasure.

I'm a big fan of sleeping and respect others' sleep as something sacred. I used to feel conflicted about waking my children up every morning for school. I thought, What can I do to ease the discomfort of waking up? I decided to wake them 10 minutes earlier than usual to give them a brief full-body massage, scratch their backs and heads, and start telling them how beautiful and strong every part of their body is. I still believe I made the right choice. Although they don't jump out of bed with joy, the tantrums and tears have stopped. My hope is that they value starting their day with harmony and love, know they deserve affection simply for being themselves, recognize the difference between well-intentioned and harmful physical contact, and are able to express affection through touch because they understand its value.

Building My Happiness: **Exploring My Physical Contac**t

1. What form of physical contact do I experience the most?
2. How are hugs perceived in my culture/family?
3. Do I habitually give hugs?
4. Would I have someone to hug every day if I wanted to?
5. How do I feel when someone hugs me? Is it pleasant, uncomfortable, familiar, strange, etc.? Why?
6. Have I explored any massage therapy? If yes, what was my experience like?
7. How could I increase my "hug vitamin"?

STRESS IS YOUR ALLY, IF...

> "The best bridge between despair and hope is a good night's sleep."
> E. JOSEPH COSSMAN

Stress is the body's automatic reaction to risk, putting you on alert and preparing you to defend yourself. Thanks to this, the human species has survived for thousands of years. The three stress defense mechanisms are: fight, flight, and appease. The reality is that stress strengthens you by helping you build greater resilience in the face of life's adversities. What actually makes you sick and leads to burnout is experiencing long periods of intense stress without recovery periods.

Avoid burnout by following a formal recovery plan that includes short breaks during the day, conscious breathing for one minute, at least three times a day, sleeping for at least 8 hours, frequent visits to your "sanctuaries" (relaxing activities), shared experiences with your "vitamin people," and paying attention to your posture.

Do you feel stressed? Have you heard that stress kills? Have you gotten used to living with stress? Sometimes the fast pace of modern life, which promotes a culture of immediacy, integrates stress into your existence until it becomes chronic. Despite being considered one of the most significant health issues of the century, stress itself isn't bad. Stress is your body's defense mechanism against situations your brain identifies as dangerous or harmful.

Psychologist Kelly McGonigal, in her TED Talk "How to Make Stress Your Friend," shared a study conducted on 30,000 people in the United States. Participants were asked two questions:

1. Rate your stress level over the past year on a scale from 1 to 10.

2. Do you believe stress is bad for you?

They tracked participants' health for 8 years and found that those who believed stress was harmful experienced far worse health outcomes and higher mortality rates than those who had high levels of stress but did not believe it was harmful. In conclusion, **changing your perspective on stress can save your life**.

Stress works similarly to when you lift weights at the gym and keep going despite muscle burn. If you don't stop, you'll eventually get injured. Was the exercise bad? Of course not! It was the excess of exercise and not listening to your body that caused harm. The same applies to stress. Therefore, **the key to avoiding burnout is recovery**.

The 12 Stages of Burnout:
- A strong need to prove yourself.
- Working harder and harder to achieve it.
- Frequently postponing your own needs.
- Experiencing conflict and blaming the situation or others.
- Shifting your values to focus more on work.
- Denying problems caused by work-related stress.
- Neglecting your family and social life.
- Your behavior changes, irritating your loved ones.
- Feeling depersonalized, no longer yourself.
- Feeling empty and confused, possibly turning to substance abuse.
- Feeling depressed, lost, and completely exhausted.
- Complete burnout, leading to physical and mental collapse.

Currently, burnout is a common experience for many people, especially women. It's crucial to acknowledge **that it's okay not to be okay**. This acknowledgment is the first step toward self-care and recovery through intentional and conscious efforts that can gradually help you feel like yourself again.

At first, taking time for yourself may feel uncomfortable or cause anxiety because you're only tackling half your tasks. But remember, you're doing the best you can — and stop! If you're not well, nothing external (work, home, car, family, garden, tasks, reports, results, etc.) will be either. The good news is that each day is a new opportunity to try again.

High performance requires rest. The best ideas, strategies, and products didn't come from exhausted, overwhelmed minds. Believing that hard work leads to success implies that if you're not successful, you haven't worked hard enough — which means you'll never allow yourself to rest.

In Western countries, we often have a culture that condemns rest. A European friend living in the U.S. shared how difficult it is to justify taking vacations longer than a week with her American colleagues. Meanwhile, her European family thinks working half of August is absurd. Which of these views do you relate to? What if you reconsidered your concept of success and started viewing a balanced life as successful?

Suggestions for Burnout:
- Reflect on your achievements. Slowing down doesn't mean you haven't accomplished anything.
- Remember that not everything on your to-do list needs to be done in one day.
- Do something that requires no mental or physical effort, like watching TV, enjoying nature, listening to jokes, or classical music.
- Listen to your mind. If it's asking for rest, you likely need it. Take a nap.
- Take it one day at a time.

- Spend time outdoors and engage in physical activity to reset your mind.
- Do something just for pleasure or self-care, like painting, getting a massage, a manicure, or dancing.
- Reach out to your support network or a mental health specialist.

Furthermore, I invite you to check your posture at this moment and reflect on the positions you frequently adopt. It's proven that not only does your brain influence your posture, but your posture also sends information to your brain about your mood, prompting it to release the corresponding body chemistry.

For instance, if you wake up feeling low and then stand up, stretch your spine, raise your arms, and look up to the sky, your posture will send signals to your brain of joy, fulfillment, or gratitude, triggering the chemicals associated with these emotions. Conversely, if you spend most of your day with your head down, looking at your phone, and your back hunched—even if you started the day in a good mood—your posture will convey signals of defeat, failure, heaviness, or fatigue, leading to body chemistry that matches these emotions.

Here are three of my favorite exercises for daily recovery:

1. Set an alarm for a mid-morning self-care break: 1 minute of conscious breathing. 5 minutes of physical stretching. 10 minutes of tidying and organizing. 15 minutes of reading.
2. Create what my teacher calls "Islands of Sanity": Dedicate 15 minutes to an activity that requires minimal physical or mental effort, but fully captures your attention so you feel like time "stopped" or "flew by," such as doing a puzzle, listening to music mindfully, coloring mandalas, dancing, or watching a TV series.
3. Spend time with your "Vitamin People": Marian Rojas Estapé defines these individuals as those with whom you can always be yourself, have a great time, and feel so secure that they help you release oxytocin and reduce cortisol levels.

Building My Happiness: **Exploring My Relationship with Stress and Rest**

1. Do I feel stressed? If yes, rate your stress level from 1 to 10.
2. Have I gotten used to living with stress, or do I suffer from chronic stress?
3. What is causing me stress?
4. Where in my body do I feel stress?
5. Before reading this section, did I consider stress to be good or bad for me?

6. How do I feel knowing that stress has protected and strengthened me over the years?
7. Do I feel or have I felt burned out? If so, up to which stage of burnout did I reach?
8. Do I believe my worth depends on my work success?
9. Do I allow myself to rest regularly?
10. Do I feel guilty when I rest, or do I believe I deserve it?
11. How can I integrate balance into my concept of success?
12. Do I have insomnia issues?
13. Do I have a nightly routine to prepare for sleep?
14. Am I able to listen to my body and recognize signs of fatigue before getting sick and being forced to stop? If not, why do I think that is?
15. Am I aware of my posture throughout the day?
16. How can I incorporate a realistic recovery plan to enjoy the benefits of stress without paying a high price or feeling burned out?
17. What commitment do I make to myself?

BREATHING

Breathing is a powerful, accessible, and free tool, undervalued in modern life. The correct way to breathe is through the nose; conscious breathing is the foundation for bodily recovery, and maintaining carbon dioxide levels within a proper range is crucial for optimal body function.

According to Anders Olsson, teacher, author, and founder of the concept of "Conscious Breathing," some documented benefits are:

- Lowers heart rate.
- Reduces sweating.
- Relieves stress by lowering cortisol levels in the body.
- Helps manage anxiety and uncomfortable emotions.
- Promotes better concentration.

Since breathing is an automatic bodily function, everyone breathes (hence we are alive), but not everyone breathes correctly. This can significantly affect your body's function and, therefore, the vitality you enjoy, so I considered it important to bring it to your attention.

The three pillars of good breathing are:

1. Breathing Awareness: Intentionally observe your breath.
2. Breathing Knowledge: Understand the proper way to breathe.
3. **Applying That Knowledge: Put this understanding into action.**

The proper way to breathe is through the nose for inhalation and exhalation. This prepares the air as it passes through your respiratory tract to reach your lungs. When air enters through the nose, it gets cleaned, humidified, and temperature-regulated. When you exhale through the nose, it prepares the nasal passage for the next inhalation.

We often think oxygen is good and carbon dioxide is bad, and we need more oxygen to improve our breathing. In reality, we need more carbon dioxide. When carbon dioxide levels rise in the body, adrenaline levels decrease. In other words, prolonged exhalations can promote calm and help us better handle adverse and stressful situations. It's worth mentioning that while excess carbon dioxide in the body is toxic, a deficiency is also problematic.

Although this text doesn't aim to dive into the technicalities of breathing, it intends to offer useful information about a free, always-available tool that requires no equipment and has been with you since your first breath on this planet. With a little willpower, you can choose to build well-being by trying any of the following recommendations:

- Engage in physical activity with your mouth closed.
- Follow a breathing routine that includes 3 to 5 breaths with elongated exhalations every 3 or 4 hours.
- Use adhesive tape on your mouth while sleeping to promote deep sleep, relaxation, and recovery (there are special tapes available online that do not harm the skin).
- Inhale as you bring food to your mouth to aid digestion.
- Meditate while walking outdoors (to absorb more oxygen), taking twice as many steps during exhalation as you do during inhalation.
- When you feel stressed, focus on your nose and lungs, and take twice as long to exhale as you do to inhale while imagining an anchor sinking deeper and deeper.

Here's a 3-step breathing exercise I learned in a class with Dr. Olsson, recommended to ensure you are breathing properly:

1. Place your hands on the sides of your waist just below the ribs.
2. Inhale until your hands move.
3. Exhale slowly.

HAPPINESS

Other breathing exercises you can try are:
- **Conscious Breathing:** Let go of everything you're doing and simply observe your breath. How does the air feel as it enters and leaves your body? What parts of your body move? What happens in your nose, chest, and throat? What is the temperature of the air when it enters and when it leaves? Did anything change?
- **Mantra Breathing:** As you inhale, repeat a phrase of your choice, such as "I trust life," and as you exhale, repeat another phrase like "I am safe and well here and now."

Building My Happiness: **Exploring My Breathing**

1. Have I observed my breathing?
2. Do I breathe through my nose or my mouth most of the time?
3. How do I feel when I try to make my exhalations longer than my inhalations?
4. What is my biggest insight after reading this section?
5. What commitment do I make to myself?

LONGEVITY

It doesn't matter how many years you live, but how you live them. Longevity is about having a long and quality life. The environment in which you develop is key to facilitating decisions and habits that support a healthy lifestyle and well-being.

It is inevitable to mention Dan Buettner when talking about longevity. As I shared, Dan is the author of The Blue Zones: The Secrets for Living Longer and the creator of the Netflix series Live to 100. He has studied regions of the world with the highest density of people over 100 years old to understand their habits and decipher how their lifestyles have led them to live so long. In March 2024, I had the fortune of meeting and interviewing Dan at the Festival de las Ideas in Puebla, Mexico — a three-day event filled with enriching talks that nourished my mind and soul like no other. Dan is a simple, cheerful, and incredibly generous man who genuinely cares about helping people create environments that allow them to live better. He believes that if you build a proper ecosystem, you can live well without even trying.

Dan shares a model of 9 key elements identified in his research, grouped into the following four categories:

1. Move naturally.
2. Have the right perspective.
3. Eat wisely.
4. Connect.

During the same event, I also had the opportunity to meet Dr. David Sinclair and listen to his lecture. He is a professor of genetics at Harvard Medical School and co-director of the Paul F. Glenn Center for Biology of Aging Research. He leads epigenetic research focused on improving human organ functionality through rejuvenation. During his talk, he shared the remarkable achievement of restoring vision in blind rats by rejuvenating their eye tissues.

Dr. Sinclair argues that aging is a disease because it naturally deteriorates bodily functions, but it is not classified as such because it is so common and affects everyone. For years, he has worked on rejuvenating his father's body, who, despite having a biological age of over 80, reports a cellular age and lifestyle similar to that of a 60-year-old.

Epigenetic technology (beyond genetics) involves changing gene expression without altering DNA sequences, focusing on how genes are turned on or off, affecting cell function and health.

Some of Dr. Sinclair's recommendations include:

- Avoid eating three meals a day.
- Move and stretch.
- Build muscle.
- Put your body in adversity mode.
- Sleep well.
- Eat plants grown under stress (natural conditions).
- Avoid sugars and refined grains.
- Follow a Mediterranean diet.
- Skip snacks and drink something warm instead.
- Measure, change, and optimize.
- Change your lifestyle gradually.

Hearing Dr. Sinclair gave me mixed emotions. On the one hand, I was amazed by human capabilities to understand and improve bodily functions, and I was hopeful for the relief this might offer to people with various ailments and pains. But on the other hand, I felt fear and anxiety about the implications of these advances for humanity. I worry they may intensify society's obsession with staying young and undervaluing age, experience, and the wisdom that comes with time.

I have friends in their 30s who already feel they're late in using Botox, and many people take pride in being told they "look young for their age," as if aging naturally were something bad. In reality, I consider it both an achievement and a privilege. You are alive!

I think of the story of Benjamin Button, where the protagonist is born old and gradually becomes younger until he turns into a baby and dies. I wonder: What if we could rejuvenate with a supplement? What side effects would there be? What would be the purpose of living 150 years or more? Are humans playing God by defying natural processes? Could the planet sustain a growing population that doubled its time on Earth?

I sincerely desire a healthy, functional body for as long as I live, but I do not wish to live beyond 100 years. Being consistent with the idea that adversity, in all its forms — including aging — is an opportunity to learn, expand, and evolve, I'm not sure it's wise to deprive ourselves of the adversity of aging.

Moreover, if we consider life as a journey, I can confidently say that 100 "well-traveled" years are more than enough. In life, less is not always more, nor is more necessarily more. Here, the way you live truly matters.

Let's avoid nostalgia for life and obsession with youth. Let's live intensely, building a life we love, focusing on quality, not quantity.

To conclude, I share a phrase from Homer's The Odyssey that encapsulates my thoughts and feelings on longevity: "Hector, don't insist; the gods envy us because we are mortal and all our moments are unique and unrepeatable."

Building My Happiness: **Reflecting on Life**

1. How many years would I like to live? For what purpose?
2. Do I think I place too much importance or value on youth?
3. What are my thoughts on aging? Does it scare me?

4. Do I believe my habits so far will allow me to live beyond 100 years with good quality of life? Why?
5. Do I feel that the environment I live in supports a healthy lifestyle? Why?
6. What adjustments can I make today to improve my environment?
7. Do I consider aging to be a disease? Why?
8. What costs would I be willing to pay to rejuvenate by 20 years? Why?
9. What emotions arise when I ask myself the previous question? What beliefs might be influencing my perception of age, youth, and aging?
10. Do I feel nostalgic when thinking about the possibility of living fewer than 100 years? Why?
11. Which of Dr. Sinclair's recommendations resonated with me, and what am I committed to implementing?

INTELLECTUAL WELLBEING - LEARNING

> "Learning is a treasure that will follow its owner everywhere."
> **CHINESE PROVERB**

A positive environment is necessary to enhance learning. Have the courage to allow yourself to be bad at something new and explore: a curious and open attitude is key to building intellectual well-being. To commit to learning what is meaningful to you, you need to know yourself and understand your strengths. Dedicate time to activities where you experience a state of flow. The most significant learning is experiential – learning should be fun, so improvise, embrace mistakes and failure as part of the process. Fail often and fail fast.

Intellectual well-being is linked to learning, satisfying that innate curiosity of humans and the desire to understand the phenomena happening around them. To maximize your intellectual well-being and your learning about the world and yourself, you must stay open to possibilities and allow yourself to be surprised.

Learning a new idea creates new neural connections, and you should know that if you don't revisit that idea within the next three days, those connections will disappear. Therefore, be consistent, question, investigate, repeat, reflect, and explore those ideas that feel like nuggets of wisdom, those "Aha!" moments or "Eureka!" insights.

The value of learning lies in acquiring tools to face life more effectively and harmoniously. In other words, when we know more, we feel more capable and empowered to handle the various situations we encounter.

Building My Happiness: **Feeling Like an Expert**

1. What am I an expert in, or what do I consider myself really good at? (If you struggle to find an answer, think about what your best friend would say about you.)
2. In what areas of my life have I received recognition, compliments, awards, or medals?
3. What subjects or activities do I feel I have mastered?

STATE OF FLOW

> "The best moments in our lives are not the passive, receptive, relaxed moments... The best moments usually occur when a person's body or mind is stretched to its limits in a voluntary effort to accomplish something difficult and worthwhile."
> MIHALY CSIKSZENTMIHALYI

The state of gratification we experience when we are fully engaged in what we are doing is called the State of Flow. In this psychological state, you are completely immersed and focused on an activity; distractions fade away, and your brain enters a rhythm and harmony so profound that you lose track of time and even yourself.

As Mihaly Csikszentmihalyi shares in his book Flow, which explores the psychology behind optimal experiences, it is not what happens to you that determines your reality, but how you make sense of it and integrate it into your life experience.

When the challenges of a task match your abilities, you experience a sense of flow and control, which creates a feeling of deep satisfaction and enjoyment. This state of flow is highly beneficial for increasing productivity and emotional well-being.

When the challenge exceeds your abilities, you will experience frustration. When your abilities exceed the challenge, you will experience boredom. However, when you engage in an activity that has just the right level of difficulty for your skills, you will maintain complete interest for a significant period, and your mind will feel at rest.

STATE OF FLOW OR FLUIDITY

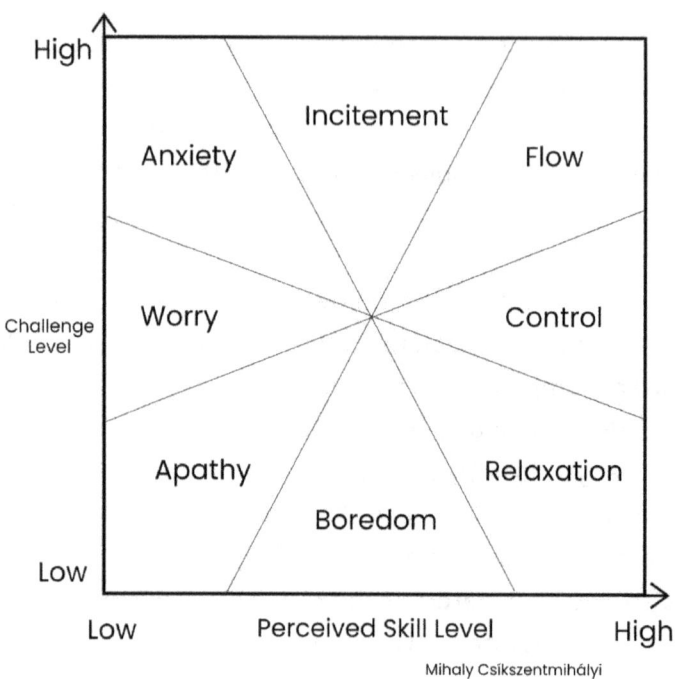

Mihaly Csikszentmihályi

It is important to promote states of flow to optimize our intellectual well-being. Therefore, once again, self-observation and self-awareness are very important, as we all have different skills and interests. When does time stop for you? At what moment do you find yourself doing exactly what you want and not wishing for the situation to end? Is it painting, making love, playing tennis, solving puzzles, speaking in front of a group, climbing mountains, or listening empathetically to someone else's problems?

Building My Happiness: Exploring My States of Flow

1. What activity do I perform when time flies by without me noticing?
2. What frustrates me?
3. Can I identify the skills I lack from my previous response that trigger the anger of feeling incapable of facing that specific challenge?
4. How can I develop those skills?
5. What bores me?
6. What are the skills I possess in excess that make the challenge insignificant and cause me to lose interest?
7. How can I increase the difficulty of the activity to maintain my interest in it?
8. What represents a challenge for me but one that I know I can overcome?

IMPROVISATION

Remember that you can think of yourself as imperfect or perfect in your imperfection. **Have fun making mistakes!** To do this, I recommend trying improvisation because it will help you lose your fear of error. "Make mistakes often" is one of the six principles of the technique, according to Patricia Ryan Madson (the other five are: say yes, pay attention, appreciate, take care, and have fun).

Improvisation is a technique that involves the spontaneous and unscripted creation of music, dialogue, performance, or any form of expression. The key is to create and respond in the moment without detailed pre-planning, which requires and develops skills such as creativity, spontaneity, active listening, and adaptability.

An important aspect of building intellectual well-being is losing the fear of making mistakes. In my experience, improvisation began when my friend Tania Rincón invited me to a workshop, and I accepted without knowing what it was about. This was because I have a personal policy of often stepping out of my comfort zone and giving myself the chance to be surprised by life, as a way to strengthen my courage muscle.

For me, attending improvisation sessions for several months was about fully embracing myself, laughing, connecting, and experiencing, in two hours, an analogy for life in its entirety. **To learn to improvise is to learn to live.**

Building My Happiness: **Exploring My Improvisation**

1. When did I feel the need to respond without being prepared?
2. What emotions did that experience generate in me?
3. What was the result of my actions?
4. Would I like to attend an improvisation workshop? Why?

ASK AND PLAY

> "Questions create our reality by sending us on a journey. They determine the course of the journey we are about to begin, What we will pay attention to, and the kind of life we will have."
> TAL BEN-SHAHAR

Your understanding of the world was shaped by your ability to ask questions and inquire. The importance of questions doesn't lie in the answers but in the next questions they generate.

Questions determine where you place your attention and what paths you follow to explain the world and life.

Asking a question in any subject can open a world of new possibilities for you. Even in scientific research, the questions determine the findings and conclusions. And in life, it is questions that create reality by defining it.

Learning arises from questions. One day, Isaac Newton asked why apples fall from trees and embarked on a journey that led him to discover the Law of Gravity. We often underestimate the power of questions.

We underestimate the power of questions, and I believe it's because of our absurd need to control everything, to have immediate certainty, to feel secure and wise, to focus on the outcome… when in reality, I think learning to navigate the uncertainty of questions allows you to embark on an uncertain process full of possibilities to be pleasantly surprised and to learn.

For example, What would happen if I considered myself brave starting today? What would happen if I chose to pursue a different career path? What would happen if I started questioning and redefining my values today? How would it feel to set healthy boundaries? What would happen if I let go of relationships I maintain despite knowing they are toxic? Why do I feel what I feel when I feel it? Who am I today, really?

You can learn not only about the world but also about yourself by giving yourself the time to ask questions—simple or complex, direct or abstract and philosophical. There are no rules. And remember, how you frame the question will determine the journey. Asking "What am I feeling?" is not the same as asking "Why do I feel depressed?" Asking your child, "How was your day at school?" differs from "What did you like most and least about your day?" versus "Did you have a bad day at school, or why do you look like that?" Each question prompts different conversations and processes.

Curiosity enriches life and helps you live not only happier but also longer and healthier. So, pay attention to how you ask yourself and others questions.

On the other hand, if you're someone who overanalyzes your life and the world constantly, I invite you to pause, rest, and focus on the quality of your questions, not the quantity. Psychologist Sonja Lyubomirsky and her colleagues studied "The Costs and Benefits of Writing, Talking, and Thinking About Life's Triumphs and Defeats." They found that while talking and writing about painful or negative situations had positive effects (because it involved analyzing them), ruminating on them had negative effects, as it was like reliving them. In contrast, thinking about positive situations brought positive effects because it was like experiencing them again, while writing or talking about them did not, since it involved analyzing them.

Therefore, when you want to share your positive experiences, it is recommended to do so in a descriptive, anecdotal manner, without overanalyzing.

What if you play with questions or questioning? Play promotes the most meaningful learning because it is experiential. I am convinced that one of the best ways to learn is through play because you live the knowledge, which makes it memorable. Play also generates pleasant emotions like joy, fun, and connection, making you want to continue and learn more—it becomes a motivator in itself.

Play isn't just for children; it promotes learning and brings physical, mental, and emotional benefits to all humans. Here are some of them:

- Cognitive Development: Helps with problem-solving, creativity, and decision-making.
- Social Skills: Encourages cooperation, communication, empathy, negotiation, teamwork, and relationship-building.
- Emotional Development: Allows for expressing, exploring, and managing emotions.
- Promotes Physical Activity.
- Reduces Stress and Anxiety.
- Improves Concentration and Attention.
- Boosts Self-Esteem and Self-Confidence.
- Fun and Entertainment.
- Social Connection.

In the 1950s, Benjamin Bloom developed an educational framework that is still widely used today to organize learning objectives into six levels. The highest level is "Create," which is experiential because, at this stage, the individual has already mastered the information, processed it, evaluated it, and is capable of creating, planning, proposing, designing, etc., based on that knowledge.

Play is an experiential form of learning because, to engage in it, you must have already passed through the first five levels of the taxonomy, integrating the information into your life.

Here is a graphic of Bloom's Taxonomy for reference:

BLOOM'S TAXONOMY

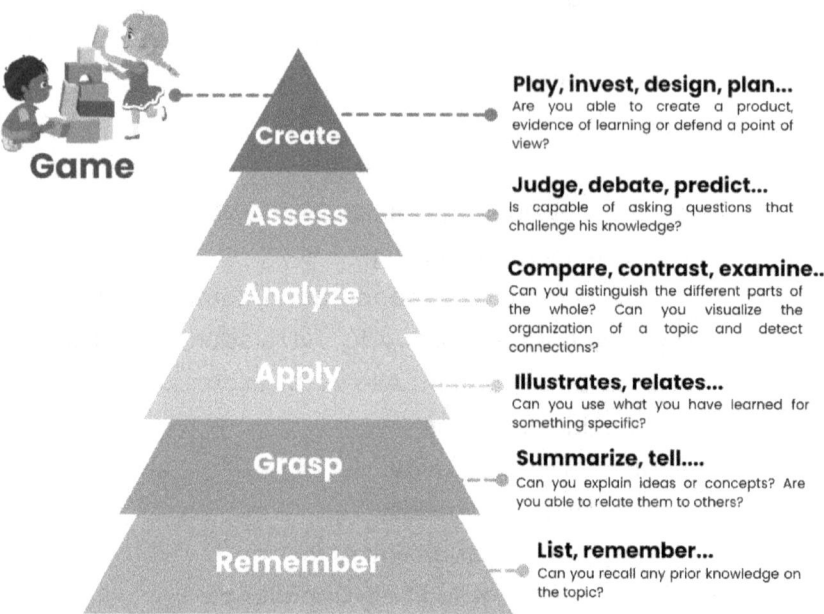

There are many learning theories, and what I take away as a common thread is the **value of action**. This conscious and intentional action (whether reading, observing, speaking, or teaching), when combined with passion, makes magical things happen. Personally, I have experienced this with Valentinamente Feliz.

While human behavior is what fascinates me the most in the world, when I began formally studying the Science of Happiness in 2019 at the Happiness Studies Academy (HSA) and launched Valentinamente Feliz on social media in 2021, during the pandemic, with the intention of sharing what I feel fortunate to know so that people could have scientific tools to better navigate the pandemic, the magic happened.

Since then, a positive, upward spiral of wanting to learn more and more to share and teach has taken hold, allowing me to contribute to a better country and world. Teaching requires mastering the subject, so the more you engage and delve into sharing what you're passionate about, the more you learn.

Here is an image showing various actions and the percentage of learning retention associated with each:

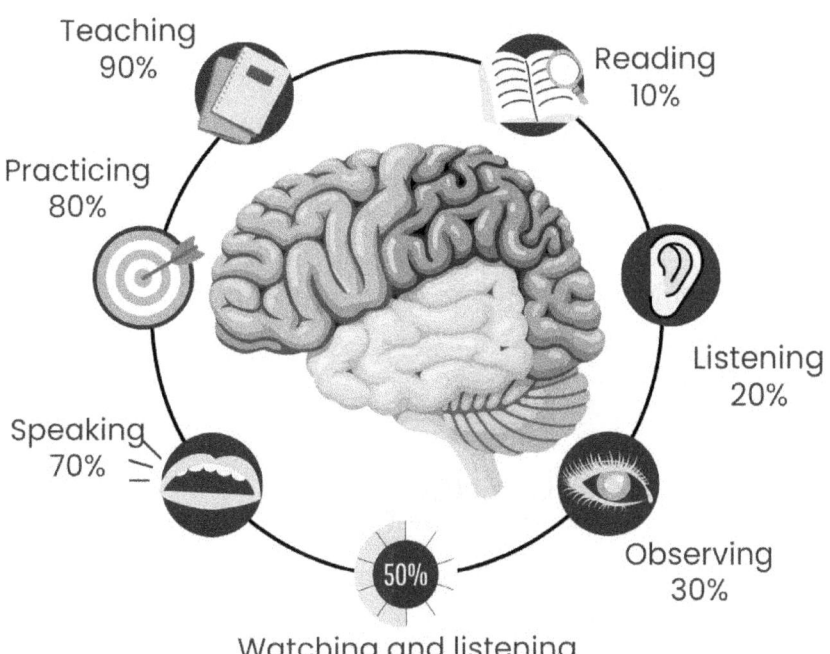

HOW OUR BRAIN LEARNS

- Teaching 90%
- Reading 10%
- Practicing 80%
- Listening 20%
- Speaking 70%
- Observing 30%
- Watching and listening 50%

Building My Happiness: **Questioning While Having Fun**

1. Have I observed what kind of questions I often ask?
2. Do most of my questions come with good intentions, or do they carry a hint of anger?
3. What outcomes do these questions bring me?
4. What areas of my life and the world do I often question?
5. What have I assumed as true and never questioned?
6. What crazy question would I like to ask myself today? You might feel fear just thinking about it... and that's okay. For example: What if I sell everything and move to another country?
7. Do I allow myself to play? Why or why not?
8. What types of games attract me the most?
9. What do I learn when I play?
10. What emotions often arise while I'm playing?

MULTIPLE INTELLIGENCES

> "Intelligence consists not only of knowledge, but also of the skill to apply that knowledge in practice."
> ARISTOTLE

Intelligence is not a generic characteristic; instead, there are many forms of intelligence. Today, when we describe someone as highly intelligent, it should be followed by the question: "Intelligent in what?" Recognizing this is essential to understanding that intelligence is not black and white but contains many nuances. This understanding helps you focus your efforts to build intellectual well-being more effectively. In other words, the question is not "Are you intelligent?" but rather "In what are you intelligent?" — opening up a world of possibilities.

In 1983, Howard Gardner, an American psychologist and educator, developed the "Theory of Multiple Intelligences," a framework for understanding the mind. For him, intelligence is not a single set of specific capabilities that can be measured uniformly. Instead, it is a network of autonomous yet interconnected sets. Therefore, each individual has a unique combination of these intelligences. There are nine types, and each develops depending on three factors:

- Biological factor
- Personal life factor
- Cultural and historical factors

Intelligence	Description	Related activities and professions
Linguistic	Effective use of words, whether in speech or writing.	Reading, writing, public speaking, and language interpretation.
Logical-Mathematical	Solving logical and mathematical problems.	Abstract reasoning, numerical analysis, and solving complex problems.
Visual-Spatial	Creating and interpreting images. Perceiving and manipulating space and objects within it. 3D thinking.	Navigation, spatial orientation, graphic design, and solving visual puzzles.
Bodily-Kinesthetic	Controlling body movements and using them in a coordinated manner.	Athletes, dancers, and surgeons.
Musical	Appreciating, composing, and understanding music.	Empathy, interpersonal communication, and building strong relationships.

Interpersonal	Understanding and effectively relating to other people.	Empathy, interpersonal communication, and building strong relationships.
Intrapersonal	Self-awareness and understanding oneself.	Awareness of one's own feelings, goals, and motivations, enabling autonomous decision-making and understanding one's behavior.
Naturalistic	Observing and understanding nature, its patterns, and systems. Recognizing and classifying different species.	Nature and animal enthusiasts, biologists, adventurers, and outdoor athletes.
Existential	Exploring the purpose of life and the unknown; interest in philosophical debates and big existential questions.	Philosophers, writers, spiritual leaders, speakers, lecturers, and meditation guides.

Although this theory has been controversial within the scientific community, sparking debate and criticism, I find it accurate and important because it offers an inclusive perspective on human differences and suggests that intelligence cannot be measured in a one-size-fits-all way.

If you want to take the free test (it will take you less than 10 minutes), you can go to IDR Labs website (idrlabs.com).

Here, I'm sharing an image with my results. I loved seeing myself reflected in them, and as I always say, these kinds of exercises don't define who you are; they simply help you become aware and recognize certain information.

HAPPINESS

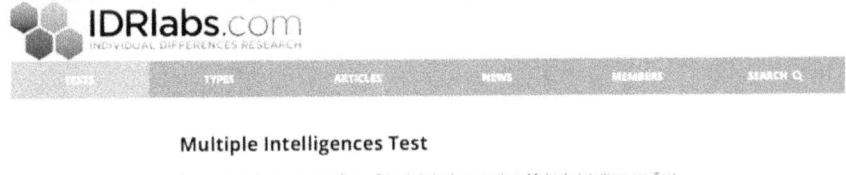

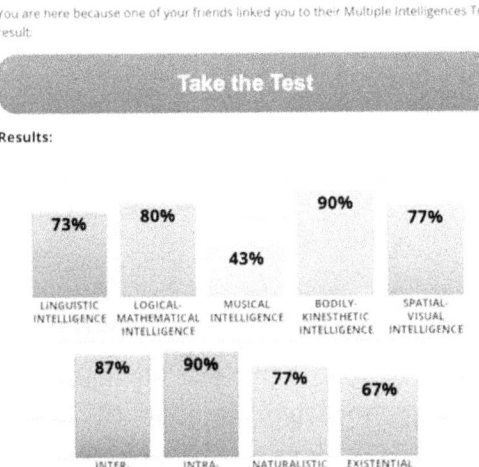

Building My Happiness: **Discovering My True Intelligence**

1. Have I considered myself intelligent throughout my life? Why?
2. Did Gardner's Theory of Multiple Intelligences help change my perspective on my intelligence? Why?
3. In which of the nine types of intelligence do I consider myself strong?
4. How have I applied those intelligences from my previous answer throughout my life?
5. Which type of intelligence would I like to develop or strengthen, and how would I do it?

6 What does this information invite me to do as father, friend, boss, colleague, etc.?

RELATIONAL WELLBEING - CONNECTION

> "It gives more strength to feel loved than to feel strong."
> GOETHE

Your relationship with yourself is the foundation of your relationships with others. The quality of your meaningful relationships impacts your well-being more than you might think; in fact, it is the #1 predictor of happiness. Your relationships are part of your identity, and **quality matters more than quantity** for relationship well-being. If a relationship robs you of your peace, it costs you too much.

Yes, you can learn how to be an effective and loving parent, and you can also improve your relationship with your partner. **Are you aware of how often you trade authenticity for connection?** Good relationships benefit mental and physical health. Having an unconditional relationship (partner, family member, or friend) can add 8 to 10 years to your life. All relationships, no matter how good, have flaws and rough patches. Remember, excessive expectations doom relationships to failure. Investing in your relationships is a great decision for happiness – choose those relationships that bring out your best self and deserve your time, resources, and energy.

Being family alone is not enough for someone to be on your list of important relationships. Any healthy relationship requires effective communication, solidarity, and kindness. The four behaviors that damage or doom relationships are criticism, contempt, defensiveness, and stonewalling. Responding actively and constructively when someone shares good news influences your relationship more than how you respond when they share bad news.

Well-being in **relationships** reflects that we are social beings. It focuses on the bond we build with ourselves and others.

Your brain perceives meeting others' expectations as a matter of life or death. Humans are physiologically wired to connect because belonging to a tribe or community has ensured our survival for hundreds of thousands of years. That's why pleasing others to belong has become a survival mechanism, even if it means betraying yourself.

Repeating this behavior throughout your life may have strengthened your disconnection from your true self, leading you to feel an emptiness and uncertainty about who you really are today. We will explore this further in the next chapter, "Freedom," when we discuss authenticity and personal liberation. **Remember, strengthening your courage is key to your happiness**.

In general, people need two things: a sense of belonging and love/connection. Your relationships make you feel part of a group, which is essential because physiologically, you are made to connect. In fact, **the #1 predictor for overcoming depression is having a community, a support network**. It is unrealistic and mistaken to think you can meet all your relationship needs through just one person. Relationships offer various benefits: fun, support, honesty, challenges, company, security, learning, growth, and sometimes intimacy.

Your relationships give you identity. They are part of who you are. As the saying goes, "Tell me who you spend time with, and I'll tell you who you are." If you surround yourself with five friends who exercise or love music, you will likely be the sixth. Quantum physics also explains how similar energies attract each other. You don't connect with who you want but with those similar to you. The best way to attract a healthy partner is to work on your own healing and self-love. "We are all mirrors." **The people around you reflect what's inside you, whether pleasant or unpleasant.**

Investing in your relationships is a great decision for your long-term happiness and well-being. To enjoy good relationships, you need to dedicate time, show care, listen with your ears, eyes, and heart, and simply be present and available, whether in friendships, parenting, work, or romantic relationships.

Routine is key in relationships – schedule regular times to meet and focus solely on connecting and enjoying each other.

In the longest-running anthropological study in history, lasting over 80 years and still ongoing, Dr. Robert Waldinger from Harvard University concluded that everyone, regardless of where they fall on the personality spectrum between introverts and extroverts, needs at least one unconditional person – someone they can trust, rely on, and express themselves to, in order to normalize their stress and cortisol levels. Good relationships have a direct impact on your health: mental, emotional, and physical. They can even extend your life by 8 years.

One of the most important challenges in building relationship well-being is understanding that life is an individual journey. Sometimes, we love so much that we want to take on someone else's learning process to spare them pain, but allowing them to experience their own journey – including the pain – is also an act of love.

For example, when our children face uncomfortable or painful situations at school, our first instinct may be to take over the problem to minimize their frustration. But by doing this, we take away their opportunity to:

- Practice their communication skills.
- Set healthy boundaries.
- Develop emotional regulation tools.

HAPPINESS

- Feel capable and confident in handling life's challenges.
- Strengthen their courage and comfort with discomfort.

Misguided expressions of love can create toxic relationship dynamics. It would be like showing up to take an exam for your child or loved one.

Building healthy relationships is a challenge and requires effort. Therefore, my suggestion is to consciously choose the relationships where you want to invest your time, resources, effort, energy, and emotions. These are the relationships that are truly worth it and have earned the right to be part of your exclusive list.

Remember, being family is not reason enough to automatically consider someone for this list or to keep them close. Maintain only the relationships that uplift you and help you become the best version of yourself.

Wherever someone brings out the best in you – that's where you belong. Wherever you don't need to "pretend" and can simply "be yourself" – that's where you belong.

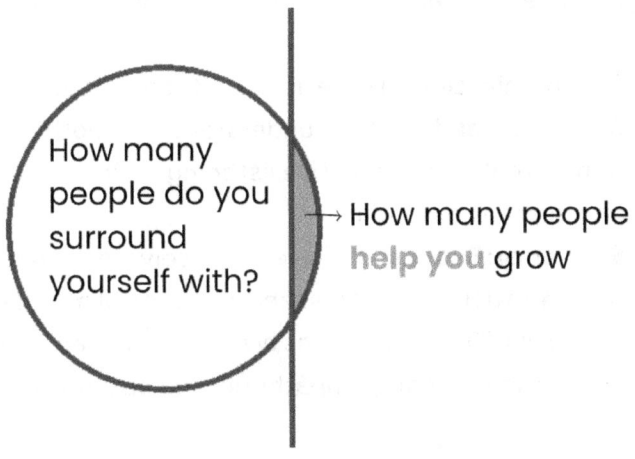

One of the most effective tools for nurturing your relationships is to cultivate what Barbara Fredrickson calls micro-moments of connection — brief moments of positive resonance: spaces to validate, listen without distractions, show interest, and acknowledge ideas, comments, or experiences related to the other person.

Some ideas she shares to create micro-moments of connection with anyone are:

- Use your body language.
- Know and let yourself be known.
- Play with fun and humor.
- Paraphrase.
- Respond in an active and constructive way.
- Engage with respect.
- Show empathy.
- Ask questions.
- Avoid judgments and giving advice.
- Take turns.

In any type of healthy relationship, there are three key ingredients:

- **Communication:** There is an effective exchange of information and mutual understanding, both verbal and non-verbal. For this, active listening (with your ears, eyes, and heart) is essential.
- **Solidarity:** Both parties give and receive in the relationship, building a dynamic of trust and certainty of mutual support.
- **Kindness:** The interactions are characterized by being loving, compassionate, empathetic, and optimistic.

Regarding communication, I'd like to share the following table, which illustrates research conducted by social psychologist Shelly

Gable on the types of responses you can give when someone enthusiastically shares good news, and how these responses contribute to or affect the relationship.

HOW DO YOU RESPOND TO GOOD NEWS?

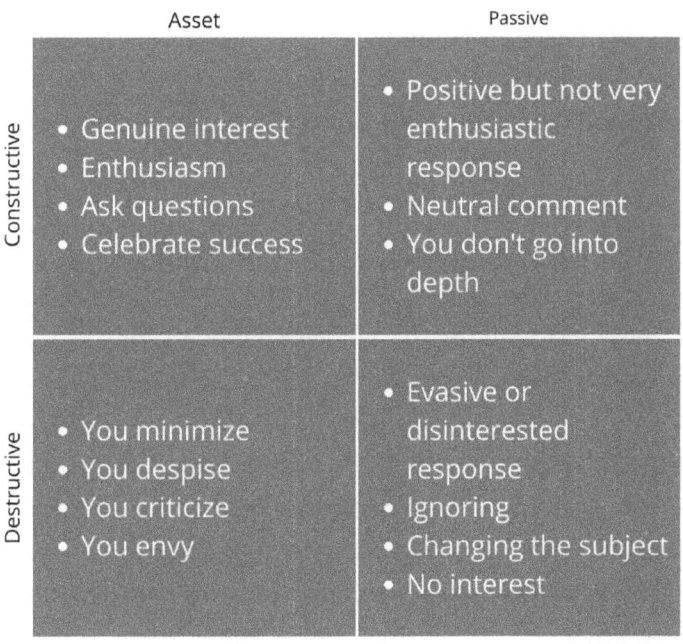

Psic. Shelly Gable

The numbers indicate the order in which each type of response might benefit your relationship. Clearly, giving an active and constructive response, showing interest, and celebrating success will make the person sharing the good news feel seen, recognized, and appreciated.

In a romantic relationship, how you respond when your partner shares positive news is a better predictor of your relationship's success than how you respond to negative news. This is because active constructive responses (number 1 in the diagram) build resilience to face negative events, which are also an inevitable part of any relationship.

Personally, I've come to believe that it might even be less damaging to have an active destructive response than a passive constructive one. In the first option, at least the other person feels seen and acknowledged.

Having healthy, positive, and strong relationships promotes:

- Emotional well-being.
- Physical health.
- A sense of community and empathy.
- A sense of belonging.
- Stress reduction.
- A support system to navigate difficult times.
- Longevity (living longer).

On the other hand, your important relationships can also be a source of misery and stress if they are destructive. Drs. Julie and John Gottman identified behaviors that doom relationships to deterioration or failure, calling them the "Four Horsemen of the Apocalypse":

- Criticism
- Contempt
- Defensiveness
- Stonewalling (Avoidance)

The Gottmans propose that each of these has an antidote, as described below:

1. **Criticism** – Focus on the behavior, not the person. Speak about your feelings using "I" statements, and then express a need. Don't attack.

2. **Contempt** – Build a culture of respect and appreciation.
3. **Defensiveness** – Don't take everything personally and accept your responsibility.
4. **Stonewalling (Avoidance)** – Take a 20-minute break, calm down, and then return to the conversation.

Emotionally engaged relationships that are perfect or conflict-free do not exist, because in the end, they are two people, two brains, and two worlds interacting—not one. **Conflict is acceptable, and even necessary, if it is approached positively**. Reasonable conflict can enrich you, help you learn from others, set healthy boundaries, get to know yourself better, and develop empathy, tolerance, and respect.

Building My Happiness: **Knowing My Relationships**

1. Do I have at least one unconditional person in my life today? If yes, write their name...
2. How many important relationships do I have in my life today?
3. Which relationships are the most significant in my life right now? How are they doing?
4. Do I feel these relationships add to or detract from my well-being?
5. Can I identify the positive things that each of these relationships contributes or has contributed to my life?
6. Which family members have I kept in my life simply because we share blood ties?
7. Do I invest enough (time, resources, energy, attention) in my relationships?

8. How do I choose to build micro-moments of connection with that important person today?

9. Which of the three key ingredients for healthy relationships (communication, solidarity, kindness) would I like to work on?

10. What type of response do I usually give when someone shares good news with me?

11. What type of response do I receive from _____ (an important person to you) when I share good news with them?

12. Which of the "Four Horsemen of the Apocalypse" (criticism, contempt, defensiveness, stonewalling) do I resort to most often? Why do I think this is my go-to response mechanism?

13. What can I do to achieve 2% more well-being in my relationships?

YOUR RELATIONSHIP WITH YOURSELF

> "Self-love is not a place you arrive at;
> it's a place you start from."
> GABO CARRILLO

Building a healthy relationship with yourself is incredibly important because it influences all aspects of your life: professional success, ambitions, the jobs you apply for, your negotiation skills, performance, perceptions of others, courage, health and self-image, ease of learning, sense of purpose, ability to set boundaries, the size of your dreams, your self-confidence… and, of course, it will determine the kind of relationships you have with others.

This reflection leads to a simple question: Are you with certain people because you want to be, or because you need to be?

HAPPINESS

For many years, I have been interested in my relationship with myself and how it impacts other areas of my life. My undergraduate thesis in Industrial Relations in 2007 was titled The Importance of Self-Esteem in Employees' Job Performance. I argued that investing in promoting team members' well-being was a wise choice for companies—a concept that remains relevant and becomes even more significant with recent research.

I'm delighted that topics like self-love, self-esteem, self-appreciation, self-concept, and self-compassion are now popular. The term "self-love" recently stood out to me in a conversation between Dr. Margarita Tarragona and Laura Chica on the podcast "Psychology and Happiness". Rather than focus on the differences between these terms, what truly matters is understanding the importance of consciously building a loving and healthy relationship with yourself, as it affects your performance in all areas of life.

Self-Esteem and Self-Talk
To build your self-esteem, you need to meet four basic psychological needs:

1. Competence – I can.
2. Autonomy – I decide.
3. Connection – I belong.
4. Self-Worth – I matter.

There are two types of self-esteem:

1. **Dependent Self-Esteem:** This relies on positive recognition from others. It's tied to results and comparison. It protects the image you think others have of you. This type of self-esteem is based on labels such as "handsome,"

"smart," "visionary," "creative," etc. These labels do not help build true self-esteem.
2. **Independent Self-Esteem:** This is based on improvement, learning, and growth. It's built on your strengths. It's linked to effort and the journey, regardless of the outcome. Therefore, nurture your passions and confidence in yourself.

Sometimes, in our desire to promote excellence in our children and instill ambition, we inadvertently send the message that who they are today isn't enough—that they will only be worthy of love and value when they become "the best" at something. The reality is that self-esteem and self-love are not about being better than others; **they are about not needing comparison to feel valuable and loved**.

Self-Worth and Society
I see a generation of fractured adults who measure their worth by their job titles, academic degrees, the brands of clothing they wear, or the cars they drive. They believe, "I am valuable as long as others recognize and applaud me." This mindset can lead to compromising one's integrity for applause and recognition.

Self-Talk
Self-talk is that voice in your mind with which you converse throughout the day. It shapes your reality. The way you speak to yourself reinforces your self-image and creates situations and outcomes that confirm your beliefs.

If you constantly tell yourself that you are unattractive, unable to make money, unworthy, or incapable, you will likely experience situations that reinforce these beliefs, creating a vicious cycle. Conversely, if you repeatedly affirm that you are attractive, abundant, worthy, capable, and interesting, you will manifest situations that support these beliefs, creating a virtuous cycle.

Whether your self-image is positive or negative, you will always find evidence to convince yourself that your beliefs are true. As Henry Ford said, "Whether you think you can or you think you can't, you're right."

CYCLE OF YOUR INNER VOICE

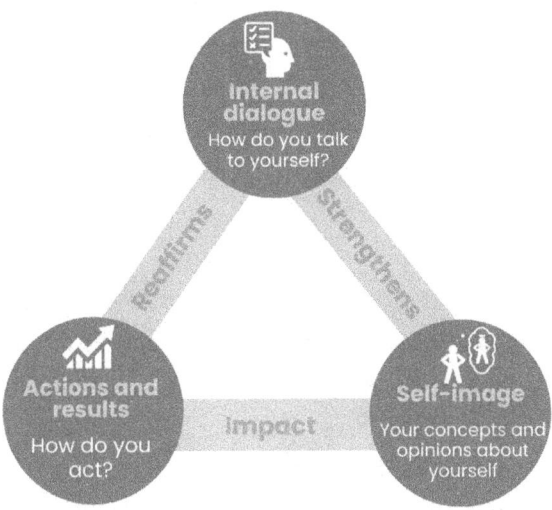

It is estimated that people have, on average, 60,000 thoughts a day, and 87% of them are negative. Yes, you read that right! It is likely that you are your own harshest critic and judge. So now, how can you become your biggest fan? Is it even possible?

Often, that inner voice is unconscious and has been programmed and reinforced since childhood. Maybe in your youth, a close adult compared you, labeled you, or made a disparaging comment that you accepted as truth. Or perhaps a situation led you to interpret a part of yourself negatively, causing you to create a self-image that is negative, unworthy, or incapable. Over time, you have repeated it so much and gathered so much evidence that you believe it to be an unchangeable truth.

Three Types of Negative Self-Talk

1. **Victim:** This person feels defenseless against life, powerless, never takes responsibility, feels life owes them, and suffers constantly.
2. **Catastrophic:** Always imagines the worst-case scenarios, tragedies, adversities, and dangers. Negative thoughts become overwhelming and relentless.
3. **Perfectionist or Critical:** Everything is imperfect, flawed, and could be better. This mindset leads to constant dissatisfaction and frustration from never meeting expectations of perfection.

According to psychiatrist Marian Rojas Estapé, negative self-talk is more frequent and intense in people who are sensitive, obsessive, depressed, anxious, have low self-esteem, physical illnesses, or have unresolved emotional wounds.

On the other hand, if your self-image was nurtured with praise, appreciation, and recognition during childhood, **you have likely built a positive self-image.** You believe yourself to be capable, valuable, and brave, gathering enough evidence over the years to consider this an unshakable truth. This doesn't mean you are perfect or good at everything (which is impossible), nor does it mean you live in arrogance. It simply means you have a positive self-image that strengthens your self-esteem, which is healthy and recommended.

True self-esteem is nurtured by self-awareness, acknowledging both your light and shadow, and lovingly accepting your whole self—strengths and weaknesses.

Improving Your Inner Dialogue
Since you spend so much time talking to yourself, make it an enjoyable experience. **The good news is that this inner voice can be**

trained. How? By living in the present, observing that voice, and correcting it gently, just as you would with someone you love. As an adult, you are responsible for creating a positive self-image and reinforcing it with words and emotions until you achieve the results you expect.

Tips to Become Your Biggest Cheerleader

- Identify how you talk to yourself. Would you dare talk to your best friend the way you talk to yourself?
- When you have a negative thought, ask yourself: Who told you that? or According to whom? This helps you separate from the thought and question it.
- Notice what you say when you look in the mirror.
- Reflect on the last time you acknowledged something amazing about yourself.
- Ask yourself: If a friend talked to you the way you talk to yourself, would you still be friends?
- Thank your body when you see it in the mirror for being your primary armor and vehicle for so many years, instead of criticizing it.
- Visualize your success and connect with the feeling as if it were happening now.
- Celebrate your own achievements and those of others.
- Show up for yourself in everything you consider important.
- Instead of being your harshest judge, celebrate what you do well and take pride in who you are.

Building My Happiness: **Strengthening My Relationship with Myself**

1. Do I love myself? Do I believe I have a healthy relationship with myself? Why?

2. Rate yourself from 1 to 5 on each of the four psychological needs of self-esteem:

   - Competence: I can _____

   - Autonomy: I decide _____

   - Connection: I belong _____

   - Self-Worth: I matter _____

3. Which of the two types of self-esteem do I relate to more? Can I identify why?

4. Does what I think of myself and my results depend on what others think of me?

5. Do I only feel enough when others recognize me?

6. When I enter a room or event full of people, do I have the habit or need to compare myself?

7. Would I dare speak to my best friend the way I speak to myself?

8. What is my inner dialogue like?

9. What phrases do I say to myself when I look in the mirror?

10. What opinion do I have of myself? Who do I think I am?

11. What evidence have I gathered to support my opinion of myself as true?

12. Where do I think these ideas about myself come from? Can I identify any situations or people who contributed to building this self-image?

13. What actions can I take to become my biggest cheerleader and build positive self-talk?

14. Which affirmation in the diagram am I committed to transforming to change my inner dialogue?

ROMANTIC RELATIONSHIPS

> "Love is not just a feeling but an act of will."
> MARIAN ROJAS ESTAPÉ

Being in a committed relationship or living as a couple is entirely a choice (even if it may seem like an obligation). A successful relationship is not defined by how long it lasts, but by whether the two people in it are happy and fulfilled, regardless of its duration. There is no such thing as a committed relationship without conflict, and that's a good thing! Conflict is necessary for growth. According to the Gottman Institute, nearly 70% of relationship problems are perpetual (they will never be resolved).

One of the biggest issues in romantic relationships is believing that feelings will always stay the same. It's crucial to let go of the idea that a successful relationship is primarily about finding the perfect partner. Instead, success depends on both partners' willingness to work intentionally toward building a long-term life of well-being, based on agreements, shared values, quality time, healthy intimacy, emotional security, and more. When you step into the "dating market," make sure you are aware of your value (what you offer), your expectations (what you seek), and your non-negotiables.

Expecting your partner to make you happy is setting the relationship up for failure by asking for the impossible. If your partner promises to make you happy, don't believe them. No matter how good their intentions are, they simply cannot fulfill that promise. Knowing your own love language and that of your partner can lead to more effective communication. Wanting to change your partner is not only frustrating but also an act of arrogance. If you prefer to change green into purple, better find purple instead... and go to therapy.

Do you feel incomplete or insufficient and are looking for your "other half"? In other words, do you believe that finding a partner will make you feel whole and enough? Looking for a partner is like buying shoes. Let me explain: When you walk into a shoe store, do you ask to see the pair that's been sitting in the window for a long time, faded, defective, missing a lace, or broken, so you can take it home and fix it? Of course not. You go in looking for the nicest and most comfortable shoes that you believe will make you feel good when you wear them.

The same goes for finding a partner. What makes you think someone would want to connect with a person who feels broken, faded, defective, and outdated? Reflect, work on your self-love, and then seek a partner from a place of wanting to share life with someone, not from dependence, toxicity, low self-esteem, or feelings of inadequacy, expecting someone else to do the work you haven't done for yourself.

Rethinking Your Relationship Beliefs

- Do you think your partner should make you happy?
- Do you believe that finding your "other half" is the only key to a successful relationship?
- Do you think love is all you need for a healthy relationship?
- Do you believe that getting married guarantees lifelong happiness?

If you answered yes to these questions, you've got it all wrong!

Many people still believe a successful relationship is one that lasts a lifetime, regardless of whether the people in it are miserable. Thankfully, more people are realizing that the goal of a relationship is not its duration but the fulfillment and growth of its partners.

A healthy and functional relationship is one where both people add value to each other's lives and feel that being in the relationship enhances their long-term happiness and well-being. In other words, it's beneficial for both to remain in the relationship.

Dr. John Gottman's research shows that 69% of relationship problems are unsolvable. You will have to learn to live with these issues if you choose to stay in the relationship. Even if you switch partners, you will encounter another 69% of problems that can't be resolved. The key is to ensure your non-negotiables don't fall within that 69%.

There is no such thing as a "perfect match". Attraction is necessary, but it's not sufficient to maintain a relationship without deliberate effort to nurture the bond. The partner you choose will require a lot of work from both of you to communicate, reach agreements, negotiate, evolve, share new experiences, set healthy boundaries, and possibly raise children if you choose to.

It's essential to eliminate magical or idealistic thinking in relationships. The key is not just in finding "the one" but in ensuring that both you and your partner are willing to work hard to build a harmonious, healthy, and lasting relationship. In short, you need to make your relationship a priority.

What you are building is a relationship with a life partner that benefits you both. To avoid misunderstandings or heartbreak, two things are crucial:

1. Engage in Personal Reflection:

- Does this relationship make me a better person?

- Is this what I've always envisioned aligning with my way of being and seeing life?
- Is it beneficial for me?
- Can I imagine living my day-to-day life with peace, harmony, and excitement?
- Do we share fundamental values?
- Does this relationship meet my criteria?

2. Have Difficult Conversations in Advance About Topics Such As:

- What are each person's expectations in the relationship?
- How do they relate to their family, and what are the expectations for family interactions?
- What childhood traumas do they carry?
- What are their financial expectations and spending habits?
- How important is religion to them?
- How do they view change – as a challenge or an opportunity?
- Are they communicative?
- If they want children, how do they envision parenting?
- What are their expectations regarding sexuality?
- Are there any significant hereditary illnesses in the family?
- What are their dreams, desires, and professional aspirations?

Currently, a couple breaks up every four minutes. The effectiveness of the "recruitment and selection process" in finding a partner is important because compatibility facilitates agreements and dynamics, but it does not guarantee the relationship will endure. Therefore, it is crucial that both partners are aware of the ongoing need to invest in the relationship for it to mature, evolve, and flourish. Both must be willing to do the work, knowing that emotions change over time. Psychiatrist Marian Rojas Estapé suggests in her book Find Your Vitamin Person that true love begins when the initial infatuation ends since hormones are no longer involved.

No one can or should be responsible for your happiness. To be happy is your responsibility, the most important one you have. It can sometimes feel overwhelming to build a fulfilling and happy life for yourself. Imagine how much more overwhelming it would be to also carry the responsibility of doing that for someone else — and the frustration of attempting something impossible.

While all relationships require compromise and negotiation, **it is essential not to lose yourself.** Excessively pleasing and compromising will lead to frustration, disconnection, and a buildup of emotional "credits" that you will eventually want to cash in. If both you and your partner work on your individual happiness and support each other, you will be fortunate to share your paths of awareness, learning, and growth, thereby nurturing the relationship effectively.

Regarding love, some authors even recommend not marrying while infatuated, as this feeling can cloud your judgment about compatibility and your ability to reach agreements.

In his book, The 5 Love Languages, Gary Chapman offers a theory that helps you ask: "How do I like to receive love, and how do I like to express it?"

He identifies five love languages:

- **Quality Time:** Consciously sharing moments and seeking new experiences together.
- **Words of Affirmation:** Actively listening, appreciating the positive, and recognizing effort verbally.
- **Physical Touch:** Expressing affection through physical contact.

- **Acts of Service:** Understanding routines, anticipating needs, and offering help.
- **Receiving Gifts:** Give thoughtful gifts and consider the details your partner enjoys.

You can communicate more effectively by identifying your love language and your partner's. Peter Fraenkel, from the Ackerman Institute in New York, talks about 60-second pleasure points — taking a minute to show appreciation, interest, or affection with a small gesture like a hug before work, a compliment, a text message, or offering help. These frequent expressions of affection help nurture the relationship.

Conflict in emotionally committed relationships is necessary because it helps them evolve and thrive. The key is having mechanisms to communicate differences and reach agreements that benefit both parties. Remember, **an agreement only lasts if it works for both sides.**

Most relationship conflicts are due to these four topics: Money and spending habits, child-rearing practices, relationships with in-laws, sex and fidelity

Having triggers (situations or phrases that provoke arguments) does not make your relationship toxic. The difference between a healthy and dysfunctional relationship lies in how those triggers are managed. Triggers should be validated and used for growth, reflection, and wisdom. However, if the triggers are repetitive, unresolved, suppressed, or lead to violence, they become problematic.

In my own life, the most significant, deep, and challenging relationship I have had is with my children's father, Antonio. We have been on this journey together for 17 years, and I consider him my life partner and the love of my life. He has been my greatest teacher, my sharpest critic, and my most optimistic cheerleader — what Emerson calls my "beautiful enemy" (someone who challenges and encourages you).

HAPPINESS

A few years ago, we faced a severe crisis. After numerous attempts at therapy, journaling, meditation, books, podcasts, and courses, I felt exhausted and hopeless. I thought it might be best to amicably co-parent our children, Lázaro and Simón, and go our separate ways.

One night, I cried myself to sleep, overwhelmed with sadness, anger, and despair. But the next morning, with a clear head and a commitment to my belief — "Focus on what you can impact and control" — I asked myself: "What can I do differently?"

I decided to start a gratitude journal for Antonio. Every night, for a year, I wrote down at least one thing I was grateful for about him. There were nights when I could hardly stand him, but I stuck to my commitment. Over time, I began to focus on the good things, the magic we created together, and the great team we made as parents and life partners.

Slowly, the tears stopped. I began sleeping peacefully and saw each new day as a new opportunity. Though not every night ended happily, I at least went to bed in peace.

Building My Happiness: **Working on My Relationship**

1. Would I want to marry myself?
2. What characteristics would I like my relationship to have?
3. In the shoe store analogy, what type of shoe do I feel like: a brand-new model or last season's leftover stock?
4. Do I believe a successful relationship is one that lasts a lifetime, no matter the circumstances? Why?
5. Do I have a clear objective for living with a partner, if that's what I desire?

6. If I'm in a relationship, do I feel that my current relationship is good for me? In other words, does it make my life better?

7. If I'm in a relationship, can I identify the perpetual problems in my relationship? If so, does any of them clash with one of my non-negotiables?

8. Do I believe that both my partner and I are aware that our relationship requires continuous voluntary work to keep it healthy?

9. Have I had any of the suggested uncomfortable conversations? Why or why not?

10. In general, do I feel that my relationship allows me to flourish, or does it stifle my essence and freedom to be myself?

11. Which of the 5 love languages do I identify as mine, and which one belongs to my partner? What can I do to improve our communication?

12. What "60-second pleasure point" (simple act of appreciation) do I plan to implement to nurture my relationship?

13. What is the main source of conflict in my relationship? What agreements can we make about it?

14. What situations or phrases trigger conflicts in my relationship? Do I know where they come from? What can I do about them?

15. Would keeping a gratitude journal for my partner help me focus my attention and energy on the good and add value to my relationship?

16. What do I contribute to my relationship, and what does my partner contribute? How can we improve our contributions?

17. Do I have clarity about what makes me stay in my relationship or what would make me leave?

(18) Which societal ideas about what makes a relationship thrive resonate with me, and which of the truly important ideas did I connect with?

EMOTIONAL WELLBEING - MESSENGERS

You are not your emotions, and you can approach them with curiosity. **Every person is responsible for their emotions;** according to Marc Brackett, there are over 1,500 emotions. **The only way to stop feeling an emotion is to go through it.** Emotional intelligence consists of identifying, understanding, and addressing what you feel to use it to your advantage. Emotional well-being requires self-awareness, courage, and a lot of work. Giving yourself permission to feel is accepting your humanity. Experiencing pain might seem like a sign of illness, but in reality, it is a sign of health (as long as you don't enjoy it); denying or ignoring your emotions only makes them grow in intensity, duration, and frequency.

Emotions – E-MOTIONS – are energy in motion. The reality is that how you feel affects everything in your life, including how your family feels and how you perform in your activities. It is important to learn about your emotions to avoid becoming a victim of them and to inhabit your own skin comfortably and harmoniously.

Your emotions are extremely important, not only because they define your mood and, subsequently, your personality and what the famous Dr. Joe Dispenza calls the state of being, but also because they impact all areas of your life: the type of relationships you build, how you take care of your body and mind, your work performance, energy levels, your activities in general... in short, they determine the quality of your experience in this life. It's important that you understand the emotional world, your emotional world, so that you are not a victim of it and that inhabiting yourself is pleasant.

Even John Gottman, a leading psychologist in the field of emotional intelligence, summarizes the importance of emotional well-being in the following brief paragraph: "In the last decade, science has discovered a tremendous amount of information about the role emotions play in our lives. Researchers have found that, even more than IQ, emotional awareness and the ability to manage feelings determine success and happiness in all areas of life." This is why it's worth dedicating time and effort to learning how to develop this superpower.

In a world numbed by screens, drugs, doing without pause, and immediacy, it's very easy to think that feeling pain is a sickness, when in reality, it is a sign of health. Feeling pain is part of being human, but you are so disconnected that pain feels so foreign to you that when it appears, it scares you... especially because of the few tools you have to manage it. At the slightest sign of any uncomfortable emotion, you perceive it as unsustainable. You believe the emotion is a monster that takes over you and that you will never see the light again.

When you were a child and went to a party with your family, your mom asked you to greet an older man with a kiss (which is common in Mexican society) – someone you had never seen before and who gave you a bad feeling. Your automatic reaction was to hide behind her and avoid the request. Of course, she pulled you out from behind her legs and practically forced you to approach the person and make cheek-to-cheek contact, so both she and you would gain recognition for having "good manners" learned and practiced in the family.

Or when you went to the pediatrician for a vaccine, and the injection hurt, you burst into tears... Suddenly, the nurse rushed for a lollipop, the doctor pretended nothing happened, and your mom, at best, hugged you and told you to stop crying. At worst, she said it wasn't a big deal, it was over, and threatened a punishment if you didn't stop crying.

In both situations, the adults' discomfort with the child's natural reaction ended up forcing the little girl to ignore what she felt and betray herself to please others and adhere to "good manners." This is how, from an early age, we learn to disconnect from what we feel and develop mechanisms to "control" (or block) our emotions. We prioritize being socially accepted over connecting with our essence, understanding what we feel, and attending to the message of our emotions.

Emotions are everything you feel, and they have two components:

1. Physiological – bodily sensations like sweating, shoulder tension, body posture, a pit in your stomach, clenching your jaw, etc.
2. Cognitive – the associated thoughts.

COMPONENTS OF EMOTIONS

Cognitive - Thoughts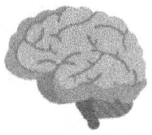

Physiological - Sensations

Emotions are neither good nor bad; rather, they are pleasurable and comfortable or painful and unpleasant to feel. Yes, you read that right: fear, envy, anger, sadness, etc., are not bad. They only have a bad reputation because they don't feel good and are often associated with inappropriate behaviors.

All emotions have a light side and a dark side. For example, it is thanks to fear that the human species has survived for thousands of years. In its light aspect, fear protects you and allows you to respond appropriately to danger and adversity. In its dark aspect, fear paralyzes you. Envy arises when you see in someone else something you wish to have in your life. In its light aspect, envy motivates you to work to achieve it. In its dark aspect, it drives you to harm or destroy others. Similarly, joy, in its dark side, can lead you to trivialize life or fall into toxic optimism, while its light side invites you to celebrate and experience jubilation.

This is why the phrase "emotions are neither good nor bad" is not just a theory but a practical truth. Emotions are simply information. To better understand this information, I highly recommend The Field Guide to Emotions by Dan Newby and Curtis Watkins. This book is a comprehensive guide to all emotions, with inquiry questions, descriptions of how they manifest in body posture, related emotions, the time frame they focus on (past, present, or future), and more. It is like a practical dictionary of emotions that you can consult to understand what your emotions are trying to tell you and why you feel what you feel.

Imagine that emotions are like a messenger or delivery person holding an envelope of information for you. If you ignore them, they will ring the doorbell persistently, shout, knock on the door, text you, call you, and do whatever it takes to be noticed. This is what happens with emotions: the more you ignore them, the more their intensity (how strongly you feel them), duration (how long you feel them), and frequency (how often you feel them) increase.

That's why when you stop to understand and address what you feel, emotions lose their intensity, duration, and frequency. In other words, when you acknowledge them and ask yourself, "What is my emotion trying to tell me?" and "Why am I feeling this, and what is it inviting me to do?", the message is received, and the invitation to work on it is accepted. The messenger or delivery person has fulfilled their purpose, and their presence is no longer needed.

All emotions are temporary. That means everything passes. In fact, this is a life mantra for me. When I experience painful or uncomfortable emotions, the first thing I do is allow myself to feel them without judgment and remind myself they are not eternal: **everything passes**. It is also important to recognize that we are not our emotions, even if it feels that way sometimes. Occasionally, we feel an emotion so deeply and for so long that we might think it's an inherent part of us. But the reality is that it isn't, and separating ourselves from our emotions helps us approach them with more objectivity, curiosity, and the ability to identify the sensations and thoughts associated with them.

The truth is that all human beings feel pain and uncomfortable emotions – the only ones who don't are psychopaths, and they are genuinely unwell. Trying to block our painful or uncomfortable emotions is an illusion, not only because it's nearly impossible but because if you succeed, you will pay a steep price. The mechanism in our body (the nervous system) that allows us to feel pain is the same one that allows us to feel pleasant emotions, like love or joy. If you numb this mechanism, you block both types of emotions. Whether you numb your life with drugs, gambling, pornography (socially condemned products), or with phones, social media, work, or a hectic lifestyle (socially accepted), the effects are the same. **Numbing the darkness of your emotions also numbs your light.**

Your emotional state is like a super GPS that we humans are equipped with – some choose to use it, and some don't. Emotions always provide information. **The key is to know yourself and be aware of them so you can interpret this information and use it to make daily decisions.**

When we previously discussed the difference between "feeling happy" and "being happy", we explored the idea of feeling seemingly contradictory emotions simultaneously, because being happy (building long term well-being) can be tremendously uncomfortable in the short term. This is not only completely normal but also quite common. From my perspective, it's fascinating because it shows the complexity of the human species, embodying infinite possibilities. For example, when someone shares a tragedy with you, you might feel anxiety, sadness, and anger for what happened, but also peace, joy, and gratitude that it didn't happen to you. Or, if you experience something unpleasant or dangerous, like a car accident, you might feel annoyed by the inconvenience but also fortunate that it wasn't worse.

HAPPINESS

EMOTIONS COMBINE

	1 Joy	2 Sadness	3 Disgust	4 Fear	5 Anger
1 Joy	Ecstasy 1+1	Nostalgic 1+2	Distain 1+3	Excitement 1+4	fervor 1+5
2 Sadness	Melancholy 2+1	Despair 2+2	Contempt 2+3	Dread 2+4	Resentment 2+5
3 Disgust	Ironic 3+1	Loathing 3+2	Abhorrence 3+3	Horror 3+4	Outrage 3+5
4 Fear	Protective 4+1	Anxiety 4+2	Repulse 4+3	Terror 4+4	Vengeful 4+5
5 Anger	Zeal 5+1	Betrayal 5+2	Hatred 5+3	Hostility 5+4	Rage 5+5

Valentinamente_feliz

The emotional world is complex and, from my perspective, fascinating because **it makes you a being in constant change**, offering infinite possibilities for learning. In general, for many years, education has focused on transferring knowledge rather than developing skills – especially emotional skills – which is very unfortunate.

It is important to recognize that exploring the world of emotions requires courage because for many, it means accepting their humanity (imperfection) and venturing into the unknown, uncertain, risky, and uncontrollable. It's like lifting a manhole cover – you don't know what will come out of it. In short, there isn't a natural inclination to allow yourself to be vulnerable.

Here are some tips to work on your emotional well-being:

- Write or talk to someone.
- Identify the story causing your emotion.
- Approach your emotion with curiosity and observe.
- Breathe and remember that what you feel is temporary.
- Be grateful for your emotion.
- Take responsibility for your emotion.
- Expand your emotional vocabulary.

One of the reasons you avoid acknowledging your emotions is the fear of getting stuck. It feels like willingly stepping into quicksand from which you might not escape. But what you don't realize is that choosing to take that step is the beginning of your liberation. Rejecting or ignoring your uncomfortable emotions makes them more intense and prolonged. Observing your emotions with curiosity is a powerful mental health exercise because, by doing so, you take the first step toward healing.

Building My Happiness: **Understanding My Emotional World**

1. Do I believe I have emotional awareness/intelligence? Why?
2. Did I learn to connect with my emotions during childhood? How was my emotional upbringing? Did we talk about what everyone felt at home?

3. How do I think my previous answer impacts my emotional skills today?
4. How do I evaluate the quality of my emotions?
5. How does my previous answer impact the quality of my life?
6. What does the emotions chart tell me?
7. Based on my findings, what commitment will I make to myself? Can I create an action plan?

EMBRACE YOUR EMOTIONS

When you recognize that part of your humanity is experiencing the full spectrum of emotions – not just the ones you like – you embrace your essence and place yourself in a good position to develop emotional skills. These skills will allow you to cultivate and promote emotions you enjoy and manage and attend to difficult, painful, or uncomfortable emotions. Remember: emotions are neither good nor bad; they simply are.

It is true that you can build new emotional habits, and three things are essential for this:

1. Living in the present.
2. Knowing yourself.
3. Intentional and consistent work.

In other words, pause to compassionately observe and understand what you feel, when you feel it, why you feel it, and what purpose it serves. Once you have an action plan, move to execution.

Consider that there are three areas that play a role in how we interpret and express emotions:

1. Universal: Common human experiences.
2. Cultural: The social and family context in which you grew up and live.
3. Personal: Your unique beliefs and experiences.

Depending on these factors – your beliefs, societal and family context, and the era you live in – your way of observing and analyzing emotions will differ.

Here's a brief and simple (though not necessarily easy) 5-step method for processing your emotions and building emotional well-being:

1. **Diagnose and Understand Your Emotion:** Identify what you are feeling and name it. Try not to judge and allow yourself to feel it. Notice when it appears, how it manifests in your body, and which thoughts are associated with it. Expanding your emotional vocabulary beforehand can be very helpful. How do you feel right now? What emotion do you feel most often? Is it pleasant, painful, or uncomfortable? What thoughts arise when you feel it? How does your body react? What is this emotion trying to tell you? Why do you feel this emotion? What past belief or situation is related to this?
2. **Plan:** Define specific activities with a timeline. What is this information inviting you to do? What should you work on regarding this information? Why are you feeling this emotion?
3. **Execute the Plan and Address Your Emotion:** Make a commitment to yourself to bring 3% more well-being into your life and carry it out for 30 days. How will you measure your progress? How will you reinforce or correct your efforts?
4. **Evaluate:** Measure your progress compared to when you started. How far are you from your goal?

5. **Decide:** Choose whether to continue, adjust, or drastically change the plan. Have your actions brought the expected results? Why or why not? What benefits you now?

When I worked at a Mexican state-owned energy company — at the time, one of the primary contributors to the GDP and a symbol of national progress — I had the opportunity to be trained in the Senn Delaney method, which aimed to foster a culture of growth and success within the organization.

I recall one of the most useful tools for me was the "Mood Elevator," which ranked a series of 19 emotions from least to most desirable. "Depression" was the least convenient state, "Gratitude" was the most desirable, and "Curiosity" was positioned in the middle. This tool suggested that simply being aware of how you felt upon arriving at the office was an achievement, and it encouraged you to elevate yourself a few levels throughout the day, aiming to feel flexible, patient, optimistic, resourceful, creative, reflective, or wise — with curiosity being the minimum state necessary.

Remember: Only by going through our emotions can we stop feeling them.

While most tools for building emotional well-being focus on helping us process uncomfortable emotions like fear, sadness, anxiety, or anger, it is equally important to focus on promoting the emotions we love to feel.

Therefore, I want to share with you a tool developed by James O. Pawelski called the "Positive Portfolio." The three steps are:

1. Choose a pleasant emotion you want to promote in your life (e.g., love, joy, serenity, peace, courage, inspiration, interest, gratitude, etc.).
2. Create a portfolio (digital or physical) with photos, poems, songs, books, quotes, images, movies, objects, etc.

3. Use it for 10 to 15 minutes a day for 10 to 15 days, and observe how you feel.

I suggest you gift yourself your positive portfolio, especially if what led you to buy this book and reach this page was feeling drained, dissatisfied with your life, and lacking in purpose. All I have left to say is that using the cutting-edge internal GPS, which is your emotions, is a choice. We all have that possibility, even you, and everyone chooses whether to use it or not. This life is yours to decide, and you choose whether to ignore and avoid it (with its associated implications) or if today you reflect and consciously work on learning to use it, re-educating it, and making the most of it to navigate your days harmoniously and lightly, for and by you.

At times, it's not easy to do the work, and like many other valuable things, building emotional intelligence requires effort.

Remember, **those who don't repress, don't get depressed**. Expressing emotions, whether in an honest conversation with someone you trust, in therapy with a mental health specialist, writing, crying, doing explosive physical activity (like boxing or running), creating a craft, or meditating, is the best way to prevent them from intensifying or manifesting as physical affliction. We are all different and inclined towards some of these options, and that's okay. Choose yours and act.

Sometimes, expressing emotions immediately after a traumatic event can increase Post-Traumatic Stress Disorder (PTSD), so, for some people, it may be better to just stay calm and allow themselves to be. It's surprising how something so normal, it can be so difficult to accompany a loved one in feeling painful emotions. Right away, we tend to want to fix it or help, minimize their pain with the famous "it's not that bad," distract their attention (changing the subject), etc. When what's important is just creating a psychologically safe environment where the person can be authentic, honest, and real, express themselves in their own way and at their own pace, and let the emotions flow without expectations.

Embracing our own and others' emotions is a real challenge, but one worth taking on to embrace your humanity and feel truly free. That's why, being happy is for the brave.

Building My Happiness: **Cultivating and Promoting Pleasant Emotions**

1. List at least five pleasant emotions that you feel frequently.
2. How can I cultivate or promote the emotions I love to feel, instead of waiting for them to just happen?
3. Which pleasant emotion would I like to explore using James Pawelski's "Positive Portfolio" exercise?

Building My Happiness: **Managing Unpleasant Emotions**

1. Do I feel like a victim of my emotional world?
2. Have I ever felt that my emotions are a monster I can't escape?
3. What is the emotion I find hardest to feel, the one that sometimes seems to take over me? How do I process it?
4. Do I think I have consciously or unconsciously tried to block what I feel to protect myself from pain? When? What were the consequences?
5. Which of the three requirements (living in the present, knowing yourself, intentional work) do I want to start with to

build new emotional habits? List at least five uncomfortable emotions you feel frequently. Choose two emotions you experience most often or those you want to work on, and apply the 5-step method (diagnose, plan, execute, evaluate, and decide) by answering these questions:

- When do I feel it? – Describe the situation.
- How does it manifest in my body? – Physiological effect.
- What thoughts do I have when I feel it? – Cognitive component.
- Why do I feel it? What is this emotion telling me? – Information.
- Why do I feel it? What is it inviting me to do? – Purpose.
- What should I work on or change? – Benefits.

6. How do I numb my uncomfortable emotions (screens, shopping, sex, drugs, work, social media, etc.)?

7. Which option for expressing uncomfortable emotions resonates most with me?

8. How do I react when someone I love shows vulnerability and expresses their pain or uncomfortable emotions to me? Does it make me uncomfortable? Why?

HAPPINESS

THIS IS HOW YOU CREATE YOUR REALITY

> "Watch your thoughts, for they will become your words.
> Watch your words, for they will become your actions.
> Watch your actions, for they will become your habits.
> Watch your habits, for they will become your destiny."
>
> MAHATMA GANDHI

Emotions are just that — emotions. And they are impermanent. The reality is that ALL emotions pass, even though sometimes they are so intense and long-lasting that you feel they will stay with you forever or even destroy you. **Your emotion does not define you** (even if it feels that way), but what you do with it does. Your emotions can change if you change the thought that generated them.

As we mentioned before, emotions are neither good nor bad. What can be judged and evaluated are the behaviors associated with those emotions.

That's why I want to share with you the reality-creation model that my teacher Tal Ben-Shahar calls The 3 E's: Event – Explanation – Emotion. I like to add an A at the end, representing Action, which sets the stage for a new event, thus creating a cycle.

This diagram can help illustrate it clearly:

REALITY CREATION MODEL 3E + A

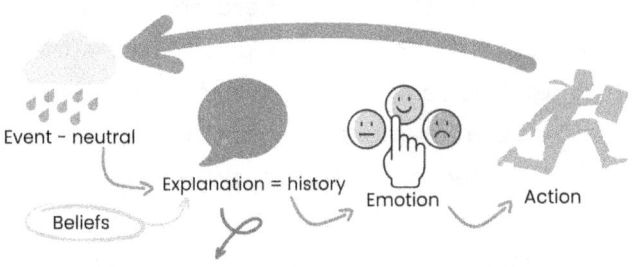

Tell yourself stories that add to you

Let me explain briefly: all events are neutral, and as an observer, you assign them meaning. Your explanation will depend on three factors: Your belief system (ideas you hold as truths), your current mood (at that moment), and your ability to filter what's important (through the Reticular Activating System).

Based on this explanation or the story you tell yourself, certain emotions are triggered — either ones you like or uncomfortable, painful ones. These emotions, in turn, lead to certain behaviors or actions, setting off a new event.

For example, Rain is a neutral event. If you interpret rain as a threat because it gets you wet, makes you sick, causes you to miss work, creates traffic, and turns the city into chaos, you will trigger emotions like anger, frustration, worry, anxiety, or fear. These will lead to actions that create a new event. But if you interpret rain as a wonderful natural phenomenon that cools the heat, cleans the environment, nourishes plants, and even lowers your water bill, you'll feel emotions like contentment, peace, wonder, or gratitude, leading to different actions and a new event.

There is a space between your emotion and your action where you can freely choose how to face the event. This choice can be either conscious (a response) or unconscious (a reaction or impulse). This is where awareness plays a crucial role.

And so it is with everything... **Your life is the result of the interpretations and stories you've told yourself about what has happened to you over the years.** Therefore, you are what you've learned from your experiences. The good news is that you have the power to reframe your stories, even if the events have already passed. Yes! You can tell yourself stories that uplift you, generate emotions you enjoy feeling, and lead to positive behaviors that help you live better.

If today you feel disconnected from yourself, overwhelmed by sadness, or afraid of life, it's a result of the stories you've told your-

HAPPINESS

self about your experiences. The great news is that you can always, ALWAYS, reframe your story, even when the experiences are in the past. TODAY is a great day to start taking responsibility for building your happiness and retelling your stories in a way where you are the protagonist, taking charge of your role, and challenging the ending.

This isn't about denying reality or living in fantasy, but about building a compassionate and constructive objectivity.

Sometimes, you've felt an emotion for so long that it becomes part of your identity. It seems like feeling it is inevitable. What happens is that you've become addicted to the chemicals that emotion produces in your body. Your body then overreacts to the slightest stimulus to generate the chemicals it has learned to rely on.

For example: If you've felt anger or rage for a long time, it may seem like it's part of your personality. Even if you try hard not to get angry, your body will trigger anger over something as small as a fly buzzing, just to produce the chemicals it needs. The same happens with sadness, anxiety, or even gratitude.

Here's a QR code for you to listen to the two-part episode of my podcast "Valentinamente Feliz" titled "You Are Addicted to Your Emotions" and try the exercises I suggest at the end. Remember you can activate the Youtube subtitles in English.

Building My Happiness: **Reframing My Stories**

1. Write the 3E+A model using an adverse situation you've faced. That is, describe an event, the explanation you gave it, the emotions it triggered, and the behaviors that followed. Event, explanation, emotions and actions/behaviors:
2. What else do I need to know about this situation?
3. What assumptions am I making?
4. What do I need to clarify?
5. What am I really feeling?
6. What was my role?
7. What is the key lesson here?
8. Now, rewrite the model by reframing the story/explanation of the same situation. Assume others have good intentions and recognize that, like you, everyone is doing the best they can with what they have. Event (same as before), reframed explanation, new emotions, new actions/behaviors.
9. What changed? What effect did this have on your emotions?

BELIEFS

> "When we finally recognize that our beliefs are this powerful, we will possess the key to freedom."
> BRUCE H. LIPTON

Of the 60,000 thoughts a person has daily, 87% are negative. Therefore, it is crucial to observe your thoughts and make an effort to train your mind to automatically: Focus on what is present rather than what is lacking. Create positive concepts and tell yourself empowering stories. Filter information consciously and make decisions based on your values and priorities.

Working on your beliefs isn't easy because, in general, you aren't aware of them. Over the course of your life, you've simply absorbed and accepted certain ideas or ways of doing things as true and absolute. Then, at some point, you experience something that makes you realize that what you considered an absolute truth is not the only reality.

However, **you can challenge your beliefs by bringing them into awareness, questioning them**, and presenting evidence that challenges them. You can choose new, empowering beliefs that help you create a freer and happier life.

For example, I grew up believing that The father in a family is the provider. The mother raises the children and manages the household. If the mother works, it's just a hobby or an additional source for personal expenses. Since the one who holds the money makes the decisions, the father's word ultimately determines plans, purchases, and investments.

These were my beliefs because that was the dynamic I experienced. I assumed this was the only true and correct way for a family to function. However, I've always loved to work and to feel that I contribute. For me, work nourishes the soul; it's a matter of life purpose, not money. Because of this, the traditional life model of marrying and having children seemed extremely unappealing to me.

When I was 20 years old, I went to live in Connecticut, United States, for over a year with the Feiner family, a Jewish family where both parents worked, provided, raised their children, and made fair agreements to make everything function smoothly. Wow! My world opened up. What I believed possible until then completely changed. My reality challenged my beliefs, and I was able to broaden my perspective.

I experienced firsthand that it is possible for both partners in a relationship to develop professionally and create a balanced dynamic to handle household responsibilities and parenting. My concepts of partnership and family broke down and were rebuilt.

On a personal level, this new concept of teamwork made much more sense to me. I believed that the sacrifices in terms of freedom and purpose were significantly reduced. I was willing to take on responsibilities but also wanted the rights. When I encountered a living example of a fair partnership that aligned with my values, I allowed myself to question and reinvent my beliefs without trying to please others.

I knew that this innovative model was disruptive and perhaps even controversial for men (and women) in more traditional regions. However, I also knew that I would never sacrifice my happiness. I was prepared to remain unmarried and childless if necessary. I knew that adopting a traditional family model that didn't align with my expectations and personal values would make me deeply unhappy. Let me clarify: it's not that the traditional model is wrong; it simply wasn't right for me.

But, fortunately — and to keep it short — when you know what you want and what you don't want, the Universe conspires in your favor. About three years later, during a quick trip to what is now Mexico City, I met a brave man willing to create a new formula — our formula.

I met the man who is now my life partner, and with whom, after 17 years, I still choose every day to grow, negotiate, embrace, adjust the formula, make plans, share investments, have conversations, disagree, reflect each other, reach agreements, raise two amazing kids, love imperfectly, explore the world and support each other and, ultimately, build our best individual versions to share with one another, living as a team, no matter what circumstances life presents us with.

Obviously, you don't have to wait for life to punch you in the face or experience something extraordinary to broaden your perspective, see that there are other ways to live, question your beliefs, reflect on their usefulness and origin, or reinvent your concepts and reinterpret your stories. For me, the three key questions in this exercise are: Why? Since When? According to whom? So, let's get to work! You might be afraid to challenge your beliefs because you feel like you are being disloyal to your roots, your society, or your story. But remember two things: **Loyalty begins with yourself, and to be happy is for the brave.**

By coincidence—or synchronicity—this morning, I wrote this section, and in the afternoon, I was invited to see the movie Inside Out 2 at the theater. Amazing! I found it highly recommendable and incredibly useful for a visual explanation of beliefs. Don't miss it!

Building My Happiness: **Changing My Beliefs**

1. What do I believe about the following concepts, and why? Happiness – Partnership – Family – Work - Money - Friends – Health – Fun - God - Your Country – Life - Your Home – Order - Self-Love – Men – Women - Your Word – Integrity – Commitment – Freedom - Courage

2. Have my beliefs about these concepts helped me live a fulfilling life?

3. Where do these beliefs come from, and how long have I held them?

4. Which of these beliefs would I like to change? (If you have many, choose two to start with.)

5. What evidence (data or stories) can I find that challenges my current beliefs and demonstrates the opposite?

6 How can I redefine my beliefs to lead a more fulfilling life?

SOME EMOTIONS...

> "Emotions are the rudder of our lives."
> DOMINIC O'BRIEN

I'm going to say something that might sound harsh: we are emotionally foolish. Learning to understand and harness emotions is a superpower that we can all develop if we work on it. It's important to **broaden our knowledge** and learn to identify the type of information each emotion carries in order to transcend the primitive perspective that uncomfortable emotions are bad, which condemns you to reject many valuable emotions needed to make effective decisions in your daily life.

As I mentioned, emotions are simply information—neither good nor bad. The behaviors you associate with emotions can be good or bad. That's why every emotion has a light side and a shadow side.

I wish we could always choose our behavior rationally, but the reality is that impulses often win, and we act without thinking. That's why **the difference between reacting and responding is consciousness**. It's in that space where you can use your inner freedom to act according to your values.

Moreover, emotions manifest differently in the body (the physiological component) and focus on different timeframes (past, present, or future), even though they are all temporary. That is, they all pass. ALL OF THEM.

Here, I share information about some of the most common ones, by way of example:

HAPPINESS

Emotions	Light	Shadow
Joy: Celebration	Gives you space for enjoyment.	Trivializes life.
Fear: Protection	Makes you competent, capable, and intelligent.	Paralyzes you and prevents action.
Anger: Injustice	Creates boundaries and protects you.	Hurts and destroys.
Sadness: Loss	Helps you let go, reflect, renew, or recover what was lost.	Isolates and depresses you.
Guilt: Mistake (Breaking a personal value)	Invites reflection, safeguards your values, predisposes you to apologize, make amends, and question your beliefs (to keep or change them).	Leads to self-punishment.
Shame: Insufficiency (Breaking a social value)	Protects your public identity, maintains order, and upholds collective values.	Makes you want to avoid judgment, being seen, or evaluated; causes feelings of incompleteness, unworthiness, or lack of belonging; leads to self-betrayal.
Envy: Admiration/Lack of self-esteem	Te ayuda a poder admirar a otros, aprender de ellos y ser consciente de tus deseos.	Breeds resentment; you want everything for yourself because you "deserve" it.
Jealousy: Disloyalty	Reconnects you with what you value, want for yourself, and fear losing (a relationship).	Generates paranoia and causes harm.
Love: Acceptance	Is the foundation of connection and weaves relationships.	Accepting others as they are could enable unhealthy behaviors; can be used for manipulation.
Boredom: Disinterest	Invites you to explore new possibilities and be creative.	Leads to stagnation and idle behavior.

Love, which is often seen as a "positive" emotion, can sometimes lead to manipulating another person. On the other hand, anger, typically considered a "negative" emotion, can help you set healthy boundaries and strengthen relationships. Therefore, it's not about rejecting uncomfortable emotions or resigning yourself to them. Instead, it's about starting an active process of acceptance where you consciously choose the course of action to understand and address the emotion, and ultimately benefit from it.

The world of emotions is fascinating and vast, and it is precisely our lack of knowledge that leads us to reject exploring it. For example, did you know there are primary and secondary emotions? Or that anger is often a secondary emotion that hides fear or sadness? This is especially clear in teenagers.

The uncertainty that emotions bring can make us fearful of delving into the emotional world. We feel it's like stepping into quicksand, losing control, and being in danger. So instead, we disguise our fear with apathy or disinterest, saying things like "That's boring," "That's cheesy," or "That's for girls." This avoids the opportunity to understand and strengthen one of the five areas of SPIRE – emotional well-being – and diminishes our chances of living fully by 20%. That's why to be happy is for the brave.

Emotional learning requires formal efforts to build self-awareness, self-regulation, a growth mindset, empathy, humility, gratitude, scientific understanding, and self-compassion. **It is a journey that, once you bravely begin, will make you live intensely and passionately.**

Building My Happiness: **Facing My Emotions**

1. Which emotion from the table do I feel most frequently?
2. How could I apply the information from the table to align my behaviors with the positive aspect of that emotion?
3. If I find myself living in the shadow side of an emotion, what am I currently sacrificing in my life because of it?

4. What has stopped me from exploring my emotional world?
5. What is the most significant insight or idea I've gained from this section?
6. What commitment will I make to myself to build emotional well-being in my life?

RESILIENCE AND OPTIMISM

> "Life isn't about waiting for the storm to pass, but about learning to dance in the rain."
> VIVIAN GREENE

Emotional well-being, in general, involves building resilience in the face of life's inherent adversity and cultivating optimism. This is crucial for developing confidence and knowing that even when challenges arise, you won't break — you'll grow from them.

Working on the different areas of SPIRE (Spiritual, Physical, Intellectual, Relational, and Emotional well-being) helps build resilience. If you are clear about what gives your life purpose, maintain good health, have extensive knowledge, a solid network of relationships, and understand your emotions, you'll be much better prepared to face tough times and thrive.

Personally, I believe exercise has been my greatest ally in building resilience. I remember recording a social media story where I shared that even though I don't wake up motivated to work out every day when I exercise despite feeling unmotivated, it strengthens my character and confidence. Exercise not only makes you healthier but also more resilient. Physical strength translates into mental strength. All SPIRE elements help build happiness and resilience during adversity and trauma.

Strengthening your optimism also improves resilience. According to Dr. Martin Seligman, the father of positive psychology, optimism depends on how you explain the good and bad events in your life. If you constantly focus on the negative, complain, imagine tragedies that never happen, live in constant fear, and experience high-stress levels, it may be time to choose differently and reframe your story with optimism and gratitude.

Optimists view adversity as a temporary challenge. They know everything passes and maintain hope, trusting that the future will improve. The good news is that optimism can be learned and strengthened, just like a muscle. No matter the source of your hardship or how long ago it happened, you can always reframe your story to build a life with greater well-being, happiness, and fulfillment.

The best opportunity to practice realistic optimism is when adversity arises. To do this, you can take the following actions:

1. **Determine the Duration:** Analyze whether the undesirable situation is permanent or temporary.
2. **Put It in Perspective:** Identify which areas of your life are affected by the undesirable situation.
3. **Assess the Risks:** Think about the worst-case scenarios and make a list. Clearly evaluate the impact/damage level and the likelihood of each item on your list occurring.
4. **Filter and Focus Your Attention:** From the previous list, separate what is within your control and what isn't.
5. **Implement Safeguards:** For the things within your control, decide what you can do to prevent them.
6. **Create an Action Plan and Execute It:** Outline specific steps and carry them out.

7. **Acknowledge the Lessons:** Reflect on what you learned and identify any positive outcomes from the undesirable situation.

Just as repeated experiences can teach you helplessness (the belief that your actions don't significantly impact your reality), they can also teach you optimism — a mental attitude that expects favorable results, even in the face of challenges, and drives you to take action.

Of course, this isn't about falling into idealism or fantasy. Optimism is meaningless if it's not paired with action plans that you actually follow through on. The key is to focus on what you can control. Personal Reflection for Optimism Personally, I like to ask myself every night:

- What was the best part of the day?
- What made living this day worth the effort?

These two questions help me remember that days don't have to be extraordinary, special, or perfect to be worth living. They also allow me to capitalize on bad days by focusing on their lessons and benefits.

Building My Happiness: **Strengthening My Resilience and Optimism**

1. Think of an adverse situation you are experiencing and apply the 7-step exercise.
2. What insights do you have?
3. What does your previous answer invite you to do?

4. What was the most valuable part of your day? (Do this every day.)

GIVING THANKS VS BEING GRATEFUL

> "Gratitude can transform common days into 'thanksgivings,' turn routine jobs into joy, and change ordinary opportunities into blessings."
> WILLIAM ARTHUR WARD

Gratitude doesn't just mean giving thanks; it goes much further. It is a deep emotion (e-motion = energy in motion) of fortune and appreciation for something specific present in your life. **Gratitude is one of those muscles that strengthens and can become a way of living.** At its fullest expression, gratitude entails actions of reciprocity.

The word "gratitude" comes from the Latin "gratia," which means grace. In other words, when someone received something from another person, they would respond by wishing them well, with grace. Gratitude involves a feeling of appreciation for what you received, whether tangible or intangible, and helps you connect with something greater by recognizing the goodness and fortune in your life.

To be grateful for something, you had to notice it and consider it valuable; you had to connect with it. That means your Ascending Reticular Activating System (ARAS) focused on that specific thing and filtered out many other stimuli and information it deemed less relevant, creating a precedent in your mind (a message like "this matters") and developing a "velcro" or "magnetism" to detect similar situations or events in the future. This is how your mind registers that something is important.

For example, a woman doesn't see as many pregnant women as when she is pregnant herself. A man doesn't see as many cars of a specific model and color until he decides that's the one he wants to buy. You don't notice as many ads for a product until you decide that it's something you need or want, etc. **When you express gratitude, you focus your attention and train your mind.** This is why gratitude also creates an upward spiral, a virtuous circle. This simple idea is the foundation of the famous "Law of Attraction" shared in Rhonda Byrne's book The Secret.

Gratitude develops your conscious and intentional observation (you see more of it) while simultaneously elevating your vibration by perceiving yourself as fortunate and blessed.

Research has shown that consciously practicing gratitude can reduce feelings of stress and anxiety. In fact, studies have found that a single act of reflective gratitude produces a 10% increase in feelings of joy and a 35% decrease in symptoms of depression.

Some researchers believe that people have a negativity bias because, for thousands of years, the human species has focused on dangers and problems to survive. In other words, if ancient humans focused on a sunrise, the jaguar would come and eat them... That's why we developed this defense mechanism that gives us "Teflon" for the good and "Velcro" for the bad. And while it allowed us to survive, if taken to the extreme, it can also make us live from a place of scarcity, dissatisfaction, complaints, discontent, and the dangers of stress...

Although there is controversy surrounding this idea, with some authors and research opposing or supporting it, I believe the important thing is to bring to consciousness the possibility that you have the **choice of where to predominantly place your attention**. Do you choose to focus on what you do have or on what's missing? Gratitude is an incredibly powerful tool for building long-term happiness and well-being because it forces us to see the glass as half full, to focus on what was pleasant and sufficient, and therefore, generate more of that.

Similarly, strengthening your habit of gratitude directly impacts your levels of hope and optimism, thereby increasing your happiness. **Hope and gratitude build a virtuous cycle and nurture each other.**

Is gratitude obvious or elusive? Gratitude can seem obvious, yet at times, impossible. It is very easy to be grateful when things are going well; it feels natural and is easy to sustain. But what happens when things go wrong? Can you still be grateful? The short answer is: Yes!

Gratitude invites you to embrace life's adversity because it helps you find usefulness even in unpleasant things and reframe situations as challenges instead of problems. For example, I am grateful for the conflict with that person because it helped me set boundaries. I am grateful for the discomfort I felt because it helped me listen to my body and rest. I am grateful for my colleague's comment, which made me uncomfortable because it showed me that I need to work on a specific aspect of myself. I am grateful for that setback because it reminds me that the adventure of living involves vulnerability and uncertainty.

Gratitude, gratitude, gratitude... **Just like hope, gratitude requires a personal commitment.**

Science says that people who express gratitude experience greater:

- Happiness.
- Success.
- Optimism.
- Kindness.
- Generosity.
- Health.
- Connection with themselves.

HAPPINESS

In September 2021, I met Masouma, a woman born in Afghanistan, then a refugee in Mexico. Beyond her story of extraordinary and inspiring bravery, effort, and hope, Masouma gave me one of the biggest "cold buckets of water" I have ever received in my life. A "tómala," as my kids would say...

A friend asked me to meet with her to get to know her and support her in whatever she might need during her stay in Mexico City. We agreed to meet at a café to get to know each other and have breakfast. After telling me her story in detail, keeping me on the edge of my seat and wiping away my tears for several hours, I asked her:

"What do you like most about my country (Mexico) now that you've been here for a few weeks?"

Obviously, I expected her to say the typical things: the food, the culture, the warmth of the people, etc. But her answer was far from that. She took a breath and, with a thoughtful look, said:

"Feeling my hair move with the wind. And second, walking in heels on Reforma" (a landmark street in the city). I was stunned, unable to say a word.

Sometimes, we live with so much privilege that we forget to appreciate the small but significant things in everyday life. And it's precisely those "little tastes of fortune" that are available to everyone (without exception) almost every day that we can capitalize on to strengthen our muscles of hope, optimism, gratitude, and, therefore, happiness.

Training your mind to focus on these "tiny details" is a great boost to building long-term well-being and fulfillment. Those details are there, but if you don't appreciate them, it's as if they weren't. Why wait until they are gone to value and give thanks for them?

Struggling to build a habit of gratitude? Does it feel strange and unfamiliar? If you don't know where to start, think about everything in your body, relationships, and life that, if you didn't have it, you would deeply miss.

Gratitude heals, energizes, changes lives, and amplifies emotions. Gratitude is one of the most powerful tools for building long-term well-being and achieving tangible results quickly. You can even start by thanking YOURSELF for everything you've done and chosen to get to where you are today... Don't take anything for granted!

And you, what are you grateful for?

Here are several tools to help you start strengthening your gratitude muscle:

- Download a free, quick gratitude exercise on my website.
- Start your gratitude journal or jar now! Every day, at the same time, write down three things you are grateful for. I like to do it at night to review my day and ask myself: "What made my day worthwhile?"
- Listen to Episode 10, "Gracias Totales," from the first season of my podcast Valentinamente Feliz, on any audio platform. I'm sure you'll find valuable ideas there.

Write Yourself a Thank-You Letter:

Start by writing: "Today, I, (your name), thank myself for..."

And take off for 10 minutes thanking yourself for EVERYTHING you are, have done, have, can do, live, etc.

Two-Minute Miracle: Take two minutes out of your day to thank someone for what they have done for you, looking them directly in the eyes.

Thank-You Letter: Write a letter to someone from a place of deep gratitude, whether or not you choose to deliver it.

Building My Happiness: **Strengthening My Gratitude**

1. What idea related to gratitude resonated with me the most?
2. What do I commit to doing to strengthen my gratitude muscle?

DIAGNOSIS: HOW HAPPY AM I?

> "What cannot be measured cannot be improved."
> PETER DRUCKER

How happy do you consider yourself today? It's important to know where you stand in your happiness levels to have a reference point for your starting place. If you decide to formally work on building your happiness, you can later measure your progress and celebrate yourself.

Therefore, I invite you to do the following exercise, keeping in mind that the results do not define you as a person; they are just a snapshot of your current perception of your life.

Working formally on your long-term well-being is the greatest act of self-love. As I always recommend, you can accompany it with a ritual. That is, if you feel like it, you can play some calming music to promote a reflective state, pour yourself your favorite drink, and light a candle or a diffuser with a pleasant scent. The intention is to engage all your senses in a state of comfort, openness, and introspection.

Are you ready to start your happiness diagnosis?

Instructions:

1. **Rate/evaluate** how you are doing today in each area of SPIRE; in the first column – How much?
2. **Analyze and briefly describe** the reasons, situations, and characteristics behind that rating for each area of SPIRE; in the second column – Why?
3. **Prescribe** or list the actions you could take to improve your well-being level in each area in the third column – How?
4. **Choose one action/effort** from all those you wrote in the previous step and commit to being consistent with it.

I suggest that you don't just focus on detailing the areas you rated the lowest, as one of the strategies of positive psychology is to leverage strengths to address areas of opportunity.

Here's an image and example (of the first type of well-being) for easy reference, as well as a QR code with the PDF and instructions.

MODELO SPIRE

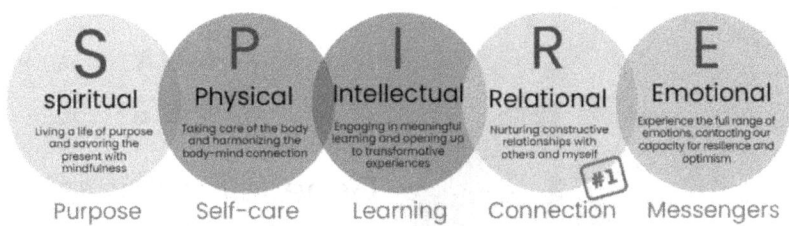

Tal Ben-Shahar, Megan McDonough y Maria Sirois

Work area #	Motives/Reasons Why?	Improvement Options How will I improve?
S		
P		
I		
R		
E		

What percentage of your happiness depends on you? In 2005, academics and researchers Sonja Lyubomirsky, Ken Sheldon, and David Schkade conducted a study to answer this question. They concluded that, under average conditions (not in survival situations like war, extreme poverty, natural disasters, etc.), 50% of happiness depends on your biology or genetics and your early life experiences (ages 0-7), 40% depends on your intentional activities or what we can call your attitude, and the remaining 10% is completely out of your control, such as what your neighbor does, the weather, government decisions, etc.

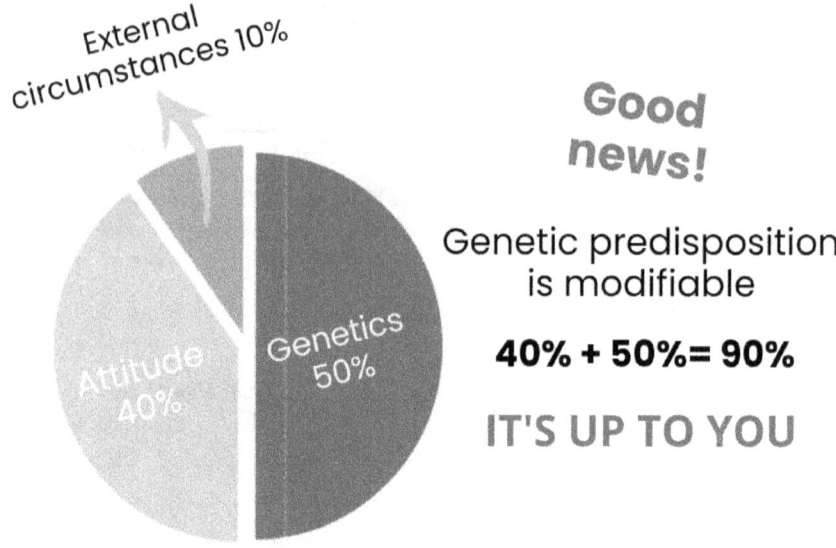

But here's the good news: thanks to neuroscience, which offers insights into the neural plasticity of the human brain, the 50% related to genetics can be modified. In other words, by building healthy physical, mental, and emotional habits, you can create new structures in your brain that counteract the genetic predisposition you were born with.

Although genetics and context are important ingredients, they are not determinants. It's like in a card game, the hand you're dealt does influence the outcome, but what you do with those cards determines the result. In other words, if your family has a genetic predisposition to depression or anxiety, there are many measures you can take from an early age to counteract the implications of that in your life, such as maintaining physical activity habits, developing optimism skills, building resilience, etc.

So, if we add the 50% you can modify, plus the 40% which is your attitude, 90% is within your power. Conclusion: **happiness is not an easy path, but it can definitely be successfully built**. I hope you give yourself that reinterpretation of your stories and start those small intentional and conscious efforts to build a little more well-being in your life every day... and in doing so, you'll start adding pieces to the Lego of your life.

Building My Happiness: **Choosing My Truths About Happiness**

1. How is my genetics? What characteristics do I observe that are repeated across generations in my family tree?
2. Which ones do I believe benefit me and which ones do not?
3. What do I commit to doing to improve the genetic predispositions that don't benefit me?
4. How has my attitude been towards life and those significant events?
5. What is definitely out of my control and I need to accept?
6. What do I commit to doing based on my findings?

IT'S A PROCESS, NOT A DECISION

Stating that happiness is a decision is false. I can decide to be happy, but if I haven't done all the work required to build a fulfilling life, I won't be. It's very important to clarify this (as harsh or cruel as it may sound) so that if you decide to be happy, you understand that building fulfillment is a lifelong journey, and you don't give up thinking happiness isn't for you just because you decided with all your heart to be happy and still aren't. **It won't be easy, but every effort, doubt, discomfort, and challenge will be worth it, I guarantee it.**

Don't believe in false expectations, seduced by the immediacy and comfort of modern life. That's why happiness isn't for everyone.

It's only for the brave who refuse to settle for a mediocre life and are willing to do the uncomfortable or frightening work, no matter how overwhelming it may seem.

If you find no meaning, feel like the wave is dragging you down, or are tired of your daily life, the truth is you don't have much to lose. Today, I believe it's an excellent opportunity to gift yourself a moment to reflect on your life. Ask yourself if you are living or just surviving, and if you're surviving, I suggest considering the possibility of choosing to be happy as the first step in a lifelong adventure. But remember, you'll need to put in effort and patience because deciding isn't enough! A marathon begins with the first step!

For many years, I even believed in the idea that happiness was a decision. Thinking that way gave me a sense of empowerment, autonomy, and agency – that a simple choice was enough to be happy. Today, I know I was wrong, and that it's much more complex than that.

In my case, I decided to work on building my happiness since I was a teenager, and I can tell you I've been in the process for over 25 years, and I believe I'll continue for the rest of my life. Today, I know that **happiness is not a decision, but a process that begins with a conscious decision, accompanied by many more decisions** tied to courage, discipline, commitment, effort, emotional management, consistency, intention, etc., which are part of the adventure of living.

Happiness is a lifestyle, accessible only to the brave. When you decide to be happy and are willing to work on building a little well-being every day, you begin to transform your presence on this planet.

For me, happiness is not a distant, abstract concept that only the "enlightened" can understand and achieve, but a concrete, practical, and ambitious idea that anyone willing to try can bring to life by being brave.

Building My Happiness: **Deciding to Be Happy**

1. Did I ever believe that happiness wasn't for me? Why?
2. Do I decide today to be happy, willing to do the work it requires?
3. How can I remind myself that happiness is a long-term process so I don't get desperate or impatient?
4. How can I achieve some quick, tangible results to build the confidence that will push me to keep going?

FORMULAS

Is there a formula for happiness? Yes, and according to scientists Lyubomirsky, Sheldon, Schkade, and Seligman (all of them leading references in the field of the Science of Happiness), it is as follows:

H (happiness) = R (set range/genetics) + C (circumstances) + V (volition).

Formula of Happiness

$$H = R + C + V$$

R: Set Range (Genetics)
C: Circumstances
V: Volition (Intentional Activities)

Lyubomirsky, Sheldon, Schkade and Seligman

The formula states that happiness is the sum of our genetic predisposition for happiness, the contextual situation in which we live, and the discretionary effort we are willing to make. **This generic formula** broadly explains the components of happiness. However, while it helps understand the factors involved, it doesn't serve much as a guide or generic recipe to start building your happiness. It is essential to be strategic in your happiness construction at different stages of your journey.

For this definition, the happiness calculator is very useful – a tool to allocate our limited resources (energy, time, money, inputs, etc.) across the 5 SPIRE areas. Suppose you only have 100 marbles (resources); choose how many you want to assign to each area based on your circumstances and current stage of life. Will you place 20 in each or make an uneven distribution to achieve balance?

For example, if I decided to run a marathon (physical well-being), I would have to adjust my current formula. Since I will be using time and energy to train for the race, I'll have to decide if I sacrifice those resources for meetings with my friends or family (relational well-being) or study less (intellectual well-being).

My personal happiness formula, in this case, would look like this:

Therefore, you must consider a **personal happiness formula**, which is the definition or combination each person makes according to their current life stage. There is no magic formula that applies to everyone or to a person throughout their entire life.

I am convinced that defining your personal happiness formula consciously, recognizing yourself as an integral being (spiritual, physical, intellectual, relational, and emotional), and adjusting it to the flow of life is key.

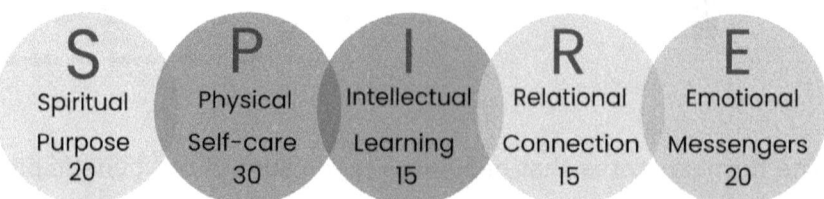

HAPPINESS

The demand to be at the top of everything, the one that makes you feel suffocated, like you're falling short in every area, letting everyone down, and feeling exhausted.

For example, it's common to focus on working toward professional success and financial prosperity, completely neglecting our relationships. Big mistake! This is a terrible decision regarding overall well-being, as the number one predictor of happiness is the quality of our important relationships. This idea is backed by extensive scientific evidence, and it was recently confirmed by the new findings from the longest documented anthropological study in human history, led by Dr. Robert Waldinger, a psychiatrist and psychoanalyst from Harvard, and co-author of the book The Good Life.

By the way, I highly recommend the book, and here's a QR code to an excerpt of the most relevant information from his conference in Puebla, Mexico, at the Festival de las Ideas in March 2024, where I had the opportunity to meet him and hear him live.

Building My Happiness: **Defining My Personal Formula for Happiness**

1. What is my current personal formula for happiness? How many marbles do I allocate to each aspect of SPIRE?
2. How did I arrive at this formula? Was it through conscious strategy or by inertia?
3. What adjustments to my formula do I commit to making with myself to live more in alignment with my current priorities and stage of life?

4. How can I give greater importance to my significant relationships (predictor #1) to maximize my overall well-being?

WHY IS BEING HAPPY SUCH A CHALLENGE?

Being happy is a challenge because it is a **process that requires courage, time, and a lot of effort**, especially since it feels uncomfortable at first. While it begins with a conscious decision, it continues with a lot of intentional and constant work that requires small daily decisions, moment by moment. You need a lot of energy, willpower, and momentum at times to make things happen, and at other moments, a lot of serenity, pause, and balance to recalibrate the compass, rethink the strategy, and adjust the plan.

Thanks to my more than 20 years of studying human behavior and my passion for the topic of happiness, I have concluded that there are 8 pillars or key aspects to work on when you commit to building your happiness. These pillars support the complex and ambitious construction that being happy entails. I love that there are 8, because it is the symbol of infinity, which, in this case, represents for me the infinite possibilities available on a personal journey toward well-being:

This graphic shows the key ideas of each pillar:

1. SELF-LOVE

> "Loving oneself is the beginning of a lifelong adventure."
> OSCAR WILDE

Have you ever thought about which relationship is the most important one you have?

The most important relationship you have is with the person who's been with you from your first cry in the delivery room and will be there until your last breath. And that person is you.

Why is self-love important?

Self-love is important because it determines every aspect of your life, including:

- Professional success.
- Ambitions.

- Jobs you apply for.
- How you negotiate.
- Your activities and performance.
- Your spirituality.
- The quality of your relationships.
- The boundaries you set.
- Your physical well-being and health.
- Your image and self-care.
- Your internal dialogue and mental health.
- Your emotional intelligence.
- The likelihood of achieving your dreams.
- Your level of resilience/antifragility.
- Whether or not you ask for help.
- Your knowledge and learning.
- How you invest your time.
- Your financial stability.

Self-love is that deep and honest connection with yourself where you recognize that you are worthy, deserving, capable, and that you belong — that you have a place in this life. From there, you respect yourself, honor yourself, celebrate yourself, and build your well-being. Can you love yourself if you don't know yourself? The answer is NO. **The beginning of self-love is self-knowledge**, and like any other loving relationship, it needs to be nurtured and cultivated.

In one phrase, self-love is connecting with your essence and feeling fulfilled by being you. It's the place where all loving words fit: worth, esteem, compassion, confidence, security, understanding, appreciation, respect, self-embrace, etc.

Self-love is doing for yourself and feeling for yourself what you would do and feel for a close friend. Self-love is looking after yourself and taking action to maintain your physical, mental, emotional, spiritual, and relational well-being.

It's hard for me to imagine that you have a pet you genuinely love with all your heart, but you never bathe it, feed it scraps, listen to it, or attend to its needs. It remains confined in an insufficient space, exposed to the elements, never gets taken for a walk, is never vaccinated, or cared for in terms of health. Love must be supported by concrete actions to truly be love. And you, do you take care of yourself? What do you do for yourself?

Sometimes, it helps to define a concept by specifying what it is not. And I believe this is one of those times. Self-love is NOT:

- Judging myself, criticizing myself, having that toxic internal dialogue that constantly makes me feel inadequate... under the pretext of wanting to improve.
- Punishing myself, mistreating myself, self-harming, feeding guilt, or engaging in addictions.
- Giving and giving until I have nothing left.
- Never setting boundaries.
- Demanding so much of myself to be perfect (even though I know I will never achieve it) until I suffocate.
- Now, what self-love truly IS:
- It is a deep and honest connection with yourself. Where you recognize that you are valuable, deserving, that you have a place, that you belong, and that you are capable of building well-being in your life.
- It is seeking relationships that add to your life.
- It is knowing how to ask for help when you need it.
- It is connecting with your essence and falling in love with yourself (with both your light and your shadow).
- It is knowing yourself and taking care of yourself.

The main enemy of self-love is shame — that deep pain of "not measuring up," of feeling that something is wrong with you, that you are incomplete and defective. Ultimately, it is closely tied to fear. Fear of rejection, humiliation (mockery), abandonment, facing your mistakes, and feeling inadequate. Shame, in its light side, as we've mentioned, helps maintain social order and invites you to build authentic self-love. But in its shadow side, it leads you to betray yourself to please others and fit in, or to feel inadequate, insufficient, or broken.

Brené Brown is an expert on the topic of shame, and I'm her fan. I've read all her books: The Gifts of Imperfection, Rising Strong, The Power of Vulnerability, Atlas of the Heart, among others. I even took her course "Dare to Lead" with Lizi Oceransky, a certified facilitator of Brené Brown, where I learned that it is precisely shame that ruins our lives and dreams because it destroys our sense of worth when we feed it and let it guide our decisions and relationships with others.

In her book The Power of Vulnerability, Brené Brown shares that 85% of the people interviewed for her research on shame remember a specific incident so shameful that it changed the way they saw themselves. When broken down by gender, body image is the most common trigger of shame for women, while for men, it is having their partner think they are weak.

Brené refers to shame as a liar and a thief of stories. If you look for evidence to feed your shame, you will find it. There will always be someone more attractive, more intelligent, wealthier, or more likable... But only you have your unique combination. You are one of a kind! So stop, and be aware that **your worth is not negotiable**.

The author suggests that courage, compassion (acceptance), and connection are ways to cultivate your worth and that the key is PRACTICE. Without a doubt, it is a reading I highly recommend.

Self-disdain, soul disconnection, and the fear you might experience today—if that's the case—are the result of the stories you've told yourself about what has happened in your life. And as

HAPPINESS

Brené Brown says, it's not about denying the story, but challenging the ending. Remember that you can ALWAYS reinterpret your story and tell yourself narratives that uplift you. In the end, your concept of yourself is a story you've been constructing over the years and repeating to yourself. In this case, your beliefs about yourself shape you too. If you believe you are brave, you'll likely take courageous actions; if you believe you are progressive, you'll raise your hand for that promotion; if you believe you are generous, you'll share; if you believe you are weak, you'll surround yourself with abusers and bow your head; if you believe you are mediocre, you'll drift through life without higher expectations, etc.

How Do You Build Self-Love?

Like any other relationship, you have to work at it. Just think about how you would build a relationship with a new friend, colleague, family member, or someone you're attracted to. You'd start by getting to know them and doing everything you can to show your best self—listening carefully, paying attention to details, being present, being supportive and kind. That's how the bond strengthens.

It's the same with you. Build a relationship with yourself, starting with self-knowledge and continuing with intentional, conscious, and consistent efforts that bring out your best version. Efforts that make you feel supported that remind you that you are your best company... until you fall in love with yourself.

Living fully in the present requires awareness, and that only happens when you're comfortable being who you are, to the point where you don't want to run away from yourself and allow yourself to just be you, here and now. Give up the aspiration of a perfect life—not only because you'll never achieve it (it doesn't even exist), but because it exhausts, frustrates, and wears you down, making you feel perpetually dissatisfied.

Be aware that toxic perfectionism is probably driven by shame. Feeling defective makes you overwork to meet impossible standards, striving to feel worthy, sufficient, and deserving.

Living for yourself, embracing your limitations, and celebrating your strengths will be a liberating and empowering process.
It's Important to Understand the Significance of Having a:
Healthy, loving, respectful, intimate, and compassionate relationship with yourself.

Having Self-Esteem Means Realizing These Things:

1. **You Belong:** You have a place.
2. **You Are Worthy:** You are a unique and incomparable being, and simply for that, you are valuable.
3. **You Deserve:** It is your right to be happy and to have good things happen to you.
4. **You Choose:** Be aware of your autonomy and freedom, knowing you will live with the consequences of your decisions.
5. **You Are Capable:** Trust in your ability and have a solid sense of self-efficacy. Some authors call this a sense of agency—the ability to act intentionally and achieve goals guided by reason. It means knowing you can take action and following through on what you decide.

Some Considerations That May Help You:

- **Self-Concept:** What you think of yourself; be flexible, avoid perfectionism, be open to listening to different opinions, review your goals and real possibilities.

- **Self-Image:** How much you like yourself (there's always something missing or in excess); there are no absolute truths—beauty is cultural.
- **Self-Reinforcement:** How much you reward or punish yourself. Ouch!
- **Self-Efficacy:** Confidence in yourself and your abilities.

The Main Enemies of Self-Esteem (Keep Them on Your Radar and Address Them):

- **Shame:** Makes you feel inadequate, incomplete, and unworthy.
- **Fear:** Can paralyze you.
- **Hopelessness:** Generates spirals of negative thoughts and can lead to victimhood.
- **Self-Pity:** Leads you to connect with others in toxic ways.
- **Guilt:** Makes you betray yourself by pleasing others and living far from your true values.

As I mentioned in the section about your relationship with yourself, one of the most important components of self-love is inner dialogue. Reflect: How do you talk to yourself? What do you repeat about yourself? How often do you fuel thoughts of hope or tragedy?

One of my greatest achievements at 41 years old, just recently celebrated, is having made my mind a safe, comfortable, and harmonious place. Today, with immense pride, I can share that I have trained my inner voice to:

- Support me
- Ground me
- Unlearn what doesn't serve me

- Absorb what is useful
- Calm me in moments of uncertainty
- Use its intuition
- Cut off destructive spirals that only fuel my anxiety
- Dismiss hurtful opinions (which say more about the giver than about me)
- Keep my shame in check
- Celebrate and motivate me
- Decide based on my values and not illusions
- Keep fear as a co-pilot
- Manage the ego

This isn't absolute, of course—there are days when I realize I need to strengthen certain mental habits. But generally, with much effort, I've managed to enjoy being in my mind.

It's common that when you start working on your self-love, you may be judged as selfish. This is how it's often perceived at first because sometimes we're raised to believe that false modesty and keeping a low profile equate to humility. True humility is not thinking of yourself as more valuable than anyone else, but not less either. Humility and self-love are not at odds; in fact, humility requires self-love.

The truth is that **formally building a loving relationship with yourself is not only not selfish—it's the greatest act of generosity for two reasons:**

1. By connecting with your essence and your highest potential, you build your **best version**, and that is the one you **share with others** and the world.
2. You become an example and **source of inspiration** so that others, seeing it's possible, are encouraged to work on their self-love too. In other words, self-love is contagious.

Working on your self-love means making yourself a priority and ensuring that in ALL the decisions you make—big or small—you are aware of your protagonist role and that you deserve the best.

I'm not saying you should think you're the center of the universe—don't misunderstand. I mean that you should know that you are valuable simply because you ARE YOU, and THERE IS NOTHING WRONG WITH YOU. You are wonderful just as you are, deserve to be happy and fulfilled, and are completely capable of achieving it.

Having a healthy relationship with yourself isn't about luck or magic. **Self-esteem and self-love are about personal work**, meaning they require intentional, conscious, and consistent efforts to build and strengthen over the long term. But remember, any marathon begins with the first step.

I know I love myself when I'm addicted to me, when I enjoy how I talk to myself, when I feel fulfilled in my own company, when I know my ideas are brilliant (sometimes) or bad (other times), and it's okay. I laugh alone, I've made peace with life (its past, present, and future), I don't need to give explanations, please others, or receive applause to feel enough. I don't allow just anyone into my life, my heart, or my skin. I shine with my own light, I am self-sufficient, I recognize my fear and don't let it paralyze me, and I don't live self-absorbed. I also acknowledge my shadow and areas for growth. I'm not selfish; I simply love myself deeply.

When it comes to social media or dating platforms, if you aren't sure of who you are and what you're worth, you run the risk of believing that likes, comments, and followers determine your identity and value.

In dating apps like Tinder, people are chosen primarily based on a photo, ignoring the integrity of the human being. In other words, it doesn't matter what a person knows, feels, has experienced, their skills, relationships, or values—only their image matters.

TO BE HAPPY IS FOR THE BRAVE

This creates horrible anxiety from the fear of not being enough, reinforcing the false idea that external factors determine your value. Conversely, it can make us fall into the illusion of acceptance, engaging in a game of fleeting affections that become a "drug" due to the dopamine they release. This may bring pleasure at first but leads to a profound sense of sadness and emptiness in the long run.

I don't demonize or condemn the use of these platforms, but I suggest that if you're going to participate, **make sure you deeply know who you are and how much you're worth first**, so you don't end up basing your self-concept on what these apps reflect back to you.

You'll find a downloadable self-love diagnostic questionnaire to help you delve deeper into building a wonderful relationship with yourself. Remember, you don't have to show it to anyone, and it's important to do it because what you don't know, you can't improve. You'll also find a self-appreciation and gratitude exercise for yourself. This might sound strange because maybe you've never truly acknowledged yourself, or at least given yourself the benefit of the doubt to explore the wonderful and fascinating being that you are—yes, even in your imperfection, or your perfect imperfection, with all your humanity. Remember, to be happy is for the brave.

Building My Happiness: Reviewing My Self-Love

1. Do I feel like I know myself deeply?
2. Do I recognize myself as the most important person in my life?
3. What do I think of myself? How do I describe myself?
4. Do I like my previous answer? If not, how can I redefine my concept of myself?
5. Do I feel that I can, belong, choose, am worthy, and deserve?
6. Which of the enemies of self-love shows up most frequently?
7. How do I treat myself?
8. Do I listen to my body? Do I honor it by giving it rest when it asks for it? Do I see it as a machine or an ornament?
9. Have I thanked it for being my armor and primary vehicle all these years?
10. Does what others think of me determine my worth?
11. When was the last time I celebrated myself?

2. PERSONAL RESPONSIBILITY

> "Living is knowing how to accept, in balance, the consequences of our decisions."
> — PAULO COELHO

Taking the wheel of your life in your own hands and being responsible for your reality is the most satisfying and empowering expe-

rience you can have. Feeling and knowing that you are the creator and owner of your life is truly the beginning of living fully.

While we have already touched on personal responsibility, it's important to delve deeper into why it is essential for building your happiness. As I mentioned, the word responsibility (response-ability) refers to the ability to respond to what happens to us to face life, including its adversity and unhappiness.

Have you thought about the possibility of owning your life and stopping the need to ask for permission or opinions to live it? How long have you let others decide your life, either directly or indirectly by valuing their opinions so highly? How many opportunities have you missed because you felt that your life didn't depend on your decisions?

Maybe the thought of having to decide your life from now on, making yourself a priority, and no longer blaming others for your mistakes and disappointments sounds terrifying. Or maybe it seems impossible if you've spent years living outwardly, trying to please everyone around you to the point where your identity has faded. In other words, you no longer know if you are truly yourself in essence or just the character others told you to be.

In the best-case scenario, the idea of living for yourself might sound thrilling, and starting today, you choose for and by yourself. In any case, remember: to be happy is for the brave.

If you acknowledge that your decisions and actions have brought you to where you are today, then your decisions and actions can also move you from there if you are unhappy. Shifting from helplessness to empowerment will give you hope — the belief in a better future.

This life is yours, even when it doesn't seem that way. So connect with your essence and stop asking for permission or opinions to live. Being happy is your responsibility. Step away from the role of the victim. Feel like the owner and creator of your life. Recognizing that you've built your present with all those small and big decisions, with both successes and mistakes, offers you the opportunity to know you are 100% capable of changing it.

WHERE DO YOUR DECISIONS TAKE YOU?

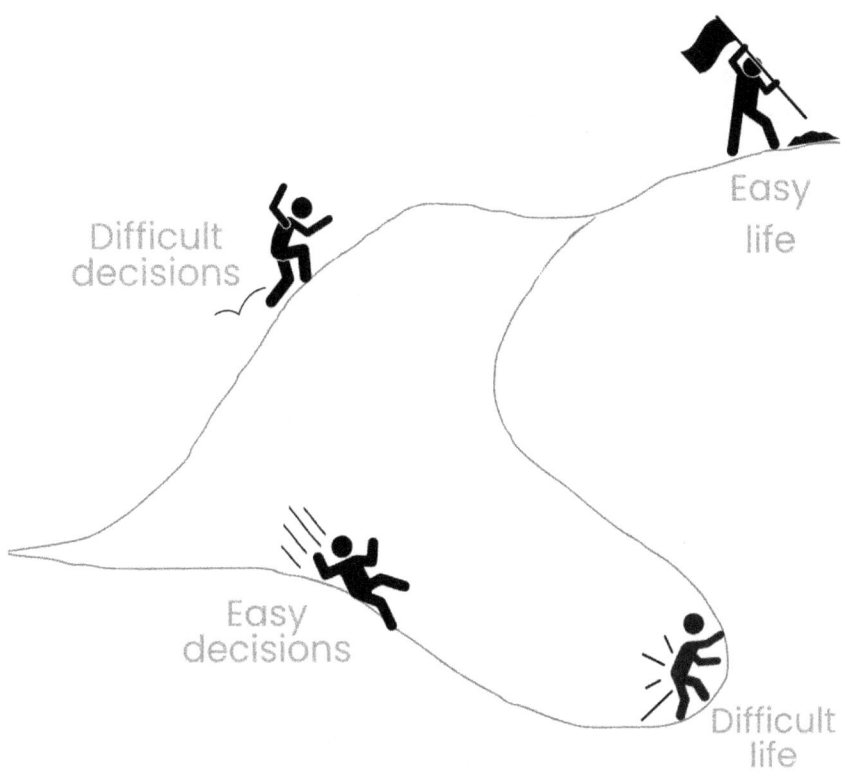

If you're waiting for your partner, your boss, the government, your children, your parents, your neighbors, or someone or something else to change for you to be happy, let me tell you: you're going to die unhappy. If even when you decide to change, it's difficult, imagine how absurd it is to try to change someone who doesn't want to change.

Sometimes, to avoid the responsibility of making mistakes, you choose someone else to decide for you. But if that person makes the wrong decision, it's still your mistake because you chose someone unqualified to decide on your behalf. **In other words, even when you refuse to decide and delegate the decision, you are still deciding. You always choose!** The goal is to make your decisions more and more conscious every day.

When you know and feel capable of responding to life, and you see the results of those small adjustments and efforts you're making, it's impossible not to get excited and passionate about living — truly living — being the protagonist of your own life.

When you understand that no one else will do the work for you and you take responsibility for your life, you can find the push you need to be brave and make the necessary efforts, even with fear. That's how **responsibility and courage are directly proportional — when one increases, the other rises too.**

Here's a chart illustrating your role:

ADVANCING IN MY RESPONSIBILITY

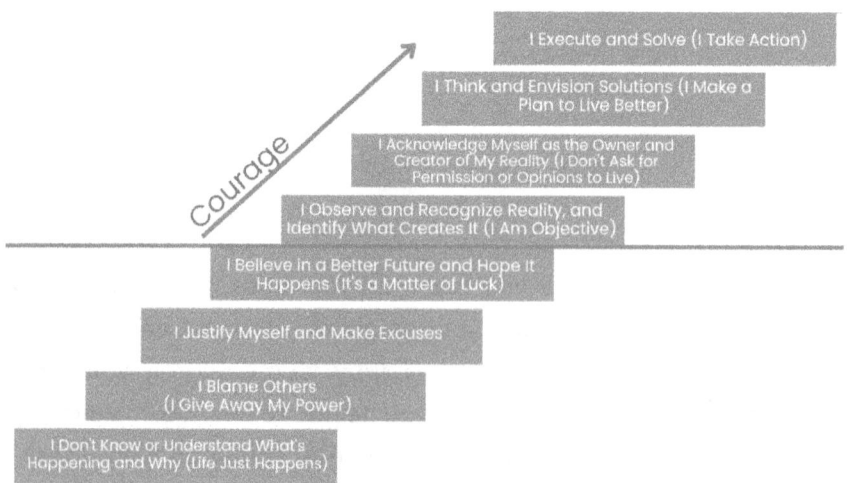

HAPPINESS

To be happy is your responsibility. Just as you are responsible for providing and doing things to make that happen by taking ownership of your responsibility, you are also responsible for paying taxes and fulfilling your fiscal obligations, just like you are responsible for your pets and do things to ensure they are well, and so on. Likewise, you are responsible for your happiness and, therefore, must do things to build it, to make it happen.

Happiness is not a matter of magic or luck, but of effort and merit. Building your happiness is a serious matter; it requires strategy (a plan) and an investment of time, effort, and resources.

So, if you are only going to remember one thing from this book, let it be: **to be happy is your responsibility.**

Here's a QR code to my podcast episode "El problema eres tú" ("The Problem is You"), which I believe can help make it clear why you are also the solution. Remember you can activate the Youtube English subtitles

Building My Happiness: **Taking Personal Responsibility**

1. Do I feel like I am merely surviving my life? Why?
2. Is it common for me to delegate my decisions to avoid responsibility? Why?
3. Do I feel like the captain of my own life? Do I acknowledge that I am in charge and responsible for my life?
4. On which step of the "Advancing in My Responsibility" chart do I currently stand?

5. Am I willing to begin my process of building happiness with EVERYTHING it implies? Why?

6. If I answered yes to the previous question, how do I move from desire to action?

3. SELF-KNOWLEDGE

> "I write because I don't know what I think until I read what I say."
> **FLANNERY O'CONNOR**

How can you give yourself more of what brings you long-term well-being — that is, purpose, health, learning, connection, and pleasure — if you don't know yourself and don't know what it is or how to obtain it? The first step to loving yourself is knowing yourself. Self-knowledge is the first rung on the self-esteem ladder, followed by self-concept, self-evaluation, self-acceptance, and self-respect. **Self-knowledge consists of looking inside yourself.**

I insist: how can you give yourself more of what you love to feel and do if you don't know what it is? If we understand happiness as having a life that you enjoy, one that provides meaning, health, learning, connection, and pleasure in alignment with who you are, then we are acknowledging that there are no recipes. What makes me happy doesn't necessarily make you happy.

For example, many people love exercising, but others detest it. **You cannot promote, do, or give yourself what brings you happiness if you don't know what it is.** That's why it's essential to be clear about your interests, motivations, strengths, dreams, resources, areas for improvement, priorities, predominant emotions, triggers for uncomfortable or painful emotions, childhood wounds, etc.

I've found that psychological therapy and coaching are excellent options for getting to know myself, and although attending regular therapy sessions doesn't eliminate the storms, it does give me tools to navigate through them.

Therapy helps because sharing with someone who makes you feel safe and connected, who you feel won't judge you and will give you good advice, allows you to tell yourself a different story about what happened — which is as good as changing the past. Therapy helps you untangle the knot of events that burden you.

Sometimes going to therapy or coaching seems strange or wrong, possibly because of negative comments we've heard or the fear of exploring that space. Although the stigma is thankfully decreasing, there is still a more challenging obstacle to overcome: having the financial resources to be consistent and attend sessions regularly. The reality is that few people can afford therapy with a specialist. It's a luxury!

An excellent alternative, which I intuitively adopted as a child without knowing its scientific basis, is journaling or keeping a diary. I remember spending hours in my childhood and teenage years lying in bed writing. I have a box with over 20 worn-out notebooks filled with writings from different stages of my life... They're dusty, and I don't read them often, but getting rid of them would feel like throwing away the experiences that shaped who I am today — like throwing away my life (absurd as it sounds! And I don't consider myself a hoarder...).

In fact, writing was undoubtedly one of the crucial tools that helped me when I moved to the United States alone at age 20. In those journals, I poured out my dreams, frustrations, sadness, and challenges...

Today, thanks to James W. Pennebaker, a psychologist from the University of Texas who demonstrated the usefulness of writing about painful and traumatic situations, we know that the **effec-**

tiveness of releasing pain through writing is undeniable. Putting your life into words clears your mind. In his study, confidentiality was guaranteed, so participants felt comfortable writing about their most intimate experiences. Initially, the participants showed an increase in anxiety levels (from "reliving" and confronting painful situations), but after a few days, anxiety noticeably decreased — even below the levels recorded at the start of the exercise.

Writing while analyzing the facts and describing how we feel gives coherence, helps us make sense of events, enhances our understanding, and releases repressed emotions.

Additional benefits beyond reduced anxiety have been documented in journaling research, such as fewer doctor visits, a stronger immune system, tension relief, fewer symptoms of depression, fewer repetitive thoughts, better socialization, and improved mood. Men reported a greater impact than women because it is more common for us to open up and share.

If you are going through a challenging moment or have been stuck with a situation (or several) that you don't know how to process, I recommend James W. Pennebaker's exercise: write without a filter about a traumatic or painful situation for 15 to 20 minutes a day for 4 consecutive days, trying to be analytical and connecting with the thoughts and emotions it generated for you then and generates now, describing the event in detail and the impact it has had on your life. Don't worry about finding the right words or perfect grammar. You can write about the same situation for all 4 sessions or different events. It's your choice. Remember that you may feel anxious during the first days, but afterward, you'll feel liberated or lighter. Write to me on my social media and tell me how it went! I'd love to read you...

Thanks to research by Chad Burton, Laura King, Sonja Lyubomirsky, and Aaron Antonovsky, we also know that writing about pleasant experiences helps us benefit from recalling, describing, visualizing, and reliving them. Just 2 minutes of writing a day can bring you these benefits... Does it sound like magic? It's science.

In addition to therapy and journaling, I believe it's important to share other safe options for diving into yourself and enjoying the benefits of self-knowledge.

I suggest that in addition to doing what you would do when getting to know someone — like observing, investing time in yourself, and asking questions — you try the following tools to get to know yourself:

- Writing a journal/journaling.
- Exploring the Enneagram tool.
- Attending retreats on topics of interest.
- Taking the free VIA character strengths test (available in Spanish) at: https://www.viacharacter.org/account/register.
- Applying the "Johari Window" exercise to identify your public, blind, hidden, and unknown areas. (I did this exercise when I was studying for my master's in Canada, and I remember being amazed by the findings.)
- Practicing silence and reflection (only when you feel safe in your mind).
- Art therapy.

You might also be interested in the Shadow's Edge app, created by The Digging Deep Project, a small non-profit organization. This tool is a game designed to build mental health; it's available in several languages and was developed based on expression, psychology, and gameplay.

Self-knowledge is serious and formal work, but it pays huge benefits. Have you heard of Lorena Ochoa, the Mexican golfer who was ranked number one in the world for over 50 weeks and retired at the peak of her career while earning millions of dollars? Well, she's been my friend since we were 10 years old. While I deeply admire her athletic achievements and the generous, brave human being she is, I admire even more the depth with which she knows herself. I believe she has such clarity about her values, priorities, boundaries, capabilities, and interests that she can lead her life with assertiveness, perform with excellence, and make titanic efforts and ambitious projects seem easy.

She works hard "without breaking a sweat" and has the ability to reinvent herself as many times as necessary, like few people can. Honestly, a story of inspiration, effort, and courage... so if you want to know more, I highly recommend her book and that you treat yourself to our unfiltered conversation in the episode "Why Quit Being the #1 in the World?" on my podcast Valentinamente Feliz, available on any audio platform or on my YouTube channel.

On this journey, you will probably discover a brilliance you've never seen before, but you will also come face-to-face with your shadow — that part your ego has tried to hide for years to protect you, the part you've avoided to pretend you're enough and worthy, the part you wish didn't exist so that the people who matter to you would never see it... Facing your shadow hurts and is uncomfortable. But remember, to be happy is for the brave.

Building My Happiness: **Knowing Myself**

1. Do I feel that I know myself well enough?

2. What brings meaning to my life?
3. What are my strengths?
4. What excites and annoys me?
5. What characteristics do the people I enjoy connecting with have?
6. What do I dream of? What are my plans?

4. AWARENESS

> "The perfect combination of humility and confidence is being secure enough in your strengths to see your weaknesses."
> ADAM H. GRANT

You cannot live better by doing the same thing, so happiness requires action. **You cannot change something you don't know exists.** To improve "something" in your life, you must first be aware that your current situation is different from the one you desire – and understand why. To perform this analysis, it is essential to be present in the present and to notice. As my mom says: "You don't realize until you realize."

It is in that space of awareness that the difference between reacting and responding lies. It is precisely in that space where you can tap into your inner freedom and choose:

- To breathe instead of yelling,
- To walk away and think rather than hurting your children or someone you love,

- To set a healthy boundary or make a decision to avoid a fight or crisis,
- To apologize instead of justifying yourself when you make a mistake,
- To choose compassion over judgment or criticism,
- To embrace the mistake instead of condemning it,
- To stay true to your values rather than seeking to please others,
- To choose "good enough" over toxic perfectionism.

Remember, to be happy is for the brave... and you are braver than you think.

Building My Happiness: **Becoming Aware**

1. Complete the sentences:
    - My best friend would say: I wish you would realize _____
    - My partner would say: I wish you would realize _____ If you have children, colleagues, or parents... continue the exercise.
2. What am I aware of today that I wasn't aware of yesterday?
3. What can I do to live more in the present and effectively choose the area to improve?

5. DISCIPLINED WORK

> "When motivation is lacking, rely on your discipline."
> LEÓN PABLO

Deciding to be happier is not enough to achieve it. That choice is necessary, but it is only the beginning of a long process of effort, change, adjustment, conscious living, and gradually adding pieces to your Lego. After making that decision, you have to do the work required to build a fulfilling life. That means putting up the framework, systems, habits, and behaviors we discussed in the "Being Happy vs. Feeling Happy" section. Remember, happiness is built and is a matter of effort, not magic or luck.

Being happy requires making changes for yourself and by yourself that no one else can make. You need to be consistent with the intentional and conscious efforts you choose to carry out to truly evaluate if the change you implemented works. Avoid being another example of the phrase: "Everyone loves transformation, but no one wants to change."

Happiness requires more action than motivation. Like most things in life that are worthwhile, happiness is a matter of work and effort. Happiness is only possible by building new beneficial and positive habits that promote purpose, health, learning, connection, pleasure, hope, gratitude, and enthusiasm for life. Breaking patterns, behaviors, and dynamics you've had for years can be very uncomfortable – that's why to be happy is for the brave.

When someone assumes during a conversation that I am happy because I was born that way or because I was lucky, they are ignoring the efforts I've had to make to be who I am and have what I have today. No one has given me anything for free –the same goes for you.

Thinking that happiness is just a matter of luck condemns you to live in your current state because it implies ignoring and diminishing the power you have to improve your life and create a happier reality. It reminds me of a scene in Disney's Inside Out 2, where Joy explodes when Anger tells her she's "messed up," and she admits that, yes, she is "messed up," showing that being cheerful and optimistic requires enormous efforts that have left her exhausted.

> Building My Happiness: **Committing to Disciplined Work**
>
> 1. What am I willing to commit to for myself to live better? (Write something concrete and immediately actionable.)
> 2. How far am I willing to go to build that fulfilling life I deeply desire?

6. BALANCE

> "Life is like riding a bicycle. To keep your balance, you must keep moving."
> ALBERT EINSTEIN

Balance is the harmony between your spiritual, physical, intellectual, relational, and emotional well-being (the SPIRE model areas). The more harmoniously these coexist in your life, the happier you will be. It's important to recalibrate your priorities and resources according to changes in your personal, professional, and family circumstances. Maintaining effective balance requires constant and conscious effort. Define what is essential for you and manage your resources in ways that support your priorities.

Balance is a personal concept that must adjust throughout different stages of life. Unfortunately, it is not something that just happens. Living in balance requires effort, awareness, and adjustments.

During a conversation with Aurora García de León, a prominent Mexican businesswoman in the housing sector, she told me that balance is like being on a seesaw forever. Imagine putting a board on top of a bottle and standing on it – maintaining balance will require constant effort. When it tilts to one side, you'll have to compensate by shifting weight to the other, and so on. The same applies when seeking balance between personal and professional life, between activity and rest, or the time spent with important people.

For example, before enrolling in my master's program, my balance was primarily working 12 hours a day, exercising, enjoying time with my husband, preparing for graduate studies abroad, traveling, and seeing my friends – and this made me feel balanced and very happy. But when I went abroad to study, everything changed. This decision prompted me to reassess my priorities and drastically readjust my personal formula for happiness.

I had to reorganize my time, review the resources I had for support, make new agreements with my husband, clearly define my non-negotiables, and determine what I was willing to give up. It was a complete life reengineering process to find peace and satisfaction with my new reality, which also brought new emotions and responsibilities. And let's not even mention when I became a mom. The hurricane named Lázaro (my first son) arrived, and I had to readjust my formula again. Then came hurricane Simón (my second son), and once again, adjustments followed. And so it will continue until I transcend.

Balance is different for everyone, and even for the same person at different life stages. The key is to allocate your limited resources consciously and in alignment with your priorities at the moment.

Balance is the midpoint between dualities, between extremes. For example, physically, while exercise and physical activity are vital, so is rest. Emotionally, I allow myself to feel fear, anxiety, sadness, and frustration, but I also permit myself to celebrate, feel joy, excitement, and peace. In relationships, I love connecting with my friends and traveling with them, spending 24/7 together – but afterward, I need some time away to breathe from their dynamics (shhh, they don't know this!).

In each of the five SPIRE areas, we can explore the extremes to identify exactly what "balance" means for our particular situation

I've identified that **taking care of my energy** is a key aspect of keeping myself balanced. That's why I'm very cautious and demanding about:

- Who I surround myself with, what I read, what type of accounts I follow on social media, what shows or series I watch, what I listen to, etc. It has become a non-negotiable for me to move my body, rest at least 8 hours every day, and practice conscious breathing to recharge.
- Working on being present, truly present.
- Observing my emotions and paying attention to the information they bring me. I practice emotional honesty, not hiding what I feel. I write, cry, and express myself.
- Prioritizing myself in my decisions.
- Making an effort to tell myself stories that empower me.
- Focusing on what I can control and letting go of the rest.

Here's a chart to help you take care of your energy:

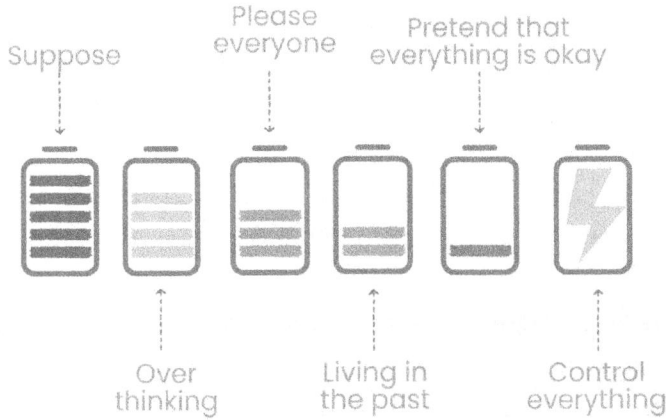

Building My Happiness: **Defining My Balance**

1. Do I feel at peace and satisfied when I think about my current dynamic? Why?

2. What percentage of resources (focus, effort, and time) am I currently assigning to each area of SPIRE based on my current dynamic?

3. What adjustments do I need to make to improve my current balance formula?

4. What commitment do I make to myself based on my findings to live in balance?

7. LETTING GO

> "Blessed be the discomfort that made you move away from places where you no longer belonged."
> DANIK MICHELL

Letting go of fulfilling other people's expectations and deciding to be loyal to yourself and your essence is not only liberating but essential to building your happiness. Avoid falling into the temptation of seeking approval, applause, and external recognition at the cost of self-betrayal – it is fundamental for living a full life. Break the predetermined mold of your life and **build your own mold**.

One of the biggest obstacles you currently face in being happy is living according to the expectations you believe others have of you. When you were born, expectations about you were already defined by your context. And while we talked about how belonging is important for your self-esteem and self-love, there's a trap here: people-pleasing. Sometimes, we misunderstand belonging and pay any price to achieve it, including self-betrayal.

In the long run, this leads to deep disappointment, disconnection from your essence, and a sense of emptiness. With the intention of belonging and connecting, we end up living a false life, a hypocrisy, a theater play where we not only lose ourselves but also disappoint and distance ourselves from the people we wanted to connect with. What a paradox! Can you think of someone who lives pretending to be who they are not? How do you recognize it? Do you connect with that person? Of course not!

How many people dedicate their lives to activities that don't ignite their passion and that they often don't even do well? How many others maintain relationships that hurt them or betray themselves simply to please people they care about or because they settle for what life puts in front of them? Or how many people value a friend or family member's opinion more than their own?

You can actually spend your days and weeks doing what you are passionate about and what you are good at. You can have healthy relationships that add to your well-being, and you can be true to yourself and authentic without guilt. **You just have to discover what that is and execute a plan to achieve it.** Remember Henry Ford's quote: "Whether you think you can or you can't, you're right."

Making your own applause the most important applause is not easy. It's a long process, a dance between observing the external world to connect and the internal world to ensure you still belong to yourself first. Question yourself, discard what doesn't serve you, and live your life by your own rules. Learn to let go of everything but yourself. That's why to be happy is for the brave...

Even review whether you need to let go of toxic behaviors (yours or those of close people) that have been normalized, such as:

- Being called boring for not smoking or drinking alcohol, or only being able to have fun if you do.
- Sharing kindness quotes on social media but being anything but kind in real life.
- Continuously sacrificing yourself for others (harming yourself) and considering it an act of generosity.
- Mocking or discrediting someone else's dreams or aspirations.
- Giving aggressive and hurtful opinions and calling them constructive criticism.
- Gossiping and talking about people who aren't present.
- Being rude in the anonymity of social media just to get likes or followers.
- Invalidating someone else's pain or trauma just because there are worse situations.

Choose whose opinions you listen to and value. Remember that a spectator hasn't earned the right to be heard and that **what others think of you says more about them than it does about you**. Their perception is based on their interpretations, beliefs, and stories rather than reality. Accept that "you are not a gold coin that everyone will like" and that, just as you don't like everyone, it's okay if not everyone likes you.

Own your life and stop asking for permission or opinions to live it. If you think about it, this isn't about an "either-or" scenario but about "both-and." The magic lies in understanding that when you stay true to yourself, you're giving your real self to the people you relate to – not a façade, a character, or a lie. And that creates connection! So, everyone wins.

Building My Happiness: **Living for Myself**

1. Do I feel that I live to please others?
2. Do I care more about certain people's opinions than my own? If I answered yes, where does this behavior come from? Who did I learn it from?
3. How can I remind myself that other people's opinions say more about them than about me?
4. How can I reframe my story to take ownership of my life?
5. What actions do I commit to taking to let go?

8. INFORMATION

> "Everyone is entitled to their own opinion,
> but not to their own facts."
> DANIEL PATRICK MOYNIHAN

When you build well-being based on science, you increase your chances of success, avoiding sabotaging yourself and losing confidence through repeated failed efforts. It is hard work.

With ups and downs, but seeing results soon proves its effectiveness and increases the motivation to keep working.

The final pillar of happiness is information, because it makes the work of building a full and happy life easier. The science of happiness provides information and tools that, having been scientifically tested, bring us closer to success when we roll up our sleeves and get to work. It offers reliable insights on what happiness is, how to work on it, what tools truly help, and what the myths are. Having a recipe to bake a cake always makes the process easier.

The uniqueness of happiness is that there are as many recipes as there are human beings. What works for you may not necessarily work for me. So, there isn't a universal recipe. You must complement it with internal exploration. This way, you can give yourself more of what brings you purpose, presence, health, self-care, knowledge, connection, pleasure, courage, gratitude, optimism, hope, and fulfillment.

Building My Happiness: **Gathering Internal and External Information**

1. What topic do I want to explore within the field of the science of happiness?

② To deepen your internal knowledge, complete this 6-step exercise:

I) Grade- How do I feel in each of the pillars from 1 to 5 (1 is minimum)?

- Self-Love: _____
- Personal Responsibility: _____
- Self-Knowledge: _____
- Awareness: _____
- Disciplined Work: _____
- Balance: _____
- Letting Go: _____
- Information: _____

II) Describe – Why did I assign each of those numbers?

III) Prescribe – What actions can I take to improve in each pillar?

IV) Select – Choose one aspect and work on it for at least 30 days.

V) Observe – What are the results?

VI) Evaluate – If it worked to build your well-being: keep going. If it didn't work: adjust or switch to another aspect.

③ Do I feel capable of building a life with well-being? Why?

④ Do I know myself well enough to understand what generates well-being for me in the spiritual, physical, intellectual, relational, and emotional areas?

HAPPY HORMONES

> "Hormones are the molecules of emotion and behavior."
> RICHARD DAWKINS

Do you know the chemistry of happiness? Hormones are the body's chemical messengers that regulate nearly every bodily process. Your body produces many chemicals or neurotransmitters that contribute to your well-being – your mental, physical, and emotional health. To simplify and make it more understandable, we will focus on 4 of them: dopamine, serotonin, endorphins, and oxytocin. These 4 substances work as a team to boost your mental, physical, and emotional well-being. All 4 are important, and the goal is to keep them balanced.

Oxytocin
Oxytocin is related to love, empathy, bonding, trust, and generosity. Some of its functions include:
- Creates emotional bonds.
- Increases trust and empathy.
- Boosts sexual arousal.
- Facilitates breastfeeding.
- Reduces stress levels.

How to Produce Oxytocin
- Listen to music and sing.
- Meditate.
- Listen attentively and practice empathy.
- Engage in physical contact with someone significant.
- Be generous and charitable with yourself and others.
- Have positive thoughts.
- Get a relaxing massage.

- Get 10 minutes of sunlight daily.
- Hug face-to-face with both arms 5 times a day.
- Laugh frequently.
- Eat fruits, vegetables, and citrus.

Its Absence Causes:
- Overeating.
- Addictions.
- Depression.
- Lack of social interaction.
- Anxiety disorders.

Dopamine

Dopamine is related to satisfaction, reward, motivation, and pleasure. Some of its functions include:
- Regulates your mood.
- Increases your energy.
- Rewards you with pleasure.
- Motivates and makes you creative.
- Helps you stay alert.
- Raises your heart rate.

How to Produce Dopamine
- Enjoy small pleasures: music, nature, flavors, etc.
- Meditate and regulate your stress levels.
- Set goals and achieve them.
- Let life surprise you.
- Exercise 3 times a week.
- Engage in sexual activity.

Its Absence Causes:
- Constant stress.

- Cravings for sugary foods, alcohol, and fatty foods.
- Oversleeping, lack of motivation.
- Procrastination.
- Not feeling pleasure in daily activities.

Serotonin

Serotonin is associated with well-being, relaxation, and satisfaction. It is commonly called the "happiness hormone." Some of its functions include:
- Regulates mood.
- Aids in intestinal movement.
- Controls appetite.
- Stabilizes emotions.
- Regulates hormone synthesis.

How to Produce Serotonin
- Practice gratitude.
- Enjoy nature.
- Recall important moments in your life.
- Exercise regularly.
- Celebrate daily achievements.
- Live in the here and now.

Tips to Boost Serotonin:
- Do 30 minutes of aerobic exercise.
- Have plants in your home.
- Practice breathing techniques.
- Seek out places with lots of light.

Its Absence Causes:
- Bad mood.
- Changes in sexual desire.

- Difficulty learning.
- Irritability.

Endorphins
Endorphins are related to tranquility, pleasure, and laughter. Some of their functions are:
- Decreases physical pain (natural painkiller).
- Regulates mood and creates a sense of well-being.
- Helps release sex hormones.
- Reduces stress and anxiety.
- Facilitates attention and memory.

How to produce them?
- Exercise or practice yoga.
- Practice a hobby.
- Dance and sing.
- Spend time with your important relationships.
- Smile at life and laugh a lot.
- Have sex.
- Eat spicy foods.

Their absence causes:
- Problems sleeping.
- Emotional imbalance: depression or anxiety.
- Chronic stress.
- Constant pain.
- Propensity to addictions.

Heads Up! Exercise Is Key. As you can see, exercise helps you produce three out of the four neurotransmitters we discussed. While endorphins and dopamine are similar, they have some differences. Endorphins' role is to dull pain; they're activated by intense exercise or a hard hit, and the result is a feeling of euphoria and well-being. Meanwhile, dopamine's role is to seek rewards; it's triggered by delicious food, winning a game, or meeting an expectation, resulting in a sense of satisfaction and feeling like you've won big.

So, boost your endorphins through exercise and find pleasure in the little things (away from screens) to keep dopamine in check.

> Building My Happiness: **Boosting My Happiness Chemistry**
>
> 1. What did I enjoy learning about my happiness hormones?
> 2. What insight resonated with me?
> 3. What can help me keep my neurotransmitters in balance?

WARNING! IT'S CONTAGIOUS

> "If you want to be in the light, help those around you shine."
> TAL BEN-SHAHAR

Happiness is contagious! Have you ever seen someone laughing, smiling, or dancing and felt the urge to join in? Or have you met up with a friend you haven't seen in months and noticed a new sparkle in her? This happens thanks to special neurons in the frontal part of your brain called "mirror neurons." As the name suggests, they reflect what they see.

When you project fulfillment, efforts to live better, optimism, health, hope, bravery, gratitude for being alive, satisfaction with who you are, excitement for living for and by yourself, etc., the people around you likely feel it, thanks to their mirror neurons, and they get inspired. Likewise, those who regularly spend time with you will see your progress and start taking action themselves.

Numerous studies also show that one person's behavior influences the behavior of others present. Two extreme examples are the "Milgram Experiment" at Yale University, which proved that most people would inflict physical harm on another person just by following orders, and the famous "Zimbardo Experiment" at Stanford University in 1971. In this experiment, young men randomly assigned roles as guards and prisoners took their roles to such extremes that the guards became sadistic and cruel, forcing the study to be halted. This research inspired the 2015 film "The Stanford Prison Experiment," a powerful depiction of how human behavior influences others.

The same applies to positive aspects like happiness. When you work on building your happiness, you share your best self with those around you and inspire them to pursue their own happiness. Have you ever started a wellness habit like eating healthier, nurturing your self-love, using your phone less, learning a new language, being kind, or reading 3 pages of a book daily, and your friends, family, or colleagues asked you what you're doing? It happens to me, too!

This ability to influence each other encourages us to surround ourselves with what Marian Rojas Estapé calls a "vitamin person" — and to become one ourselves. So be careful: happiness is contagious!

Building My Happiness: **Spreading Happiness**

1. Who spreads happiness, joy, optimism, hope, etc., to me most of the time when we are together?

2. Who brings me down (spreading hopelessness, negativity, complaints, pain, etc.) most of the time when we are together?

3. When have I felt pressured to act in a certain way to meet the expectations of my environment or the people present, even betraying myself?
4. How can I avoid emotional or behavioral hypocrisy?
5. What can I do to avoid giving too much power to my environment or others, and stay true to myself?

DOES EVERYONE HAVE TO BE HAPPY?

The short answer is NO! Being happy isn't easy; the costs are high (though lower than resigning yourself to unhappiness), and not everyone is willing to put in the work required to build a life of fulfillment. If you know someone who isn't willing to work on their happiness, I suggest you respect that.

Happiness is personal, and no matter how much you love that person, you cannot build happiness for them. Likewise, even though there are people who love you with all their heart and would be willing to do the work for you, they can't do it.

We all have the capacity to be happy, but the journey begins with a personal choice and continues with work that only you can do for and by yourself.

Building My Happiness: **Accepting and Respecting**

1. Who have I wanted to make happy? Why?
2. Who have I wanted to make me happy?

3 What do I commit to with myself based on my previous answers?

THE HAPPIEST COUNTRY IN THE WORLD

They say you don't find Bhutan; Bhutan finds you. And here I am! Exhausted from walking over 12 kilometers to visit the Taktsang Palphug Monastery, better known as the Tiger's Nest Monastery, perched on a cliff at 3,120 meters above sea level, 10 kilometers from the city of Paro. I'm soaked, my boots are full of mud, and I find myself sharing a breaded cabbage (with a crunchy orange coating that stains your teeth) and a cup of buttermilk tea with a local family and two Buddhist nuns who have come down from the temple to spend the weekend resting with their families in the city.

They don't speak Spanish or English, and I don't speak Dzongkha (the national language), so we rely on gestures and common sense. What the three of us did share during the hour-and-a-half descent down the mountain was the language of empathy, compassion, and generosity. What a joy to feel their peace! They offer me a mint.

I hesitate because the packaging looks like medicine. They insist. I'm brave and try it. My heart bursts with gratitude, and I feel a special connection with the mountain, with them, the country, or life itself. I don't even know anymore! The past and the future don't matter. Only this moment exists.

It was my last day of the trip. Tomorrow, a nine-day excursion that made me cross the world (there's nothing farther from Mexico) will come to an end and has allowed me to know and connect deeply with Bhutan. What if happiness were a place?

HAPPINESS

That was the phrase that captivated me and turned this experience into a dream to fulfill. Today, I am here. It is a reality.

Bhutan means the Land of the Thunder Dragon. It has less than 800,000 inhabitants and covers an area of 40,994 km². It is located in Asia, between two giants: China (the Tibetan region) and India. It is one of the smallest and least populated countries on the planet, and its territory is divided into twenty districts. It is a constitutional monarchy with a parliament as the legislative body.

The uniqueness of its history, culture, and environment makes it one of the few places on Earth where humanity and nature still coexist in harmony. In fact, it is the only country with a negative carbon footprint – meaning it cleans the planet more than it pollutes it. They even charge a fee of about $140 per day to compensate for the environmental damage caused by your visit.

There is evidence suggesting the first settlements in Bhutan date back to 2000 B.C. However, in modern history, there isn't much written. In 1949, India and Bhutan signed the Treaty of Peace and Friendship. In 1952, under King Jigme Dorji Wangchuck, Bhutan slowly began to emerge from isolation and initiated a program of planned development. It became a member of the United Nations in 1971.

In 1972, Jigme Singye Wangchuck (the fourth king) ascended the throne at the age of 16. Despite his youth, he was a visionary who emphasized modern education, government decentralization, hydropower development, tourism, and rural development. He recognized that development has many dimensions and that economic goals (Gross Domestic Product) are not enough to measure progress. He is internationally known for his philosophy of "Gross National Happiness" (GNH).

From my perspective, something that clearly reflects his human greatness is his detachment from power. Satisfied with Bhutan's transitional democratization process, he abdicated in December 2006, leaving the throne to his son, Jigme Khesar Namgyel Wangchuck, born in Nepal in 1980 and better known as the Dragon King of Bhutan (Druk Gyalpo). This made him the youngest reigning monarch in the world at the age of 28. The Bhutanese people and the world know that, although the fourth king keeps a low profile, he still advises his son.

Bhutan is a magical country, full of legends and mysticism. When we arrived, we found an entire delegation of elegantly dressed cadets, a red carpet, and majestic decorations at the airport. Ready to be amazed after 30 hours of travel, I thought this was how they welcomed tourists. But what a surprise I got when I saw the kings of Lesotho, an African country, disembark from the same plane for a state visit! Moments later, the airport staff rolled up the red carpet before the rest of us passengers disembarked. Oh, what a disappointment!

I experienced Bhutan as a young country, primarily rural, except for the cities of Paro and Thimphu, where there were signs of modernity. For example, there are no traffic lights, just one in the city of Thimphu, and it's human-operated. Yes, you read that right! There's a traffic officer inside a kiosk directing the flow of cars. Naturally, as good Mexicans, we waved to him to challenge his skill... and yes, he waved back! Fortunately, no accidents occurred.

Until a few years ago, the Bhutanese began adopting the use of toilets, brushing their teeth, and refrigerating food. Before 1999, there was no television or internet. The use of currency is relatively recent, and in many communities, bartering is still common practice.

The king has an international vision, having studied in Boston and London, and he seeks to gradually bring modernity and prosperity to the country without neglecting the values, culture, and sustainability that define them. For example, despite polygamy being deeply rooted in their traditions, he chose monogamy with Jetsun Pema. The people love their king! They see him as a sensitive, consistent, and inspiring leader. You'll find photos of him and his family in every house, temple, restaurant, hotel, and store. Virtually all Bhutanese affirm they would give their lives for their king and his family.

I believe that, rather than delving into facts about the country, which you can easily find online, I'd like to share my experience and perception.

I find it incredibly valuable that the government takes the happiness and well-being of its citizens seriously. "The government's role is not to make citizens happy, but to create the conditions for them to make themselves happy," shared Thakur S. Powdyel, a former Minister of Education. A wise man deeply knowledgeable about public policies, he was the architect of the educational system in Bhutan's first government. We had the opportunity to converse with him and delve deeper, thanks to the efforts of the World Happiness Foundation.

The philosophy of prioritizing holistic well-being is easy to perceive. All government programs refer to Gross National Happiness (GNH) and are tied to one of its four pillars, divided into nine domains measured by 33 indicators. In the business sector, they have a GNH certification program, and when organizations don't meet the criteria, they receive guidance to close the gaps and achieve compliance.

Schools have robust programs in mindfulness, emotional well-being, and sustainability. Everyone in Bhutan understands happiness as long-term holistic well-being – not just a fleeting emotion, but something taken very seriously.

They still don't value possessions, materialism, brands, or status the way we do in Western societies. I believe they have the triad of being – doing – having well aligned. I didn't perceive hunger.

And despite having few possessions, they don't feel poor or disadvantaged. They are aware of their dignity, and the end does not justify the means. Their spiritual practice, rooted in Buddhism, leads them to practice detachment and to connect deeply with themselves and with nature. **They believe in the power of intention, karma, the common good, and the strength of community and collective efforts.**

When I ask myself if they are truly happy, my short answer is: Yes! As I've mentioned, happiness is fulfillment, satisfaction, and having a life that, in general terms, feels worthwhile. This idea has the core component of expectations. I believe their recent openness to the world still keeps many possibilities, outlooks, lifestyles, and options unknown to them, which also results in high levels of satisfaction. **The challenge will be to maintain that satisfaction as expectations shift.** In fact, one issue shared by former Minister of Labor Dorji Wangdi was that young people who leave to study abroad no longer want to return.

Being in Bhutan was an experience I will carry in my heart forever. There was everything, from taking forest baths at the foot of the Himalayas, speaking with Rinpochés, learning about the Black-Necked Crane conservation program (a bird that migrates from Tibet to Bhutan every year and symbolizes prosperity) in Gangtey, sharing meals and prayers with monks at their university temple, visiting the Golden Buddha, singing karaoke, enjoying a sound healing session with the Thunder Dragon Gong, visiting markets and local restaurants with spicy food, witnessing the changing of the royal guard, and participating in a Bhutanese naming ritual (my name was Choki Zangmo, meaning prosperity and spiritual excellence) in Punakha, where they worship fertility and there are sculptures and souvenirs of phalluses everywhere.

I also learned about the methodology, statistics, and formal measurement behind GNH directly from the director of the Center for GNH Studies in Bhutan. We visited the ELC School (Educating for Lifelong Citizenship) and met Tim, the Director of Well-being; Madame Deki, the school principal; and Kinley, a delightful and brave 9-year-old girl whom we invited to come to Mexico on an exchange.

I was amazed that all the children played the way I did when I was a child. They don't have cell phones or iPads.

I was fascinated by the energy of collective intention, compassion, generosity, and gratitude. Those days invited me to question my entire world, values, plans, priorities, routine, how I use my time, relationship with my parents, created needs, overvaluation of productivity, immediacy, instinct, religions, politics – everything.

I felt like I visited a neighboring planet, like in the Star Wars movies, where many things seem delayed because we in the West experienced them years ago (like the power of negotiation and marketing in commerce), but many other things feel like the recovery of a loss because we've forgotten them even though they are so important (like respecting ancestors and listening to your internal climate).

Bhutan is a country without haste, where calm, compassion, love for nature, and presence take top priority. There is no malice. Everyone is willing to help tourists. They are very conscious of "chogshey", which means the knowledge of sufficiency.

In conclusion, if it's possible for happiness to be a serious matter for a country, then it's possible for the whole world. I sincerely hope that Bhutan finds you one day.

Building My Happiness: **The Country of Happiness**

1. What if happiness were a place? What would it look like for you?
2. What information resonated with you the most from this section?
3. What commitment can you make to yourself to live better, based on what you've learned about life in Bhutan?

03 FREEDOM, AUTHENTICITY, AND COURAGE

WHAT IS FREEDOM?

> "Happiness is liberating,
> but only when you have the courage to live it."
> **DAVID SCHNARCH**

Being free means consciously choosing how to live your life and acting in alignment with your essence, breaking away from expectations and pre-established norms. This is essential for building a full and happy life.

Freedom is the ability to choose. It sounds so simple, yet it's so complex and important. The significance of freedom is captured in Manuel Azaña's phrase: "Freedom does not make men happy; it simply makes them men," because freedom not only promotes happiness but also affirms your humanity. Your existence loses meaning if you are not free.

And I'm not just talking about the possibilities and opportunities offered by the context or culture in which you live, but also the mental prisons we often construct for ourselves. The purest form of expressing freedom is through choice.

Do you enjoy choosing how to dress, think, speak, work, love, and where and how to live? In short, do you exercise your right to choose and decide your life? I hope your answer is a resounding YES! Because that is what it means to be free. Being free is knowing and feeling capable of deciding who you want to be and what you want to do. Love your freedom! Love it so much that you're willing to do whatever is necessary to defend it.

To be happy, you need to be free for two reasons:

1. Choosing to build your happiness is a decision you must make without pressure. (You don't work on it because someone imposes it on you.)
2. It requires authenticity — feeling free to be yourself and live in alignment with your essence.

Exercising your freedom allows you to shape your days and your life according to your priorities and values, so you can build a life that, overall, is worth living and makes you feel at home in your own skin = Being happy. As my friend Leonardo Curzio, a renowned journalist and political commentator in Mexico, says: "Freedom belongs to those who work for it."

By the way, I recommend our conversation in the podcast episode, "How to Be Outrageously Happy," one of my favorites. Here's the QR code for easy access and remember you can activate Youtube English subtitles if you prefer.

To build a life of fulfillment, you need to choose it freely, feeling that you deserve it, because only then will you be able to take the actions required by and for yourself.

FREEDOM, AUTHENTICITY, AND COURAGE

In her book Freedom is an Inside Job, Salbi, like Viktor Frankl in Man's Search for Meaning (which is my favorite book in the world), refers to the fact that inner work requires living truly free. They speak of the idea that you can always choose who you want to be in response to what happens to you. And that freedom, no one — NO ONE — can take away from you.

This awareness allows you to **respond** instead of **reacting** to what happens to you — the former being conscious and the latter automatic and irrational.

Yes, it is possible to be free and become a little more free each day. Freedom, like many valuable things in life, is a muscle that grows stronger through action. Yes, it is possible to live the way you've dreamed, to achieve what you long for, to impact the world and leave it better than you found it. Yes, you can... you just need to be brave. **Being free means having the guts to give yourself the chance to experiment and create your own rules.**

Take my friend Masouma, for example. Coming from a culture in Afghanistan where arranged marriages govern relationships, and women are seen as property, she allowed herself to experience a different kind of relationship — first with a Mexican and years later with a German, creating her own path. Or my friend Eufrosina Cruz, who defied the fate of girls in her community in Oaxaca, where they are often sold and condemned to motherhood at a young age, deprived of the right to dream. She was willing to pay the price, choosing to study, work, become a single mother by choice, and dedicate herself to politics and public service, challenging the destiny that was laid out for her.

Philosophers have pondered the nature of freedom for thousands of years. There are hundreds of books and dozens of authors who write about freedom, and there wouldn't be enough pages to explore all the arguments in detail. So, let's keep it simple: **Being free means choosing your path and owning the consequences.**

The key to happiness is freedom, and the truth is that to be truly free requires courage.

Long-term holistic well-being (happiness) cannot be built through imposition or obligation. If you are not convinced that you want to be happy, and yet you start efforts with that intention, you would be falling into complacency. In this case, the interesting part would be discovering the reason why you are not committed to working on your happiness. Do you feel you don't deserve it, or are you using your unhappiness to punish, control, or manipulate the people around you?

Building My Happiness: **Reflecting on My Freedom**

1. When have I truly felt free?
2. What decisions do I still feel incapable of making? What do I need to do to make them?
3. When have I challenged my environment and created my own rules?
4. How can I be a little freer?

AUTHENTICITY

> "Authenticity is the daily practice of letting go of who we think we are supposed to be and embracing who we really are."
> BRENÉ BROWN

Authenticity is essential for a fulfilling and happy life. Living according to others' expectations or suppressing who you truly are in the

FREEDOM, AUTHENTICITY, AND COURAGE

name of acceptance can ultimately lead to misery and personal disconnection. True happiness arises from living in alignment with your essence and desires. **Authenticity is the freedom to be — the freedom to be truly you.** Authenticity exists when there is harmony between theory and practice, between being and feeling, between thinking and doing. **Being authentic means living in alignment with your essence and having the ability not to let others define you.** Learning to live authentically is important because you will not build your best version by pleasing others. Can you really be happy if you sweep your essence under the rug and live as someone else told you to be, or as you think others expect you to be? The short answer is: No!

Freedom is essential for building a life that feels worthwhile to you. Imagine a good life (whatever that means for you): let's say you have a good job, a good partner, you do interesting activities, and you live in a "normal" country. But none of those things were chosen by you. In other words, you live in country "A" when you prefer country "B," you work as a doctor when you'd rather be a lawyer, you married Laura when the love of your life was Leticia, you have two healthy kids but never wanted a family, you love sports but instead spend two afternoons a week playing chess and dominoes.

In reality, you would likely feel miserable because, although the circumstances are not bad, they simply aren't the ones you would choose, and they are not in alignment with your essence.

You may think that choosing a "good but inauthentic life" wasn't a mistake because when you chose, whether consciously or unconsciously, to betray yourself for approval, you received applause, acceptance, and appreciation. That made you feel like you belonged, and it made you feel good.

But in the medium and long term, the effects of that self-betrayal will start to show. Maybe you'll try to ignore them, but little by little, they will scream at you and make you feel so disconnected from yourself that it will be undeniable. The discomfort you feel will force you to face them.

Freedom has an important limit: the freedom of others. In theory, as long as you don't affect anyone else, you should be able to choose what suits you best, but in reality, our decisions are often limited by the expectations of others (thanks to the trap of people-pleasing for belonging, which we've already discussed), to the point that we can confuse what we truly want and are, with what we've been told we should want and be. Remember that fitting in requires you to change something to be part of the group, and truly belonging, you don't need to change.

And just as my friend Leonardo Curzio says, freedom is for those who work for it, so is authenticity. The main work mostly consists of not falling into the trap of fitting in. Is it hard? Yes, very hard. Does it scare you? Yes, it scares a lot.

Why? Because unconsciously, we interpret that disappointing others makes us worth less and that we don't belong. That's why to be happy is for the brave.

You will probably quickly discover that much of what you say and do has nothing to do with you; it is just your old programs or ideas that you absorbed from past contexts or other people, but you use them as a defense mechanism to fit in, connect, or impress. Clichés are easy to use because they won't usually be questioned or criticized. And if they are, they won't be directed at you because you didn't create those ideas. There's no responsibility.

On the other hand, when you dare to express and act genuinely, even though you risk being criticized, feeling pain, and going back to the clichés or recipes, there is also the possibility of succeeding and celebrating yourself. Being authentic is a risk, but we don't think that not being authentic is a greater risk: letting life pass you by in your comfort zone and never discovering what you are truly capable of doing and being. No one has greater potential to be your

FREEDOM, AUTHENTICITY, AND COURAGE

best version than you. Not living authentically is adopting the victim persona and falling into the irresponsibility, helplessness, and hopelessness that it entails.

Freedom has an important limit: the freedom of others. In theory, as long as you don't affect anyone else, you should be able to choose what suits you best, but in reality, our decisions are often limited by the expectations of others (thanks to the trap of people-pleasing for belonging, which we've already discussed), to the point that we can confuse what we truly want and are, with what we've been told we should want and be. **Remember that fitting in requires you to change something to be part of the group, and truly belonging, you don't need to change.**

And just as my friend Leonardo Curzio says, freedom is for those who work for it, so is authenticity. The main work mostly consists of not falling into the trap of fitting in. Is it hard? Yes, very hard. Does it scare you? Yes, it scares a lot.

Why? Because unconsciously, we interpret that disappointing others makes us worth less and that we don't belong. That's why to be happy is for the brave.

You will probably quickly discover that much of what you say and do has nothing to do with you; it is just your old programs or ideas that you absorbed from past contexts or other people, but you use them as a defense mechanism to fit in, connect, or impress. Clichés are easy to use because they won't usually be questioned or criticized. And if they are, they won't be directed at you because you didn't create those ideas. There's no responsibility.

On the other hand, when you dare to express and act genuinely, even though you risk being criticized, feeling pain, and going back to the clichés or recipes, there is also the possibility of succeeding and celebrating yourself. Being authentic is a risk, but we don't think that not being authentic is a greater risk: letting life pass you by in your comfort zone and never discovering what you are truly capable of doing and being. No one has greater potential to be your best version than you. Not living authentically is adopting the victim persona and falling into the irresponsibility, helplessness, and hopelessness that it entails.

How many times have you wanted to appear richer, younger, wiser, or more fun? How many times have you given up being yourself just to fit in? What triggers your shame? How many times have you laughed at a joke that actually offends you or supported an idea you disagree with? Why?

In this world of social media, toxic perfectionism, competition, and individualism, it's incredibly easy and tempting to live for external validation, applause, or likes, thinking that they affirm who you are and what you're worth. Going against that and living authentically is an act of courage because it means overcoming the fear of rejection or criticism. So, acting from the heart has become the most original way to do things.

You can't live an authentic life without being brave, and you can't be brave without disappointing some people. The good news? Those who are disappointed by your authenticity don't deserve to have you in their lives.

One idea that has been key in my journey of practicing courage to connect with my authenticity and feel genuinely free is this:

When I try to appear a certain way, I give up being who I really am, assuming that my essence is wrong or not enough.

Ironically, every time you choose to pretend, you are feeding the persona you've created. Ultimately, you'll disappoint the very people you wanted to impress, because no one likes hypocrisy, lies, or false fronts.

We all crave deep connections with others, and the only way to achieve that is through essence, truth, authenticity, and genuineness.

FREEDOM, AUTHENTICITY, AND COURAGE

But how can you live in alignment with who you truly are if you don't even know yourself?

If you don't know what you like, what motivates you, what interests you, what hurts you, what inspires you, what triggers you, and what your strengths and weaknesses are – you'll easily fall into the trap of fitting in to feel an illusion of belonging.

That's why, to work on your authenticity, you first need to know yourself. Here's an exercise to get you started right away:

1. Try to distance yourself from your thoughts and opinions (especially the ones that feel odd); separate them from you.
2. Pause and approach them with curiosity.
3. Observe your body and see if they make you feel strong or weak.
4. If they make you feel weak, it's because they are not aligned with your essence; they lead you to self-betrayal, and they are not authentic but adopted to fit in.
5. Identify the reason. Ask yourself: What am I seeking in exchange for this?
6. Try to rephrase it in a way that feels more congruent with you.
7. Repeat this process for at least two weeks.
8. Observe and evaluate.

Once you have worked on the conscious and rational part of authenticity, you can also give your soul a hug by following these steps:

1. Find a quiet and peaceful place.
2. Take a deep breath, place your hands on your heart, close your eyes, and repeat:
   - "I allow myself to be different.
   - I allow myself not to fit in.

- I allow myself to be me, even if others don't always like it.
- I acknowledge that loyalty starts with me.
- It's okay to be who I am."

Or explore some of the following tools to strengthen your authenticity:

1. **Know Yourself:** Explore any of the self-knowledge tools we shared in the previous chapter.
2. **Meditate:** Give yourself moments for introspection and mental silence.
3. **Reflect:**
    - What did I dream about as a child?
    - How did I envision myself as an adult when I was 12 years old?
    - Do the versions of my dreams resemble my current reality?
4. **Listen to podcasts** or follow social media accounts that add value and inspire you. Filter out those that promote stereotypes, make you feel insufficient, and cause you anxiety.

Building My Happiness: **Strengthening My Authenticity**

1. What do I need to re-discover myself today?
2. What am I willing to do to live more as my "authentic self" and less as the character I've created to fit in?
3. What action am I committing to in order to begin reconnecting with my authenticity?

ATTENTION AND PERCEPTION

> "Your attention educates your intellect."
> JORDAN PETERSON

Attention is the ability to direct your energy; where you place your attention, you place your energy. Perception is the process by which you interpret and organize information to understand your environment. Your reality depends on where you put your attention **(Attention -> Perception -> Reality)**. You react or respond to your perception of reality (the story you tell yourself about what's happening), not necessarily to reality itself. This simple idea can change your life if you apply it by learning to train your mind. We've touched on this a little in the sections "Presence," "How You Create Your Reality," and "Self-Love," but I believe it's important to delve deeper into perception as a process of your mind.

Imagine you're in an apartment you rented, and on your first night there, you start hearing some noises. Everything feels unfamiliar; you look out the window, but you don't see anything. The noises intensify. What do you feel? What thoughts and physiological changes do you experience? What do you think is the source of the noise? Did you think of a thief or a cat or some other animal? The story you tell yourself will determine your reality, your experience.

Perception involves a series of complex steps through which the brain receives, processes, and interprets external stimuli. Here are some steps: Sensory Reception (receive), Transduction (electrical signals), Neural Processing (integration), Interpretation and Organization (organize and make sense), and Perceptual Awareness (conscious experience and understanding). **Perception is not a passive process; it is influenced by various factors, including attention, expectations, past experiences, culture, and emotional state.** These factors can affect how you interpret stimuli, how you perceive reality, and how you interact with the world. If it weren't for this, we would all perceive a person or movie in the same way.

Here lies the magic of gratitude: it helps you train your attention (the Ascending Reticular Activating System) to focus on what you appreciate, what was enough, and what you feel fortunate to have, be, or have experienced. I quote Dr. Joe Dispenza: "By combining the feeling of gratitude with a clear intention, you emotionally embody the new event: the thought changes your brain, and the emotion changes the chemistry of your body. You are now in a new future in the present moment."

Wow, how powerful! As we've already discussed, the effectiveness of meditation lies in training your mind to focus your attention in ways that add value to your life. Can you choose where to place your attention? The short answer is Yes! Like any habit, training your mind to focus on what serves you is a process, and as such, it requires time and effort.

While facts exist, and things happen in the world, you can't absorb everything and put it into a calculator that determines whether the balance is positive or negative. You know there are events, some better than others, and most of them don't depend on you. But what depends on you is where you place your attention and energy because that will determine your perception and, therefore, your reality. It's as if your attention were a magnifying glass, and wherever you place it, it magnifies. When you change the way you see things, the things you see begin to change.

That's why it can become so dangerous to place your attention on what you lack, comparing yourself and believing that everyone is better than you, focusing on mistakes, or worrying about what others think or say about you, or holding onto prejudices and stereotypes that make you feel insufficient... Try to bring your attention inward, to your values, your projects, to everything that is in your control or that adds value to your life.

FREEDOM, AUTHENTICITY, AND COURAGE

What if you stopped thinking about life and started living it? **90% of the things you worry about never happen.** They're not real, but since your **brain doesn't differentiate between imagination and reality**, they have a direct effect on your body.

The brain doesn't distinguish between reality and fiction. **We feel what we think.** And although life isn't as you think it is, it is as you think it is. So, if perception is reality, how do you make your perception more favorable? If you learn to understand why and how you perceive things, you'll be able to tell yourself more favorable stories and recognize that what you think is just a possibility.

Thought is just a proposal from your brain, not a fact. You treat someone a certain way based on what your brain suggests—like the memory of your last encounter with that person, or what you assume about them if it's the first time you're meeting them—not based on reality. In fact, that person has already changed since that day... What if you paused to adjust that proposal in a way that serves you, allowing you to live lighter and happier? Can you imagine living without taking things personally or trying to please others? Do you realize what it would be like to perceive yourself as brave and fully in charge of and responsible for your life?

A person, place, animal, or thing does not have the ability to make you feel; it is the idea your brain associates with them that triggers your emotion. That's why, by training your brain and being able to choose what you think automatically, you'll have thoughts that bring you peace, confidence, security, and hope, instead of fear, anxiety, anger, and shame.

For example, can you imagine changing your perception of your flaws and seeing them as strengths? Imagine that an area of opportunity for you is actually a strength that you haven't been able to refine. I read a long time ago that flaws or weaknesses are really strengths taken to the extreme, and that the key is finding balance. While research shows that focusing on improving our strengths is the most effective way to achieve excellence (because focusing on working on our areas of opportunity can only lead us to a moderately satisfactory performance, at best, since that's not where our talent lies), it is also not suggested to completely ignore weaknesses. What if we combine the concept of perception with the knowledge of our strengths? How can we distinguish a black swan or a rough diamond from the rest of the elements if we disqualify many of our characteristics right off the bat, without questioning that perhaps, deep down, they are strengths taken to the extreme?

In my case, I remember the issue of frankness. I am a sincere person who values language and the meaning of words, who likes to say things as they are, and who is not afraid to call things by their name straightforwardly. But Mexico is a Latin American country that values being politically correct, prudence, and pleasing others; it is perceived as violent to use short, assertive phrases. I even had a boss who, jokingly, called me Violentina instead of Valentina. For example, here it is common to ask a waiter at a restaurant: "Excuse the inconvenience, when possible, could you please bring me a little glass of water with ice?" While for me, it's normal to say: "Can you bring me a glass of water with ice please?"

My way of communicating often caused friction and problems, to the point that I even started giving a disclaimer before some conversations to clarify that I speak briefly and directly, but that I am friendly and harmless. My intention is to be clear because I greatly appreciate clarity and brevity. However, it is common for Mexicans to focus on the emotional component and prioritize the form of communication over the content. My challenge has been—and still is—to keep my frankness in check so it doesn't cause misunderstandings and is not perceived as rude or harsh.

Another fascinating experiment to explain the importance of perception is the "Counterclockwise Study" conducted by Ellen Langer in 1979, where she took a group of older men to a week-long retreat. The location was decorated to resemble 1959. The newspapers, music, products they used, everything, corresponded to the reality of 1959. The participants were even required to act as if they were really living in 1959. What was the surprise? The participants came out rejuvenated, reporting significant improvements in their physical and mental health, visual sharpness, hearing, memory, strength, and flexibility. Even the appearance of some participants changed; they looked younger after the experiment.

Once again, reality is determined by your perception, and that, in turn, is determined by your attention, among other factors.

Building my happiness: **Improving my attention and perception**

1. Do I generally see the glass half full or half empty? Why?
2. What has led me to my current habits of attention and perception?
3. How do I feel about that?
4. Am I aware that I can choose where I place my attention?
5. What do I commit to doing to focus my attention on what adds to me?
6. What do I commit to doing to remind myself that my perception is only a suggestion from my brain (a possibility), not the truth?

REINVENT YOURSELF

You always have the ability to reinvent yourself. Resigning to live unhappily or mediocrely is actually harder than facing your fears and making the difficult decisions to reinvent yourself and build a better life. You can always stop being or doing something to be or do something new. Is it easy? No, not at all! It's scary. But it's possible! And as many times as you want…

Not reinventing yourself is the famous "better the devil you know than the devil you don't," which condemns you to merely survive your days. Much of this is your ego trying to protect you from the risk, uncertainty, and discomfort that comes with any significant change or transformation. Whether you want to change jobs, start a business, change some part of your body or appearance, end or start a relationship, redesign your life philosophy, or learn something disruptive, let me tell you that you're not too late. No matter your age, gender, or past, you always, ALWAYS have the ability to reinvent yourself.

You might believe that you have to continue with certain activities or a lifestyle that no longer serves you because you made certain decisions in the past, but that's not true. Do you remember when we talked about beliefs—those ideas that are just ideas, but we live them as absolute truths? Well, thinking about sacrificing yourself or "carrying your cross" is a belief of self-punishment. It's okay to change direction! You are the sculptor of your life, so you can always choose what to adjust in your masterpiece, which is simultaneously a finished project and a work in progress. Yes, even if it sounds crazy! It's part of the famous duality we humans embody.

While we always have to face the consequences of our decisions, it's also okay to change your mind. **If you don't let life happen to you and instead create it consciously, you will find the courage**

FREEDOM, AUTHENTICITY, AND COURAGE

to act on those inner desires that tell you "something is missing or needs to change."

How do you transcend that fear that holds you back from reinventing yourself? With small steps, in safe environments. Don't jump into the void! I believe in not letting go of one vine until you grab another. For example, one way to start the process of reinvention is by taking a new course, class, or diploma, or opening yourself to information or experiences that broaden your perspective. Education makes you free because it increases your options and allows you to choose with more information.

I remember four years ago, during the pandemic, when we believed COVID meant death, when we made enormous efforts to keep the business afloat without having to reduce the team, when I lived one day at a time dealing with the overwhelming negativity of the environment, when the fragility of life was reminded to me every moment, generating a personal crisis of purpose... I philosophized about life and my existence quite often. And on one occasion, while in therapy with Carmen, she asked me: "If you were to die tomorrow and could leave a message to the world, what would it be?" I asked her to clarify the question, to which she repeated the same words: "If you were to die tomorrow and could leave a message to the world, what would it be?" After thinking for a few minutes, I answered: "I would put speakers in every corner of the world and shout: **To be happy is your responsibility.**"

Since I was a child, I have felt deeply in my heart that much of the world's unhappiness comes from people living in the role of the victim, waiting for someone else to do the work (which involves building a fulfilling life) for us. And it is exactly that which condemns us to the misery of joy, to mediocrity, and unhappiness. For me, the key is to take full ownership of your life and see yourself as the creator of your reality. We are asleep, waiting for the outside world to change so that we can be happy, and in the meantime, life slips away.

I remember that moment in therapy as if it were yesterday, and it was that burst of energy that triggered my most recent reinvention (because I have had several throughout my life). It was that very idea that gave rise to the core message of Valentinamente Feliz: Being happy is your responsibility. After piecing together the puzzle, looking for signs, taking action, and working hard, I have been able to build a project and a community that today fills me with purpose and makes my heart dance. Still, I do not cling to what is, but rather open myself to the infinite possibility of reinventing myself, always true to myself and my values.

I invite you to periodically check in with yourself, with your essence, and make sure that you still want the things you always thought you wanted. Remember that you are possibility, that you can always reinvent yourself, and that being happy is for the brave.

An exercise that helped me a lot in my reinvention process was the "Best Possible Future" exercise by Laura King, a researcher and professor of positive psychology. It consists of imagining and visualizing the best possible future for yourself, writing it down, and working backward to make it happen. In other words, creating a plan to build that future.

Building My Happiness: **Reinventing Myself**

1. What dream do I have? Why do I want this dream?
2. How can I build this dream?
3. When, where, and with whom can I progress in this dream?
4. If I traveled through time and could look back on my life, what happened for this dream to become reality?
5. How do I feel living this "best possible future"?

FREEDOM, AUTHENTICITY, AND COURAGE

MONEY AND HAPPINESS

I placed this section in the chapter on freedom because that's what financial stability gives you: freedom and flexibility in your decision-making.

Is money important for happiness? The short answer is: Yes! You can't think about living fully if your basic needs like food, clothing, shelter, medical service, and security are not met. First, you have to survive in order to think about flourishing and building your best version. But just because money is necessary for happiness, it doesn't mean you should sacrifice anything—like health, relationships, authenticity, or purpose—for money once you have some stability.

How is happiness related to money?

When we talk about the relationship between money and happiness, it was once thought that earning above $75,000 a year (research based on the U.S. population) no longer brought significant benefits. Therefore, the question shouldn't be how much money do I need to be happy? **But how should I use my money to maximize my well-being?** And what am I sacrificing (opportunity costs) to get the money?

Today, we know it's not about income but how it is used: savings and experiences.

Have you ever changed jobs or positions for a higher salary, and after a while, you still don't have enough money?

People tend to quickly adapt to new income levels, which means financial gains can only have a temporary impact on happiness. This phenomenon is known as hedonic adaptation.

The reality is that when we talk about financial well-being, income is not as important as spending habits. In other words, **it is much more important how much you save and where you spend it than how much you earn.** Science has repeatedly studied whether money buys happiness, and upon delving into their findings, it is found that having savings brings peace, freedom, and flexibility in your decision-making because it allows you to pass on certain opportunities in favor of your long-term well-being. On the other hand, spending on experiences—such as travel, concerts, meals with friends, a massage, or donations and gifts—will bring you greater well-being.

It may sound paradoxical, as we might think that an object lasts much longer than an experience, but experiences are emotionally engraved in you, allowing you to relive, feel again, and produce favorable chemicals when you recall them. Remembering your meaningful experiences makes you embody the pleasant emotions they generated, over and over again. Experiences provide memories and social connections that material goods cannot. Likewise, sharing with others can enhance feelings of connection and purpose. In conclusion, **having savings and investing in experiences or gifts are favorable decisions for being happier**.

It is important to keep in mind that happiness is a much broader idea than money or financial stability. While financial stability offers freedom, flexibility, and peace, and allows you to do many things that promote important ingredients of your personal happiness formula, it is not necessary to sacrifice the possibility of being happy today, regardless of your economic circumstances, conditioned on a certain amount in your bank account or financial growth, as long as your basic needs are met.

It is also important to mention that the relationship between money and happiness can vary significantly between cultures and socioeconomic contexts. Some cultures more strongly associate wealth with status and happiness than others.

Some ideas to remember about the relationship between money and happiness:

- **Money is a means, not an end.**
- Living paycheck to paycheck creates a lot of stress, no matter how much you earn.
- Savings give you freedom, flexibility, and control to take opportunities and let others go.
- Be aware of when it is wise to spend and when to save.
- **Think about the cost of opportunities (what you miss out on) and the trade-offs in your decisions.**
- Use money in ways that maximize your long-term happiness or well-being.
- **Invest.** Be willing to delay immediate rewards for a greater one in the long term.

Remember, as James Clear, author of Atomic Habits, says, true wealth is not about money, but about not having to attend meetings, not having to spend time with idiots, not being caught up in status games, not feeling like you have to say "yes" and please, not worrying about others demanding your time and energy. **True wealth is about being free.**

While we've already discussed that financial stability has more to do with your spending habits than your income, if there is no income, there is nothing to save or spend. So, here are 15 ideas to generate income:

1. Rent an asset (house or car).
2. Be a passive partner in a business.
3. Loan money.
4. Online sales.
5. Sell your audiobook.
6. Start a YouTube channel.
7. Create or buy an app.

8. Buy long-term stocks.
9. Put ads on your car.
10. Run a subscription service.
11. Invest in real estate.
12. Sell products on Amazon or eBay.
13. Start a car wash.
14. Sell promotional or on-demand catalog items.
15. Recommend services or products and earn a commission.

Building a good relationship with money will probably require you to make uncomfortable decisions in the short term, but those decisions will greatly benefit your long-term well-being. I understand it's not easy, but remember that to be happy is for the brave.

Building my happiness: **Reflecting on money**

1. Do I have enough resources to cover my basic needs: food, clothing, shelter, and security?

2. Have I lived considering money as an end or as a means?

3. Do I live in peace with my financial situation, or is it something that worries me?

4. How can I improve my spending habits to use more income for savings and experiences, and less on material goods?

5. What am I committing to do to maximize the well-being that money brings to my life?

FREEDOM, AUTHENTICITY, AND COURAGE

COURAGE

> "Courage is the most important of all virtues."
> MAYA ANGELOU

I'm so glad you've reached this section because it's one of my favorites—thank you! What I'm writing here aims to help you connect with your courage and push yourself to embrace discomfort, make the effort, and pay the price required to build a full and happy life. And yes, you're braver than you think!

Many times, people have told me that my courage comes from my name: Valentina. The truth is, it doesn't. **Courage is one of those muscles that gets strengthened.** While it's a reminder I've had since birth, the reality is that being brave has cost me sweat, tears, blood, relationships, and a lot of exhaustion. In fact, it still costs me! Every day, when I find myself refusing to do something, I question myself and push myself to be brave and act in alignment with who I truly am, regardless of expectations, the environment, the algorithm, others, standards, or trends. Is it easy? No! Even this act of writing and publishing my book involves a conscious act of bravery for me, because it makes me vulnerable, puts me in the spotlight, in the arena, to be evaluated and judged. My ideas, my writing style, the number of copies sold, the sales ranking, the book design, its length, etc. are aspects that can be judged and are directly linked to me because I chose them. Is it easy? No! I've had to talk to myself many times to convince myself that, even though this book may not be perfect, it is worth sharing because it can inspire you and many others to start working on building a better life. I'm not seeking recognition, but to help. Just like with my social media, my podcast, my audiobook, every lecture or workshop I give, **today I write with the sole intention of helping you build a freer, more authentic, and happier life.**

And no, I'm not enlightened, I don't have all the answers, and I'm not Mother Teresa of Calcutta—honestly, I do this because sharing what has worked for me fills my life with purpose, connection, learning, joy, and gratitude. "In giving, we receive."

Well, let's dive in. This chapter on courage, of course, has to start with fear. I hope it serves you and that you enjoy it!

WHAT IS FEAR?

Fear is an emotion that appears when you feel in danger. It's neither good nor bad; it's simply information, like all emotions. What is bad is living in a constant state of alertness because you've gotten used to interpreting every stimulus as dangerous, condemning yourself to high levels of cortisol (the stress hormone), burnout, or panic and anxiety attacks.

Just think: when a furious dog comes running towards you, it is fear that activates your alert systems and makes you run so it doesn't bite you, grab a stick, or shout for help. So, was the fear bad or good? Obviously, it was beneficial, because it made you react to a danger and do what was necessary to protect your physical integrity. Fear should be in the passenger seat, kept in check, so it doesn't control you, but never try to eliminate it, because that would be like firing your bodyguard or canceling your alert system. While you don't want to see every dog as a life-threatening danger, you also don't want to blindly trust that every dog is friendly.

I remember one time I went for a run with my dog "Ferrari." I was listening to a podcast by Esther Perel, enjoying the path, and suddenly, in a matter of seconds, without expecting it, I saw an open mouth between my feet, a furious dog trying to bite my dog, a very friendly Goldendoodle (a Golden Retriever and Poodle mix). Before I knew it, my dog had crossed to avoid being bitten, and the leash got tangled around my feet. I made a tremendous landing! Even though I tried to jump over the leash like an Olympic athlete, I tripped and fell with my knees into a curb designed to prevent cars from speeding. Covered in mud and unsure of what had happened, I turned around and saw that the owner of the ferocious dog had lost control of the leash and was now flat on his stomach being dragged by the dog towards me. All this happened in a few seconds. I was shaking (literally) and arguing with the dog owner, expecting an apology, but not only did I not receive an apology, but he told me it was my fault because I should have been running near my house, not in those streets. Yes, you read that right! He felt entitled to the public space! That's how absurd the scene was. After the rude man made a couple of calls for help, a woman (I assume his partner) came and took the angry dog in a car while the man returned to his building. That's how, in panic, after a police officer passed by and couldn't do anything because there were no injuries to send me to the hospital for more than 14 days (absurd laws), I grabbed my phone with the shattered screen, pulled my dog—who was wagging his tail like he was enjoying the drama—and went home with my clothes torn and dirty, and my knees swollen like grapefruits, crying from anger and worry about not being able to run for a while.

As we discussed in the "Emotional Well-being" section, what's important with emotions is understanding what kind of information they bring us. Fear, in its light side, seeks to protect you, and in its shadow side, it paralyzes you. Many times, people believe that brave individuals don't feel fear, but the truth is that ALL humans feel fear, except for psychopaths and the dead. Fortunately, you and I feel fear! If we didn't, we wouldn't be here.

MY FEAR AND I

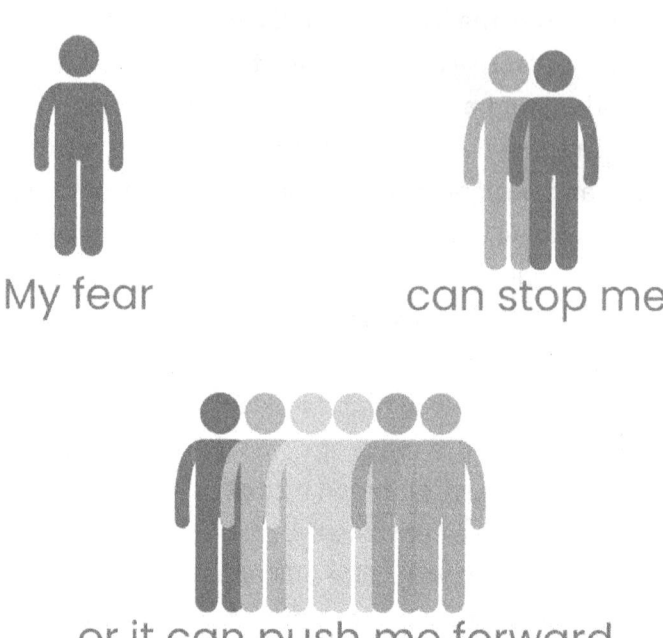

Lose the fear of fear! Thinking that fear is bad is wrong and even ungrateful. Fear is an unpleasant emotion to feel, but when we stop to understand "why" we are feeling it and address it, its existence makes total sense, and we might even end up thanking it. The key is to get to know yourself and learn to identify your fears, understand why you feel what you feel, know what they want to tell you, perceive their distinctions, recognize their temporality, and use it as part of the wonderful GPS system that emotions can be.

A long time ago, in a course, I heard that the word "fear" in English, FEAR, was the acronym for False Evidence Appearing Real. That is, fear is the response to a false piece of evidence that appears real. Your fear makes you boring because it leads you to always seek

FREEDOM, AUTHENTICITY, AND COURAGE

certainty and security. You have been programmed by evolution to feel fear, and it stays alert and hyper-vigilant all the time because its function is to overprotect you, seeking your safety and certainty, regardless of the costs you pay. 90% of the things you worry about never happen; they are products of your imagination and affect your body, mood, and relationships. That's why what's important with fear is understanding the information it has for you and using it in your favor. That is, learning to manage fear, so you can take advantage of its light side and let it protect you, but keep it in check so it doesn't paralyze you and condemn you to inaction. As Liz Gilbert says, "I find that the less I fight with my fear, the less it fights back." Here I highly recommend revisiting the sections "Attention and Perception" and "How You Create Your Reality."

Sometimes, we feel fear even when we're enjoying ourselves. Has it ever happened to you that when you're happy and laughing a lot, someone tells you, "don't laugh so much because tomorrow you'll cry"? Or that you feel fear because if you're happy today, surely a tragedy is coming? One of the hardest things to feel is joy because we fear that at some point, it will end. Brené Brown, an American researcher and academic, shares that **the way to combat the fear of joy is through the practice of gratitude**. So, when you catch yourself going from joy to discomfort because of this belief, recognize it and immediately move to gratitude. That way, you'll put your attention and energy on what works, what you like, what you have in life, and all those reasons to celebrate it. Remember, adversity will eventually come because it's inherent to life, nothing more. So, while there are moments and reasons to celebrate life, take advantage of them and enjoy.

In the face of fear, there are three types of responses: fight, flight, or freeze (the famous fight, flight, or freeze in English). When we are in truly dangerous situations, where our prefrontal cortex (key to rational thought and emotional regulation) shuts off, and we are under the control of the amygdala, we enter a survival mode where reflection, willpower, and planning have no place. Recently, some authors have mentioned a fourth response to fear: pleasing.

In the anecdote I shared about the incident running with my dog, both the man's prefrontal cortex and mine were shut off. I was terrified, definitely went into survival mode, and in retrospect, I think my response oscillated between fight and freezing.

A radio interviewer once asked me, "What should you do with 'absurd' fears?" She expressed that she thought there were justified fears and others that were unjustified. To which I replied, "I believe no emotion is absurd, and although it may lack rationality, the emotion is still completely real and valid for the person experiencing it." Remember that the brain doesn't distinguish between imagination and reality.

The emotion of fear can be the result of telling ourselves a story of danger that hasn't been well thought out. However, let's remember that in the process of perception, the factor of our past experiences plays a role, so something that makes a lot of sense to me may not make sense to you at all—for example, the fear of flying in an airplane. If we analyze the probability of something happening to you when you get on an airplane (affected passengers versus the total number of passengers), it's a low index, but if someone close to you in your family passed away in a plane crash, flying is likely to trigger a lot of fear in you, and the data may be of little help to manage your fear. While we experience emotions at different intensities and frequencies, it is important to validate them so we can understand and address them, especially the uncomfortable or painful ones.

The time I felt the most fear was when, three years ago, my 2-year-old son Simón had surgery to open his tear duct. The surgery was essential because, since he was born, every 2 or 3 months his eye would get infected, and we had to put antibiotic drops in it.

FREEDOM, AUTHENTICITY, AND COURAGE

Until one day, the ophthalmologist told me, "We've run out of antibiotic types, he's gotten used to them, and if he gets used to this one, we won't be able to remove the infection with drops." Anyway, seeing the fear in my eyes, we sought several expert opinions, and they all agreed: surgery was necessary. They explained to us that it was a low-risk procedure, but since general anesthesia was required, we had to sign a document accepting the possibility that he could die, releasing the doctors and the hospital from any responsibility. Boom! My world turned upside down! The thing I love most was at risk. I remember feeling the worst panic of my life, mixed with sadness, when I carried him and placed him on the operating table. He tried to fight back, resist, while crying and screaming intensely, but immediately they placed gauze with a substance on his nose that made him fade in seconds. I had only one thought: Please come back! Please wake up! They told us the surgery would last 45 minutes, but it turned into more than 2 hours, which felt like days. I don't remember ever crying as inconsolably as I did that day. I only begged God and life that he would wake up and that I could take him home. The thing I loved most was in danger!

It may seem exaggerated to you, or you may think my terror was unjustified. But remember that we have different "lenses." I, knowing up close the case of a little one of the same age who died from tonsil surgery, couldn't stop thinking about the possibility of a fatal scenario. And although, fortunately, the surgery was successful, and today I know it was the right decision (although very difficult), I remember that day as the worst day of my life.

It may be that deciding to build long-term well-being scares you. You may fear rejection, criticism, isolation, shame, or failure, but trust me, it's worth taking the risk because it's the only way to live fully. That's why to be happy is for the brave.

Building my happiness: **Facing my fear head-on**

1. Do I consider myself fearful? Why?
2. Do I feel like I live in fear or a constant state of alertness? Why?
3. What am I afraid of? Make a list.
4. What are my fears trying to protect me from?
5. Which of these fears might seem unfounded or irrational? Where do they come from?
6. What fear is stopping me on my path to build a better life?

WHAT IS COURAGE?

> "There is no man so cowardly that love does not make him brave and transform him into a hero."
> PLATO

Courage is acting in alignment with yourself despite feeling fear. Many times, we believe that brave people are those who are fearless, bold, daring, and emotionally strong, and who don't feel fear. In reality, that's impossible. All human beings feel fear. Only psychopaths and the dead don't feel fear.

So, the next time you feel fear, you'll have two reasons to be happy: because you're alive, and to confirm that you're not a psychopath.

In reality, what distinguishes the brave from the cowardly is action. Because it's not that the brave person doesn't feel fear, it's

FREEDOM, AUTHENTICITY, AND COURAGE

that they accept their fear, look it in the eyes, take it by the hand or throw it in the backpack... **but they act**, fear and all.

This idea is crucial because it allows you to recognize yourself as brave. No matter how old you are or your story, you've definitely experienced adversity in any of its forms, and if you're here reading, it's because you've overcome it. So, you are braver than you probably think.

The antidote to fear is courage; it's a muscle that is worked and strengthened in both small and large opportunities and scenarios. The brave are willing to give up their comfort in pursuit of a benefit. When they repeatedly **feel comfortable in discomfort, they can identify "mature courage."** Sometimes stepping out of the comfort zone is voluntary with a specific goal (you make the decision), but at other times, life throws you into the ring and suddenly, you're forced to be brave. Here's a heads up! Watch out for being comfortable in discomfort **within** the comfort zone. That is, by resigning yourself to it, feeling helpless, or believing you deserve a mediocre life. And even if you pretend not to see your dissatisfaction or act like you've gotten used to it, sooner or later your truth will catch up with you...

I confess that for many years I thought brave people didn't feel fear, and I was frustrated by feeling it, but when I understood that it's okay to feel fear, that I can leverage it and keep it in check so it helps me measure risks but doesn't paralyze me, my courage muscle strengthened much more easily and quickly. Understanding this was a big "Aha!" moment for me, or as we say in Mexico, "it clicked." I stopped feeling defective for my humanity, embraced my fear, and now we act together daily to do things that make me nervous, embarrassed, anxious, or whatever you want to call it... which, in the end, is fear; whether it's speaking to a celebrity on a TV set or daring to be vulnerable in public by sharing a personal story.

TO BE HAPPY IS FOR THE BRAVE

Acting with courage helps you trust yourself. There is no courage without action, creating a virtuous circle of trust.

You are brave when you speak your mind, regardless of what others think, when you start or end a relationship, when you travel or go to the movies alone, set boundaries, learn something new, work on your emotions, reframe your stories, ask for help or forgiveness, accept your imperfection... In other words, **while you act with discomfort and awareness toward a goal, you strengthen the muscle of courage, which is the main trigger for happiness.**

Deciding to work formally on your happiness can be scary or overwhelming, because you've spent so long surviving your life that this state has become your comfort zone, and it's hard to step out of it into the unknown. Choosing to make conscious and consistent efforts to build well-being in any of the five areas of the SPIRE Model may confront you in the short term with failure, criticism, rejection, guilt, shame, conflict, abandonment... In short, with pain in any of its forms. That's why happiness requires courage.

Without courage, there is no happy and fulfilling life. You need to be brave to defend your freedom and build a life aligned with your true self. **To be happy is uncomfortable in the short term, and it's precisely courage that drives you to take action** in those small adjustments that bring you a 2% increase in your sense of purpose, presence, health, learning, self-love, connection, and pleasure.

In English, courage comes from the old French "Corage" and Latin "Cor," which means heart, referring to the state of the heart, that is, bravery and strength of character. **Courage is that inner fire** that we all have, which drives us to do the work required to live fully.

Once, while traveling in Puerto Rico, we went on a canopy tour, which is a zipline route through the jungle. After paying for the excursion, traveling almost two hours by bus, and walking through the jungle for 45 minutes, we arrived at the starting point of the tour. Upon seeing the first segment, a girl in the group decided she wouldn't try it. We all tried to convince her, even an elderly tourist went before her to show her it was safe, a gentleman with a significantly robust physique also went, my father-in-law and husband insisted, and even teased her about the money she had already spent. I tried to motivate her... but despite the social pressure, no human power could make her continue with the adventure. At first glance, it seemed like the girl was cowardly, and the rest of the tourists were brave. But if we think about it more deeply, she was actually the brave one because she acted in alignment with herself despite the teasing, criticism, lost money, and judgment.

In this anecdote, the girl took action by renouncing the experience to stay true to herself.

Apparently, bravery is always perceived as doing things, but true bravery includes an essential ingredient, which is **congruence with oneself**. It's pointless to do things to meet others' expectations while betraying our true interests, values, and beliefs. Courage without congruence with yourself is called complacency, and it's a common trap that leads to disconnection and emptiness in the long term.

TO BE HAPPY IS FOR THE BRAVE

In a world that urges you to pay high costs for applause, followers, and likes, you must be brave and face the fear of rejection, abandonment, ridicule, contempt, criticism, humiliation, etc. Because only then will you be authentic and, therefore, truly free.

If courage is a muscle that can be exercised, what better way to do it than in safe environments with controlled risks? **Practice being brave in small doses frequently, and you'll build a sense of capability.** You will prove to yourself that you can embrace your fear and move forward. To be happy is for the brave.

Building My Happiness: **Recognizing My Courage**

1. How has my concept of courage changed after reading this information?
2. When have I lacked courage to be true to myself and not give in to the pressure of the environment?
3. What small act of courage can I take immediately to build confidence in myself, and how can I make it a habit?

YOU'RE BRAVER THAN YOU THINK

> "Courage is not the absence of fear, but the fear walking."
> SUSAN DAVID

You might not easily resonate with the idea that you're brave, either because you had a mistaken concept of courage and thought it meant not feeling fear, or because you hadn't reflected on all the times you've acted (voluntarily or involuntarily) in alignment with yourself despite feeling fear. But do you know why there's bravery in you? It's simple! You're brave for two reasons:

1. You're alive! You embody the vulnerability inherent to being human.
2. You've overcome adversity, regardless of your age or circumstance.

Today, I invite you to recognize your bravery, celebrate it, and commit to working formally to strengthen it. Remember that **courage is the main trigger of happiness** in human beings, and it's necessary to improve in any of the 8 happiness pillars we discussed, in any of the five types of wellbeing from the SPIRE model, as well as to defend your most authentic self and live in alignment with your essence.

> Building My Happiness: **Strengthening My Courage**
>
> 1. In what past adversity was I brave? How did I impact the situation?
> 2. What did I do? What characteristics did my behavior have?
> 3. What do I commit to doing to celebrate my bravery?
> 4. What do I commit to doing to strengthen my bravery?

TYPES OF COURAGE

What comes to mind if I ask you to think of someone brave? We commonly imagine a superhero, a mountaineer, a firefighter, a soldier, or someone who practices extreme sports, but the reality is that courage is also giving your opinion while being introverted, it is listening openly to viewpoints that contradict your own, it is gathering energy and taking a bath when you feel depressed, it is voting when you know in advance that the election will be a fraud, it is approaching your friend or partner after a strong disagreement and seeking connection, it is going to therapy to face your shadow and discover why you repeat patterns in your life, it is encouraging... learn a new hobby even though you know it's not where your strengths lie, it's leaving your house to work at a café to meet people and make friends, etc.

As we said, **courage is acting in alignment with yourself despite feeling fear.** So, courage can have different characteristics. It can be very stoic, reckless, and loud, or more silent and reserved; it can be impulsive or responsive, introverted or extroverted, voluntary or "involuntary," planned or spontaneous, rational or intuitive... and that's okay.

In the chart on the next page, I share examples of courageous actions. The further to the right of the spectrum, you'll see more silent and less stoic manifestations of courage, but equally valuable.

When you doubt yourself and think you can't, just close your eyes and connect with your intuitive courage, with that flame inside you guided by the wisdom of your soul, with that part of you that feels right when you listen to it in silence. Design a plan to transform your courage into conscious action.

Building My Happiness: **Getting to Know My Type of Courage**

1. When I've been brave, what type of courage has it been?
2. How do I feel recognizing my type of courage and knowing it's okay to be this way?
3. What do I commit to doing to strengthen my type of courage?

FREEDOM, AUTHENTICITY, AND COURAGE

Spectrum of Courage

Stoic Courage
- I save the world
- I take risks voluntarily
- I lift weights
- I dare to learn something new
- I am shy but I speak my mind
- I feel there will be fraud, but I still vote
- I am angry but I seek connection
- I seek therapy and get to know myself
- I am depressed but I get up
- I feel overwhelmed but I ask for help

Silent Courage

HOW TO STRENGTHEN THE COURAGE MUSCLE?

I can't find a way for you to truly be free without connecting with your authenticity, and that is an act of courage. The freedom of purpose, action, thought, expression, the ability to fight for your dreams, relate to whom you choose, and behave in ways congruent with the emotions you experience is directly connected to your essence. These characteristics of your soul and integral being are what truly make you unique and hold the greatest potential for your time on Earth. These are the particularities you must connect with to build your best version and feel free and whole in your own skin. I know it sounds nice, but it's not that easy because it requires courage. So, the question is: How do I strengthen my courage?

Building a happier life requires you to experience and not know the outcome; uncertainty is scary. That's why it's essential to light the match of courage in you that will ignite your fire of happiness and fulfillment.

Here are seven ways to work on your courage:

1. **Remind yourself of the true meaning of courage** and choose your place of fear, knowing that it's normal to feel it. But act!
2. **Allow yourself to experiment.** If it doesn't work, go back to what you were doing before and embrace the error. It doesn't always work on the first try.
3. **Recognize courage in others.** Appreciating courage in others always gives you a boost in yours. It connects you with behaviors that inspire you to be brave in your daily life.
4. **Practice.** Disagree out loud, set healthy boundaries (learn to say "no" and "enough"), learn to travel alone, make yourself a priority, empathize (approach others' pain, sadness, frustration, or those uncomfortable emotions they might

be feeling with the intent to help), or embrace your uncomfortable emotions (acknowledge your humanity and give yourself permission to be human).
5. **Commit emotionally to another person.** Love truly.
6. **Surround yourself with brave people.** Be inspired, learn, and share. In fact, I confess that this has been one of my big secrets: consciously choosing to surround myself with incredibly brave people with stories full of action outside their comfort zones.
7. **Learn something new.** Give yourself the chance to be bad at something new. How many times have you hesitated to take a risk on something you really want to do for fear of not being good enough? Dare yourself!

Here between us, I'll share that I have a personal policy of experimenting with strange things or things that push me out of my comfort zone.

For example, sometimes I buy clothes that seem a bit "strange" or even ugly, so when I wear them, I force myself to feel comfortable being myself and not valuing myself by my appearance, but by who I am. Or another time, my friend Tania Rincón invited me to take an improvisation workshop, and I said yes without knowing what it was or where I was going.

In a world that promotes disconnection from the soul, superficiality, disdain for what's different, emotional dishonesty, filters, surgeries, botox, ozempic, the "enlightened" people's magic recipes, etc., in favor of fulfilling social standards, absurd and outdated stereotypes, and magical happiness, we consciously and unconsciously betray ourselves to gain recognition, external acceptance, and a fleeting superficial sense of wellbeing (which is actually pleasure). Our physiology is made to connect, and that causes us to automatically prioritize belonging over essence, thus ignoring our "authentic self." We do this repeatedly for years, even decades, until we reach the point where we no longer recognize ourselves. There's so much fog between our essence and the image we project or the persona we were told we had to be, that we feel lost, directionless, hopeless, or without meaning.

Most adults live on autopilot, anesthetized by routine, resigned to react to whatever the day throws at us, surviving. Sometimes, we dream of a radical change that brings positive emotions, dynamism in activities, prosperity, etc., but when we think about taking action, fear shows up, which sometimes paralyzes us.

Being brave means prioritizing congruence with your being over pleasing others and seeking external recognition, even if it brings confusion to the subconscious for going against the mechanism of pleasing that you developed to survive.

It may be that your brain interprets satisfying other people's expectations as a matter of life or death. To re-educate it, you must first recognize that this resonates with you and forgive yourself because, until now, it was the best way you found to survive, even though you paid a high price for it. And if today you choose to do it differently, keep in mind that it will take work, and that it will be worth every effort because it's the only way to live fully.

Courage has many faces, stories, and shades. Personally, I deeply admire brave people, those who have the courage to face adversity and create their life, not letting life happen to them. And I've realized that bravery is a common trait among my friends, all of them brave in their own way. For example, Eufrosina Cruz challenged her culture and what life had prepared for her, refusing to marry as a minor and going to study, to become today an accountant, teacher, and a recognized figure in the world of politics and activism for indigenous groups in Mexico.

Or my friend Loretta Valle, who redefined her story of voluntary confinement in a prison "for love" to become a recognized

FREEDOM, AUTHENTICITY, AND COURAGE

therapist in the world of high-risk relationships (emotional dependence, narcissism, psychopathy, etc.). Or my friend Lorena Ochoa, who, from a very young age, gave up the comfort and security of living with her family in Mexico to pursue her dream of being the best golfer in the world, and when she achieved it, she adjusted her formula and retired, staying true to herself despite the controversy of her decision. Or my friend Dafna Viniegra, who transformed her history of childhood sexual abuse into an association that prevents this situation by providing support to individuals at risk of becoming perpetrators. In short, bravery has many facets, and one constant: Acting with all your fear. **Dare to be uncomfortable until you feel comfortable outside of your comfort zone**, and if you have children, help them dare as well.

One time, we were traveling in the United States, and my oldest son, Lázaro, was 5 years old. A very tall and sturdy waiter, with a somewhat unfriendly attitude, served us at the restaurant. Suddenly, Lázaro said to me:

— Mom, can you ask for a straw for me?
— Ask him yourself.
— But I don't know the waiter. I'm scared.
— I don't know the waiter either. If you want it, ask for it.

Eventually, he raised his hand, and after being ignored for a few minutes by the waiter, I called him over. I pointed to my son when he approached, indicating that he should listen. Lázaro repeated in English the sound I had taught him to ask for a straw. The waiter, with his unfriendly attitude, looked at me to let me know he hadn't understood, so with a firm look, I opened my mouth and said in English with a tone of celebration: "Excellent Lázaro, you were able to ask for the straw you need. The waiter will bring it to you in a moment!"

Bravery is acting in alignment with yourself despite feeling fear. **Brave people aren't born that way; they develop this ability.** Bravery is a muscle that strengthens through practice.

It's extremely important that as parents, bosses, guides, mentors, partners, companions, friends, etc., we make the other person feel that they are capable of facing the fear provoked by difficult situations. At the end of the day, what you're doing is encouraging that person you care about to practice bravery in a safe environment. This will strengthen them to be ready when things get a bit more difficult. As Eleanor Roosevelt said, "Do something every day that scares you."

> Building My Happiness: **Strengthening My Courage**
>
> 1. What do I feel when I exercise courage as a muscle I can strengthen? What changes?
> 2. Which of the 7 ways to work on courage resonated with me the most?
> 3. How do I commit to bringing it into my life? What small intentional, conscious, and constant adjustment will I make to become 2% braver?

CHANGES AND HABITS

> "If you take changing your life seriously, you will find a way. If not, you will find excuses."
> JEN SINCERO

Are you one of those who loves transformation but is not willing to change? Do you want to live better doing the same things? It's absurd! There's a saying that everyone loves transformation, but few are willing to change. Your current habits are perfectly designed

FREEDOM, AUTHENTICITY, AND COURAGE

to bring you your current results. If you don't like something about your life today, just think about what habits or actions created it and change them. Transformation always begins with becoming aware.

The reality is that deciding to put in the effort and work required to build a life of fulfillment is as straightforward as the following diagram:

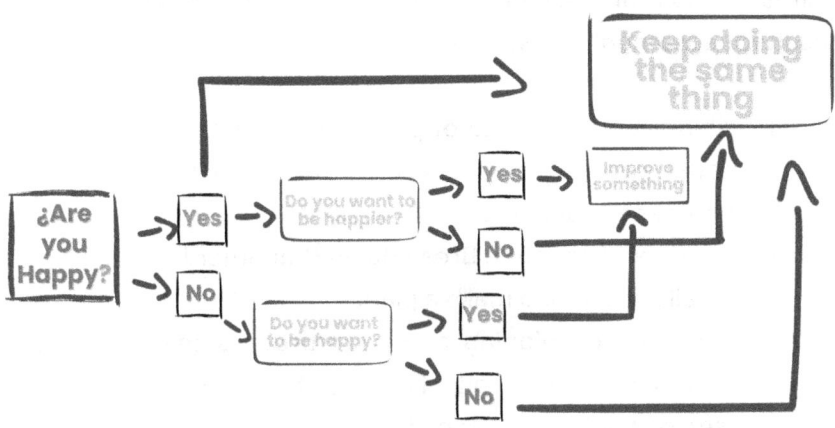

We cannot talk about significant change without talking about habits. Your habits directly determine your lifestyle and level of well-being; those repeated actions that you often don't even question and just do. You have many habits, some that add to your well-being and others that subtract. There are spiritual, physical, intellectual, emotional, relational, financial, etc. habits. For example: your routine of waking up or going to sleep, whether you say good morning or prefer to act as if the other person didn't see you, your self-care routine, the way you relate to yourself and others, your spending habits, any addiction, the emotions you're used to feeling, the time you spend using screens, how much you tip, what you have for breakfast, the seat you select, the type of conversations you have, where you focus your attention, whether you're grateful or complain, your inner dialogue, living in calm or rushing, etc. In short, your life is full of habits. And often, you're not even aware of them. That's why the first step to changing a habit, whether you want to build a positive one like exercising or destroy a negative one like smoking, is to become aware **(you don't realize it until you realize it)**.

Sometimes we wish change were immediate, and thinking it requires a whole process creates resistance. So, forget about the result for a moment and start with 3 things:

1. Think about the kind of person you want to become, because every action you take is a vote for the type of person you want to become.
2. Divide and conquer. Break down that ambitious result into small actions and make a plan.
3. Focus on developing a system/process that allows you to embody the habit. That is, think about the system (set of habits) you can design that will take you in that direction (identity).

As we reviewed in the section "This is How You Create Your Reality", one of the most effective ways to create lasting change is by re-signifying the stories you tell or have told yourself, through one of the following two ways:

1. Question your beliefs: Ask yourself, according to whom?
2. Take responsibility for your life: Take on your active and protagonist role.

Both strategies generate different behavior in you, impacting your reality. But you can also improve your life in a third way by directly changing your behavior, having repeated actions, and being consistent — that is, building habits (automatic behaviors) of well-being that generate different results, as shown in the following image:

REALITY CREATION MODEL 3E + A

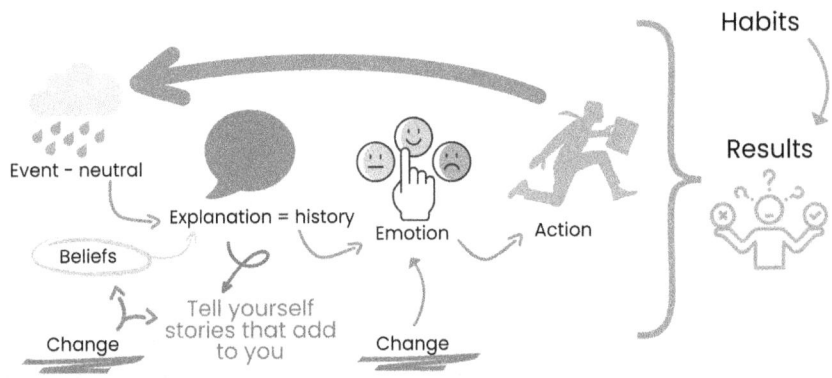

Currently, in a society that promotes the immediacy of results with minimal effort, surgeries and medications are more popular than the building of healthy habits that transform people's lifestyle. However, these measures are often not sustainable in the long term and turn out to be an illusion.

When I read Atomic Habits by James Clear, there were two ideas that made total sense to me: "Your current habits are perfectly designed to bring you your current results," and "You don't rise to the level of your goals, you fall to the level of your systems (habits)." It's not enough to wish for and have dreams; sustained actions over time are required to achieve them. Small changes bring big change if they are constant and maintained over time. For example, thinking about reading books if you've never been a fan of reading may seem very difficult, and therefore, unsustainable. But thinking about reading three pages every day is attainable, and in 3 months, you'll have finished a book.

Change, as a process, has phases, and it's important to know them to create awareness and manage your expectations. Here are the phases:

1. The Call to Adventure – What do I need to learn?
2. Resistance/Denial – The shift from being a victim to taking responsibility.
3. Fear – Embracing your humanity and giving fear the place of co-pilot.
4. Darkness – What is not learned in the light is learned in the darkness; what do you need to become aware of or let go of?
5. Transition – What new habits do I need to build, who do I need to support me? Decide and take action on a plan. Overcome obstacles.
6. Change – I have a new normal.

Change is generally difficult at first, chaotic in the middle, and liberating in the end. That's why using scientific tools can be extremely helpful. As we've mentioned, thanks to neuroscience, we now know that we can modify the physiology of our brains by creating different habits.

To build a habit, it's necessary to create the neural connections that trigger the behavior habitually, for which repetition is essential. Imagine that each repetition is like a hammering of the new path that will connect your neurons. The more repetitions (hammering) you make, the faster they will connect. The problem is that if you leave it to memory, your repetition will be seriously compromised. So, here are some **options for reminders that can help you consolidate the frequency of the behavior**, which, by the way, is much more important than the intensity.

TYPES OF REMINDERS

 Post it
 Tattoo
 Bracelets
 Alarms

 Photos
 Accountability partner
 Signs
 Wallpapers

Here I share a QR with some of the reminders I use in my day-to-day life:

For example, if you want to build the habit of movement, it's much more useful to walk 15 minutes 5 days a week than 2 hours one day, or if you're working on self-love and want to build a positive inner dialogue, it's much more useful to keep a self-appreciation journal and write three things you're grateful for every night than to write 50 things in one day.

This way, the behavior you want to establish becomes your new automatic, your natural way of doing things.

A tip for building new positive habits is to make the action obvious (make the interest you're attracted to visible), easy, interesting, accessible, satisfying, fun, simple, inevitable, and attractive. On the other hand, for negative habits you want to break, you can do the opposite: make the activity impractical, invisible, difficult, boring, unattractive, uncomfortable, expensive, and complicated.

Another tip is to "anchor" the new behavior to an existing habit. For example, when I started taking vitamin supplements, I decided to put them next to my toothbrush and place a little jar with water and a glass in my bathroom. Brushing my teeth is already an established habit for me; I don't even think about it; I do it automatically. So when I go to brush my teeth, I see my pills and take them right away. This has allowed me to be very consistent and get the results I was seeking by complementing my diet with some supplements.

Here's a 1-minute capsule, hoping it encourages you to change for a better life. Remember you can activate the Youtube English subtitles:

It's not by motivating yourself or reading a lot that you will be happier, but with ACTION. That's why it's essential to create and strengthen well-being habits. There isn't one habit so important that, once achieved, it will build your happiness, no matter how important it is. Instead, it's those small adjustments in different areas of your life that can make you happy and live in fullness. Just as one behavior can benefit multiple areas.

Beware of old bad habits, because since the "old neural pathways" still exist, it's very easy to fall back into undesirable behavior. Stay vigilant! They are always latent.

Some authors agree that there are factors that determine the likelihood of success when you decide to change. Here are the factors described below:

- **30% Clarity in objectives:** Define specific and clear goals.
- **20% Detailed planning:** Develop a detailed plan with concrete steps.

- **15% Personal commitment:** Show dedication.
- **10% Adaptability:** Be willing to adjust according to circumstances.
- **15% Social support and resources:** Have a solid support system.
- **10% Unpredictable variables:** Aspects beyond your control.

This means that 90% is in your control. Focus on those factors!

In fact, according to a study by Dr. Gail Matthews, psychologist and professor at the University of California, she concluded that you have a 42% greater chance of reaching a goal simply by writing it down.

It's also worth mentioning that the intensity of the impact of change depends on the person's ability to adapt. That is, change is subjective. Remember that we are all different, and what may be incredibly easy for you to automate may be very difficult for me. However, I believe this pyramid shows 5 phases we go through during a significant change process:

PYRAMID OF TRANSFORMATION

Knowing them allows you to understand where you stand and take action. Is it easy? No! On average, people try 7 times to make a change before succeeding. That's why achieving quick wins is incredibly helpful for building confidence, which feeds your courage and motivates you to continue taking action. Manifesting quickly to strengthen your sense of agency and the power to create your reality based on your will is extremely powerful. You will certainly face challenges and obstacles to overcome, but remember that what matters most is how you rise, not how many times you fall.

Most efforts for change do not lead to lasting impact and simply produce the "honeymoon effect." This means that an improvement is shown at the beginning, but soon after, it returns to the previous state. To achieve lasting change, we need the belief that change is possible (a growth mindset), adjustment (alignment with strengths), hard work (persistence), and guidance (instructions, coaching). It is estimated that when there is an intervention, such as a workshop, session, conference, retreat, etc., 5% of participants will show no change, 80% will have a temporary change (improve but revert after a while), and only 15% will experience lasting change (improve, and although they may backslide, they never return to their initial state). Knowing this, the idea is that when you participate in such efforts, you are aware that it depends on you which group you will belong to. Not everyone resonates with every instructor, method, information, or tool, and that's okay. No matter how much effort the instructor or author puts into promoting change, it depends on you. **Remember, happiness is a personal construction.**
In conclusion, here are 8 points to build a healthy habit:

- Take action: action is more important than motivation. Starting is the first and most important step.
- Make it easy, convenient, fun, attractive, and simple: a habit must be established before it is improved.
- Anchor it to an existing habit.
- Use reminders: notes, bracelets, cushions, photos, alarms, clothes, etc.
- Embody the identity.
- Consistency is more important than intensity.
- Announce it and share it to increase your commitment.
- Track it: what gets measured is easier to improve.

Building my happiness: **Working on my habits**

1. Do I want to live better doing the same things?
2. What habit have I tried to build or change and not succeeded? Why?
3. Make a list of my habits and classify them into positive and negative.
4. What habit would I like to build or change? Choose one
5. What reminder will I apply to trigger the repetition of that new habit?
6. What valuable finding do I consider from this section and how do I commit to applying it?

TAKE CONTROL OF YOUR LIFE

> "I will not rescue you because you are not helpless.
> I will not fix you because you are not broken.
> I will not heal you because I see you as whole.
> I will walk with you through the darkness while you remember your light."
> WOMAN MEDICINE PRAYER

Don't settle for being unhappy! Are you tired of living a mediocre life? Tired of surviving or motivated to start living?

One year after returning from the United States, I decided that I wanted to experience another culture and once again face the challenge of living alone and being autonomous. I got a scholarship to go to Spain to study for a semester of my career. At that time, I had a boyfriend with whom I had been for five years, and everyone

FREEDOM, AUTHENTICITY, AND COURAGE

was telling me: "He's probably going to give you the ring and ask you to marry him." I was 22 years old, and every time someone suggested it, I felt an overwhelming anxiety. I thought, "How strange. I should be happy and excited when they talk about the ring. Why do I feel this horrible anxiety? Of course, because I don't want to get married!"

Apparently, getting married was the perfect plan because it satisfied the expectations of our families and friends. It was a "perfect" relationship: we loved each other, had a lot of fun, shared values, were highly compatible in interests, tastes, and activities, loved doing sports together, and our families got along and enjoyed each other's company. A perfect story. However, there was something that didn't allow me to feel excited about the possibility of formalizing. The very thought of it made me very anxious. In the mix of emotions, there was a good amount of fear. I feared hurting someone who had only given me wonderful things, disappointing my family, especially my parents, and many of our friends. I feared making a mistake, fearing the uncertain future, having to reinvent myself after having been in such a symbiotic relationship for 5 years, and possibly feeling alone... Fear, fear, a lot of fear.

I realized that the plan to go live in another country was, in a way, a tactic to postpone that decision that troubled me so much. I spent days reflecting on what could be causing such anxiety. After a couple of months, I discovered that what overwhelmed me was the possibility of taking an "irreversible" step in the wrong direction: a traditional provincial lifestyle. I mean, formalizing the relationship meant giving up many dreams, like studying for a master's degree abroad, continuing to explore the world, and realizing myself as a professional.

In the stereotypes of the early 2000s, in a provincial setting, most "good" wives dedicated themselves to the home, sacrificed their dreams for their families, didn't challenge their husbands' authority, weren't financially independent, and absorbed the full responsibility of raising children, if any. Just the thought of picturing myself in such a scenario gave me chills. But I had two choices: betray myself and what I felt or betray others.

When I told him about the exchange, he replied: "You already went to the United States. And I waited for you. Now you're going to Spain and I have to wait for you. How many more times do you want me to wait for you?" And boom! I thought: "You're absolutely right. None. This is over. Thank you very much."

It was chaos. My mom was crying, my sister was crying, the housekeeper was crying, everyone was crying. My sister said to me: "You're such a fool! I went with him to buy the engagement ring, and it's beautiful."

When she mentioned that, I felt liberated. Just in time! Phew! Better to run here than stay here! Yes, it was very difficult, and it hurt a lot because our separation wasn't due to a fight, a lie, or a significant difference according to the "standards" we had set for the relationship or what society expected back in those days, but because our paths were incompatible. He wanted to get married, and I had a thousand things to do before. So, I went to Spain...

I learned to live for myself, to read my emotions, to prioritize loyalty to myself... I took control of my life and stopped asking for permission to live it. And since that moment, I don't allow anyone or anything to decide for me.

Is it selfish? Of course not. In my decision-making criteria, empathy, solidarity, consideration for others, and compassion are present. However, there is absolute awareness, and although I may decide that someone else chooses for me (though I confess, I delegate little), I am still making the decision. I always decide! I create my reality, by action or omission, I am the artist of my destiny. Feeling the helm of my life in my hands is one of the most fascinating sensations I've ever experienced, and one I will never give up.

I invite you to try taking control of your life for a week and stop asking for permission to live it, and as my mom says: "Try it, and if it doesn't work, go back to the previous way." **To be happy is for the brave.**

Building my happiness: **Taking control of my life**

1. Do I feel in control of my life?
2. Do I still ask for permission or opinions to live according to my values and interests?
3. If I answered yes, what do I need to take control of my life?

VALENTINAMENTE FELIZ

Embrace every moment with gratitude, and you will see how your world transforms, not because what surrounds you changes, but because you decide to change the way you see it. **Being bravely happy is the only way to live fully.** I used to dedicate my time to stabilizing the company and being a mom to two (Lázaro, 6 years old, and Simón, 1 year and 5 months). In the midst of the turmoil of the pandemic, I also went through an existential crisis. I felt that I was really good at running the company and consulting with our clients, I was doing well. But I accepted that I wasn't overly excited about what I was doing, and that if I weren't getting paid, I wouldn't continue doing it. At that moment, the alarms went off! I thought, "Now more than ever, life is fragile (COVID was equal to death at that time), and I'm spending my days professionally on something that doesn't make me wake up with enthusiasm."

TO BE HAPPY IS FOR THE BRAVE

I had been trying for days to decipher my discomfort, and it was in a class with Tal Ben-Shahar, one of the classes we have once a week and have had for years, that I dared to share the crisis I was going through. After listening to me carefully, he reminded me that the hardest decisions are the ones where both paths are good, and he recommended that I calmly read the poem "Our Deepest Fear" by Marianne Williamson, which turned out to be a turning point in my life. Here it is shared with you:

> Our deepest fear is **NOT** that WE ARE INADEQUATE. Our deepest fear is that we are **POWERFUL BEYOND MEASURE**. It is our LIGHT, not our darkness, that most frightens us. We ask ourselves, Who am I to be BRILLIANT, GORGEOUS, TALENTED, AND FABULOUS? But actually, who are you NOT TO BE? You are a CHILD OF GOD. Playing small does not serve the world. There is nothing enlightening about shrinking so that other people won't feel insecure AROUND YOU. We are all meant TO SHINE, as children do. We were born to make manifest the GLORY OF GOD that is WITHIN US. It's not just in some of us, it's in everyone. And as we let OUR LIGHT SHINE, we unconsciously give other people permission to do the same. As we are liberated from our own fear, our presence automatically **LIBERATES OTHERS**.

The pandemic made time and existence take on new meaning, and the true priorities became evident. Humanity confronted the fragility of life and stopped being willing to waste its days on activities or jobs that brought no meaning or well-being, only money in exchange. Working from home highlighted the value of flexibility for much of the workforce.

I had been enrolled for several months in the Certification in Happiness Studies at the Happiness Studies Academy (HSA), and having that resource was a blessing to navigate those difficult times. I was learning tools and recalling much relevant information I had studied years earlier. Additionally, the community was a safe place where I could share emotionally honestly and feel heard. I loved taking classes with Tal, perceiving him as human, sensitive, congruent, compassionate, and real. Honestly, I have fond memories of those days of great resilience. I also enjoyed sharing information and tools with friends, and I realized they found them revealing and very useful for managing their anxiety, creating strategies to manage the kids at home, improving communication with their partners while we were all in lockdown, and so on.

I remember that social panic grew, and it was expected that the government and big business leaders would rescue the country from what seemed like a disaster. I thought, "It doesn't work like that. There aren't enough businessmen nor enough government capacity to rescue everyone. That's impossible! If we first take care of ourselves individually, then our small family circle, and after that share or help a little with strangers, and everyone does the same, that's how we'll get through this."

My passion for helping became evident to me, and my knowledge of human behavior (from more than 20 years of study) and change management seemed like a scarce and in-demand asset. I perceived that some of my friends, women with many years of study, travel, financial stability, and a strong support network, among many other privileges, were feeling overwhelmed. I couldn't imagine how women who were the heads of their households, with much less flexibility to make decisions and no support, must have felt. That's when I realized the value I could contribute by sharing what I knew. And it was feeling a moral obligation to share what I felt fortunate to know and had applied for many years that I started my Instagram profile as a brave experiment, with the sole intention of helping those who resonated with it navigate the crisis of the pandemic in a slightly more empowered, optimistic, and harmonious way.

I wanted a name that conveyed action. In the end, the science of happiness is useless if it stays only in theory and doesn't help you live better—happiness is a personal journey. So one day, while showering, the idea came to me to turn my name into an adverb to spark action: Valentinamente.

I wasn't sure whether to call it well-being or happiness. In the end, it's a never-ending debate in the world of scientists and authors. On one hand, the word **happiness** has a bad reputation, it's perceived as joy, toxic optimism, superficial, and unserious, while the word **well-being** sounds more grounded, formal, and scientific (but also more boring). Personally, I think the word happiness is much more emotional and inspiring, and as long as we remove the idealism and romanticism born from misinformation, it's a much more ambitious concept. Who wants to be happy? Everyone. Who wants to have well-being? Hmm... it would take more time for them to raise their hands. It's harder for me to connect. I don't know. I think it might be my courage making itself present and seeking the risk of disruption. I feel that "happiness" aims to win, while "well-being" aims not to lose.

So, I decided on Valentinamente Feliz, where I am happy in my own way and work on it every day. I created a space where I share (from different platforms) scientific information and tools for living better, along with some testimonies of how I apply them to my daily life. I repeat, I don't consider myself a guide for anyone; I just try to show you that if I can, you can too.

The information was well received, and the profile began to grow. Later, I was invited to speak on the radio and television (on morning shows and news programs), then to write for a digital magazine, to share in many podcasts... Then I created my own podcast. In short, this is how I've been sharing on national and international forums, with both young and old, with women deprived of freedom (some physically and others mentally), with parent associations, with non-profit organizations, and with large multinational companies. **I love sharing that to be happy is possible if you work seriously on it.**

In Valentinamente Feliz, I always remind you that to be happy is your responsibility, and that happiness is a personal construction

FREEDOM, AUTHENTICITY, AND COURAGE

that no one can do for you, nor can you do for anyone else. Likewise, I provide valuable information and testimonies to inspire you and motivate you to take action. I work hard and unleash my creativity and that of my team to make the information accessible and easy to apply. All with the intention of helping more and more people know that yes, it is possible to be happy if you put in the work it requires. In the end, I am convinced that it's not that we don't want to be happy, but that most people don't know how to do it or where to start. We believe that happiness comes when adversity goes away, and that keeps us away from the possibility of being happy. Life is inherently adverse, and you can't change that, but you can choose who you want to be in the face of it. That's why it's revealing to know that you can learn to be happy, and that there are sciences to help with that.

    I don't have all the answers, but I do know where to look. I offer my willingness to accompany you on the journey and help in any way I can. CLARIFICATION: It's important to remind you that I don't do anyone else's job. The truth is that I am very busy and focused on doing mine. "Pulling my own cart" is often hard and tiring, let alone pulling yours. Just as I don't ask anyone to rescue me, I don't rescue anyone. I gladly share what I know and what has worked for me. I give you tools, I listen to you, I celebrate you, I cheer you on, and I suggest things, but the work is yours. I don't do anyone else's job!

    Until today, Valentinamente Feliz has been a wonderful three-year adventure in which I have been able to reinvent myself and find my life's purpose. It is where I venture, practice bravery frequently, and take my message to every corner that invites me, because I am convinced that it is by taking responsibility for your life and being brave that you can build a life worth living, a life perfect in its imperfection, an authentic,

free, full, and happy life. I am sharing with you a QR code to a short video about how to be happy is for the brave. Remember you can activate Youtube English subtitles.

Building my happiness: **I transcend my deepest fear**

1. What version of myself scares me so much that just thinking about it makes my hands shake and gives me a feeling of emptiness in my stomach? Why?
2. When have I made myself small to avoid discomfort?
3. How can I recognize my right to shine immeasurably, and in doing so, give others the right to do the same?
4. What information resonated with me in this section and how can I take it into action?

TO BE HAPPY IS YOUR RESPONSIBILITY

> "No one can build a better world without improving people. Each one must work on their own improvement."
> MARIE CURIE

Thinking that to be happy is not your responsibility condemns you to helplessness and, therefore, distances you from the possibility of being happy. Taking responsibility for your life is the first step toward being brave and taking the step, those steps, the ones that scare you, and at times paralyze you, but they are precisely the ones that make us uncomfortable in the moment, but bring us closer to our flourishing afterward.

FREEDOM, AUTHENTICITY, AND COURAGE

Recognize yourself as the protagonist of your life. Because if I could, and I can do something in this life of mine, you can also do it in that life of yours.

I wish that on your path to building happiness there is:

- **Gratitude**, to focus on and appreciate what you have and who you are.
- **Courage**, to know yourself and work on your shadow.
- **Humor**, to lighten adversity.
- **Smiles**, when you're sad.
- **Comfort**, on tough days.
- **Rainbows**, to value the rain.
- **Self-compassion**, to embrace your humanity in the worst moments and love yourself in the sorrow.
- **Sunsets**, to comfort your heart.
- **Strength**, so you rise completely (no matter if it's fast or slow).
- **Hugs**, to hold and contain you.
- **Scientific information**, so you don't fall for charlatanism.
- **Friends**, with whom to celebrate life and cry deeply.
- **Faith**, to keep believing.
- **Adventurous spirit**, so you play to win, not to avoid losing.
- **Confidence**, when you doubt yourself.
- **Patience**, to accept what is and lower your expectations.
- **Self-love**, to recognize yourself as unique and wonderful.
- **Time**, to experiment and adjust.
- **Generosity**, to share your best version with others.
- **Bravery**, to make those difficult but necessary decisions.

Building my happiness: **Taking responsibility for my happiness**

1. What do I need to know and feel 100% responsible for building my happiness?

IDEAS FOR ACTION

- To be happy is for the brave.
- To be happy is your responsibility.
- You can learn to be happy.
- Happiness is having the courage to build a life with purpose, presence, health, learning, connection, and pleasure, in alignment with your essence.
- Courage is acting in alignment with yourself, despite feeling fear.
- Happiness is achievable; it starts with a decision and continues with hard work.
- Choose to stop surviving and start living. Yes, you can!
- Own your life and stop asking for permission or opinions to live it.
- Don't let life happen to you, create it.
- Life is inherently adversarial, yet you can still be happy.
- In the midst of adversity, happiness boils down to resilience/antifragility.
- In the face of adversity, there are two paths: break or grow stronger. Which one do you choose?
- You are braver than you think.
- Courage, self-love, hope, gratitude, compassion, resilience, freedom, and optimism are muscles that grow stronger.
- "Feeling happy" is a momentary mood associated with joy.

FREEDOM, AUTHENTICITY, AND COURAGE

- "Being happy" is a state of long-term fulfillment and satisfaction.
- Don't call it a dream, call it a plan.
- For transformation, action is more important than motivation or information.
- Self-knowledge is the foundation of a healthy relationship with yourself.
- A healthy relationship with yourself is the foundation of healthy relationships with others.
- What you love, you take care of.
- Learn and reinvent yourself. You're not too late!
- It's okay to be yourself.
- Loyalty starts with yourself.
- When motivation is lacking, rely on discipline.
- Happiness is contagious.
- There's nothing great about shrinking yourself to avoid discomfort.
- Gratitude and generosity are effective "shortcuts" to well-being.
- Everyone can be happy, but not everyone "should" be. Don't waste energy trying to convince. Focus on yourself and remember that the path is individual.
- What gets measured is easier to improve. Periodically assess your happiness to evaluate changes and progress.

I invite you to apply a diagnostic tool again. Preferably, use the same one(s) you used when you first started reading this book. This way, you'll have a reference for your well-being levels when you began and now, weeks or months later. Compare and observe. What changed? What improved or worsened? Why? What can you do about it? How can I build an extra 2% of presence, purpose, health, learning, self-love, connection, or pleasure?

I hope you're surprised by your findings and find enough inspiration to continue on your path to building your happiness.

Remember this diagram that summarizes the proposal of this book, and remember, you are braver than you think:

MODEL: BEING HAPPY IS FOR THE BRAVE

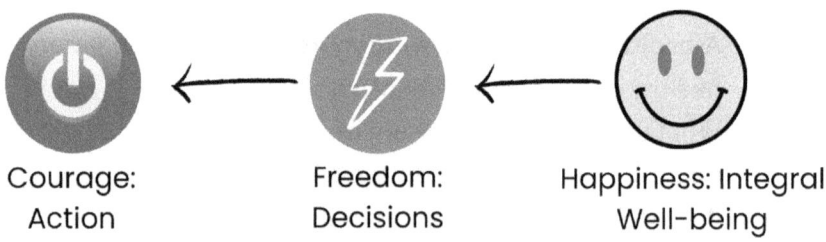

Courage: Action ← Freedom: Decisions ← Happiness: Integral Well-being

Keep in mind that happiness is not a destination, but a way of traveling. Ah! Also, traveling with company can be convenient, if you wish, and I'll be happy to share the journey with you. To be happy requires constant effort until you die, and that doesn't have to be tiring or overwhelming; you can make it exciting and enjoyable. In the end, that's what you came to this life for: to live!

Finally, if I could wish you something, it would be that you may love yourself, with or without a partner, that you surround yourself with people who celebrate your light, accept your shadow, and make you feel valued, heard, safe, understood, and unique, that you have the courage to leave the victim persona behind so that you can take control of your life and put in the effort required to build a happy life, that you stop thinking and start doing, that you embrace your most authentic version (the one that might seem crazy), that you allow yourself to feel fully, even with fear, that you are conscious that you deserve the best of this life (which is yours, even if it may not seem like it), and that you never settle for less than your best possible version.

FREEDOM, AUTHENTICITY, AND COURAGE

Thank you for reading me and sharing with me the most valuable thing you have: **your time**.

You can reach me at contacto@valentinamentefeliz.com or on my social media @valentinamente_feliz. I will be honored to cheer you on whenever you need it. This is not a goodbye, but a see you soon!

Always remember: to be happy is your responsibility, to be happy is for the brave.

BIBLIOGRAPHY

Boyce, C. J., Brown, G. D. A., & Moore, S. C. (2010). "Money and happiness: Rank of income, not income, affects life satisfaction". In Psychological Science, 21(4), (pp. 471-475).

Brickman, P., & Campbell, D. T. (1971). "Hedonic relativism and planning the good society". In M. H. Appley (Ed.), *Adaptation-level theory* (pp. 287- 302). Academic Press.

Brown, B. (2012). *El poder de la vulnerabilidad: Enseñanzas sobre la autenticidad, la conexión y el coraje.* Urano.

Buckingham, M. (2007). *The Truth About You: Your Secret to Success.* Thomas Nelson.

Bucay, J. (2003). *Déjame que te cuente: los cuentos que me enseñaron a vivir.* Océano.

Burrow, A. L. (2020). *The Ecology of Purposeful Living Across the Lifespan.* Springer.

Chopra, D. (2008). *El libro de los secretos: Desbloqueando los misterios ocultos de tu vida.* Penguin Random House Grupo Editorial.

Csikszentmihalyi, M. (1997). *Finding Flow: The Psychology of Engagement with Everyday Life.* Basic Books.

Diener, E., & Biswas-Diener, R. (2002). "Will money increase subjective well-being?" In Social Indicators Research, 57(2), (pp. 119-169).

Dunn, E. W., Aknin, L. B., & Norton, M. I. (2008). "Spending money on others promotes happiness". Science, 319(5870), (pp. 1687-1688).

Gottman, J. M., & Silver, N. (1999). *The Seven Principles for Making Marriage Work: A Practical Guide from the Country's Foremost Relationship Expert.* Crown Publishing Group.

Kahneman, D., & Deaton, A. (2010). "High income improves evaluation of life but not emotional well-being". In Proceedings of the National Academy of Sciences, 107(38), (pp. 16489-16493).

Killingsworth, M. A. (2021). "Experienced well-being rises with income, even above $75,000 per year". In Proceedings of the National Academy of Sciences, 118(4), e2016976118.

Langer, E. J. (2009). *Counter Clockwise: Mindful Health and the Power of Possibility.* Ballantine Books.

Lyubomirsky, S. (2007). *The How of Happiness: A Scientific Approach to Getting the Life You Want.* Penguin Books.

McGonigal, K. (2015). *The Upside of Stress: Why Stress Is Good for You, and How to Get Good at It.* Avery.

Neff, K. (2011). *Self-Compassion: The Proven Power of Being Kind to Yourself.* HarperCollins.

BIBLIOGRAPHY

Oishi, S., Diener, E., Lucas, R. E., & Suh, E. M. (1999). "Cross-cultural variations in predictors of life satisfaction: Perspectives from needs and values". *Personality and Social Psychology Bulletin,* 25(8), (pp. 980-990).

Powell, J. A. (2012). *Racing to Justice: Transforming Our Conceptions of Self and Other to Build an Inclusive Society.* Indiana University Press.

Ratey, J. J. (2013). *Spark: The Revolutionary New Science of Exercise and the Brain.* Little, Brown Spark.

Robinson, K. (2009). *The Element: How Finding Your Passion Changes Everything.* Penguin Books.

Seligman, M. E. P. (2002). *Authentic Happiness: Using the New Positive Psychology to Realize Your Potential for Lasting Fulfillment.* Free Press.

Seligman, M. E. P. (2011). *Flourish: A Visionary New Understanding of Happiness and Well-being.* Free Press.

Sinclair, D. (2019). *Lifespan: Why We Age—and Why We Don't Have To.* Atria Books.

Taleb, N. N. (2007). *The Black Swan: The Impact of the Highly Improbable.* Random House.

Van Boven, L., & Gilovich, T. (2003). "To do or to have? That is the question". *Journal of Personality and Social Psychology,* 85(6), (pp. 1193-1202).

Walker, M. (2017). *Why We Sleep: Unlocking the Power of Sleep and Dreams.* Scribner.

RECOMMENDED BOOKS

Ben-Shahar, Tal (2021). *Happier, No Matter What* (Más feliz, pase lo que pase).

Ben-Shahar, Tal (2012). *Choose the Life You Want* (Elige la vida que quieres).

Brualdi, A. C. (1996). *Multiple Intelligences: Gardner's Theory* (Teoría de las inteligencias múltiples de Gardner). ERIC Digest.

Brown, Brené (2010). *The Gifts of the Imperfection* (El regalo de la imperfección).

Buettner, D. (2023). *The Blue Zones Secrets for Living Longer: Lessons From the Healthiest Places on Earth* (Los secretos de las zonas azules para vivir más tiempo: Lecciones de los lugares más saludables de la Tierra). National Geographic.

Chapman, G. (2011). *Los cinco lenguajes del amor.*

Clear, James (2018). *Atomic Habits (Hábitos atómicos).*

Covey, Stephen R. (1989). *Los 7 Hábitos de la Gente Altamente Efectiva.*

Csikszentmihalyi, Mihaly (1990). *Flow* (Fluir).

Dispenza, Joe (2014). *The Placebo is You* (El placebo eres tú).

Doyle, Glennon (2020). *Untamed* (Indomable).

Dweck, Carol (2006). *Mindset* (Mentalidad).

Eyal, Nir (2019). *Indistractable* (Indistraible).

Frankl, Victor (1946). *El hombre en busca de sentido.*

Gardner, Howard (1999). *Intelligence Reframed: Multiple intelligences for the 21st century* (La inteligencia reformulada: Inteligencias múltiples para el siglo XXI).

Haidt, Jonathan (2006). *The Happiness Hypothesis* (La hipótesis de la felicidad).

Rojas Estapé, Marian (2021). *Encuentra tu persona vitamina.*

Rojas, Enrique (2023). *Comprende tus emociones.*

Riso, Walter (2012). *Autoestima: enamórate de ti.*

Salbi, Zainab (2018). *Freedom is an inside job* (La libertad es un trabajo interno).

Seligman, Martin (1990). *The Hope Circuit* (El circuito de la esperanza).

Tarragona, Margarita (2012). *Tu mejor tú.*

Waldinger, Robert (2020). *The Good Life* (La buena vida).

INDEX

INTRODUCTION 7
    Who I am 10
    To be happy is for the brave 14
    Triad = Courage -> Authenticity/freedom -> Happiness 14

1. ADVERSITY: LIFE 17
    Being happy 17
    A low blow 19
    Paths 24
    Personal responsibility 26
    Doing and trusting 32
    The vaccine 33
    Antifragility 35
    Growth mindset 38

2. HAPPINESS 41
    Happiness without secrets 41
    Being happy vs. Feeling happy 44
    What is happiness? 49
    You can learn to be happy 51
    The science of happiness 53
    Spire model 59
    Spiritual wellbeing - purpose and presence 62
    Strengths 64
    Meaning 70
    Values 74

Presence 76
Dreams 82
Physical wellbeing - health 83
Nutrition and microbiota 86
Exercise 89
Sleep 91
Touch 94
Stress is your ally, if... 97
Breathing 102
Longevity 105
Intellectual wellbeing - learning 109
State of flow 111
Improvisation 113
Ask and play 115
Multiple intelligences 120
Relational wellbeing - connection 124
Your relationship with yourself 132
Romantic relationships 139
Emotional wellbeing - messengers 147
Embrace your emotions 155
This is how you create your reality 161
Beliefs 164
Some emotions... 168
Resilience and optimism 171
Giving thanks vs being grateful 174
Diagnosis: how happy am I? 179
It's a process, not a decision 183
Formulas 185
Why is being happy such a challenge? 188
1. Self-love 189
2. Personal responsibility 199
3. Self-knowledge 204

- 4. Awareness...209
- 5. Disciplined work...211
- 6. Balance...212
- 7. Letting go...216
- 8. Information...219
- Happy hormones...221
- Warning! It's contagious...225
- Does everyone have to be happy?...227
- The happiest country in the world...228

3. FREEDOM, AUTHENTICITY, AND COURAGE...235
- What is freedom?...235
- Authenticity...238
- Attention and perception...245
- Reinvent yourself...250
- Money and happiness...253
- Courage...257
- What is fear?...258
- What is courage?...264
- You're braver than you think...268
- Types of courage...269
- How to strengthen the courage muscle?...272
- Changes and habits...276
- Take control of your life...286
- Valentinamente feliz...289
- To be happy is your responsibility...294
- Ideas for action...296

BIBLIOGRAPHY...301
RECOMMENDED BOOKS...305